Haney-Lopez,
race in the lega[l]

*look at the role of legal history

West of Sex

Time:
critical for
understanding Mexican American

⌐ standard to exclude
⌐ middle class Mex-Am
using the "standard"
to exclude lower class Mx,
immigrants... etc. anything
→ differentiate
→ recreating structure

Neither Hell No[r] + How Racis[m] made in

- combination
  of Hist.
  MEX AM w/ Hist of sex
  → establishing the
    intersection btw the two
- 1800'- Progressive era: "Americanization"
    Middle class protestant → change America
    red cross, YMCA, service-type non-profit
    "Fixing societies problems"
    Reformers → teach them "hygain"
- Americanization of school cimulum
    redefining the person in order
    to better control the individual
    CA → policies to mimick Jim crow
       dynamics of punishment (corporal
                                punishment)
Power of humiliation 2
   - Family attacked
getting rid of racism → randtications
   - modern patterns of education → mentorestlip
      - English/edu → through vocational learning
         NOT through hilosophy/literature

West of Sex

Making Mexican America, 1900–1930

PABLO MITCHELL

Studies of sex
- dismantling idea of sexual neutral"
- gendered component to our ideas of citizenship
  category of Mex. Am → being shaped
- gender/sexual component: cult of
  "true womanhood" and domesticity
  — 19th century → white middle class women
  only once considered
  woment of virtue

The University of Chicago Press
Chicago and London

- Belief in science "rationalism"
- scientific management/taylorism → mechanize
  things
- factory model → removed knowledge
  of
  ↳ model for all aspects of life
- Bell system → teaching how to follow orders
  pedagogy of training students to become
  ⊕ blue collar workers

Pablo Mitchell is associate professor of history at Oberlin College. He is the author of *Coyote Nation: Sexuality, Race, and Conquest in Modernizing New Mexico, 1880–1920* (UCP, 2005). That book won the Ray Allen Billington Prize from the OAH (best book in frontier history).

The University of Chicago Press, Chicago 60637
The University of Chicago Press, Ltd., London
© 2012 by The University of Chicago
All rights reserved. Published 2012.
Printed in the United States of America

21 20 19 18 17 16 15 14 13 12   1 2 3 4 5

ISBN-13: 978-0-226-53268-4 (cloth)
ISBN-13: 978-0-226-53269-1 (paper)
ISBN-10: 0-226-53268-2 (cloth)
ISBN-10: 0-226-53269-0 (paper)

Library of Congress Cataloging-in-Publication Data

Mitchell, Pablo.
    West of sex : making Mexican America, 1900–1930 / Pablo Mitchell.
        p. cm.
    Includes index.
    ISBN-13: 978-0-226-53268-4 (cloth : alkaline paper)
    ISBN-10: 0-226-53268-2 (cloth : alkaline paper)
    ISBN-13: 978-0-226-53269-1 (paperback : alkaline paper)
    ISBN-10: 0-226-53269-0 (paperback : alkaline paper)   1. Mexicans—
Sexual behavior—Southwest, New—History—20th century.   2. Trials (Sex
crimes)—Southwest, New—Cases.   3. Sex crimes—Southwest, New—
History—20th century.   4. Sex—Social aspects—United States.
5. Mexicans—Southwest, New—Social conditions—History—20th century.
6. Southwest, New—Race relations—History—20th century.   7. Marginality,
Social—Southwest, New—History—20th century.   I. Title.
    HV6592 .M58 2012
    364.15'309790904—dc23

                                                                    2011031181

♾ This paper meets the requirements of ANSI/NISO Z39.48–1992
(Permanence of Paper).

For Beth

CONTENTS

ACKNOWLEDGMENTS

This project is indebted to a host of programs, institutions, and individuals. A postdoctoral fellowship from the Sexuality Research Fellowship Program (SRFP) of the Social Science Research Council, with funds provided by the Ford Foundation, provided much-needed financial support, as well as a wonderful cohort of engaged, intellectually stimulating sexuality scholars. Diane Di Mauro, the director of the SRFP, was an incomparable source of enthusiasm and inspiration during and after the fellowship. The Nord Professorship at Oberlin College also provided important financial support for this project.

This book would have been impossible without the knowledge, assistance, and labor of government workers from across the country. I am grateful to the staffs of the Lorenzo de Zavala State Archives and Library, Bexar County Courthouse, New Mexico Supreme Court Archives, California Historical Society, California Supreme Court Archives, Los Angeles County Courthouse, Alameda County Courthouse, Oberlin College Library, and the outstanding public library systems of Bay Village, Cleveland, Lakewood, and Westlake, Ohio.

For over a decade, Oberlin College has been unceasing in its support of my research and writing. Thanks especially to the students at Oberlin and my coworkers in the Comparative American Studies Program, the History Department, the Office of Sponsored Programs, and the Multicultural Resource Center. I am also grateful to the following friends and colleagues: Rick Baldoz, Adrian Bautista, Yeworkwha Belachew, Jan Cooper, Judi Davidson, Sean Decatur, Nancy Dye, Eric Estes, Michael Fisher, Meredith Gadsby, Charu Gupta, Brenda Hall, Heather Hogan, Daphne John, David Kamitsuka, Kathy King, Clayton Koppes, Gary Kornblith, Wendy Kozol, Carol Lasser, Shelley Lee, Joe Lubben and Griselda Rondon, Greggor

Mattson, Gina Pérez, Charles Peterson, Baron Pineda, Meredith Raimondo, Renee Romano, Ari Sammartino, Len Smith, and Steve Volk. Moon-ho Jung, Paul Kramer, Shelley Lee, Natalia Molina, and Renee Romano offered much-appreciated advice on material in the book. Thanks as well to Allison Chomet and Elizabeth Supp for research assistance.

As I was revising the manuscript, I had the great fortune to be involved in the "On the Borders of Love and Power" workshop sponsored by the William P. Clements Center for Southwest Studies at Southern Methodist University and the Center for the Southwest at the University of New Mexico. Thoughtful comments and suggestions by workshop participants came at a critical point in the writing of this book and were enormously helpful in clarifying my arguments. I am especially grateful to cofacilitators Crista DeLuzio and David Adams.

The warmth, enthusiasm, and good cheer of Douglas Mitchell at the University of Chicago Press sustained this project for many years. I am honored and fortunate to have him as my editor. Thanks also to the wonderful work of Tim McGovern and Katherine Frentzel at the Press. Two anonymous reviewers provided careful, detailed, and judicious comments on multiple versions of the manuscript. Their comments improved this book in multiple ways, and I hope that I have done justice to their professionalism and wisdom.

Like so many, I am indebted to the generosity and good will of Ramón Gutiérrez. He has been an unswerving source of advice, rigorous critique, and encouragement. Maria Montoya, Virginia Scharff, and Carroll Smith-Rosenberg also deserve special mention. They too are gifted mentors. They cleared precious space for me and my work in their lives, space that I know is dear and not easy to part with, and for that, and much more, I am grateful. Pawan Dhingra has cheered this project from nearly its beginning. The underbrush of liberal arts colleges can be a little dense at times, and Pawan helped me find a clearing or two where I could try to become both a teacher and a scholar.

Another set of teachers has been no less critical to the completion of this project. The staff at the Oberlin Early Childhood Center and the Westshore Montessori School played an important role in raising our children and allowing me the time and peace of mind to write this book. I am especially grateful to Kathy Tracey, Sharon Blotzer, and Missy Sinka for their commitment, creativity, and love. Thanks also to the numerous Oberlin College students and former students who cared for our children and whose love, energy, and commitment to radical politics animated our lives and our home.

My parents, Beatriz and Philip Mitchell, were my first and best teachers. I'm still learning how to be a grownup (honestly, who freakin' isn't?) and I'm grateful that they're still willing to help me light the way. Ben Mitchell is my brother and I aspire to be what he has become: a father, a teacher, and a gentle man. Other family members have also helped bring life to this project: Sharon Braman, the Butkevich family, the Cadavid family, the late Ruth Kipp, the McLaughlin family (Alex, Ginger, and Noah), the Mitchell/Gallegos family (Ben, Julianne, and Estella), Jennifer Orr, the Orr/Lozier family (Lisa, Luke, and Jack), and James and Susan McLaughlin.

Ruby McLaughlin Mitchell and Tayo Mitchell McLaughlin were born in Fall 2004. I've been working on this project for most of their lives. During that time, I've tried really hard not to prioritize this book over them, but I know there were times when I was distracted or pissy or impatient (or distracted, pissy, *and* impatient) because of the book, and I apologize to them for that. Since they have lived with this book as much as just about anyone, I want them have a chance to say something in writing. Tayo would like to say that "school is fun and I really like sports." Ruby says, "I like science and soccer."

I am most indebted to Beth McLaughlin. This project would be lost without her, and so would I. She has been a research assistant, a firestarter, and my best critic. I am extraordinarily lucky to have spent the last two decades with her. Every day she inspires me to be a good worker, a good parent, and a good partner, and every day I love her more. This book is for her.

ONE

Introduction

There's a restaurant chain in Pittsburgh with fancy Mexican food and a racist name. The chain advertised heavily, and one billboard was especially raunchy: "Take your tongue south of the border," it counseled passersby. I saw this billboard a lot when I lived in Pittsburgh and it always gave me a jolt, and a thrill.

"South of the border," of course, is Mexico, where tourists and outlaws on the run go, both seeking, in their own way, freedom: freedom from posses and overeager sheriffs, freedom from the banal and the boring. Mexico here is framed as a place of racial and national difference and, as the phrase suggests, culinary and sexual possibility.

"Take your tongue West" is not quite the same as "Take your tongue south of the border." Still, "goin' West" suggests a similar set of flights, from bad luck and bad choices, and similar new lands, marked by repeated ruptures in racial and sexual norms. The American West, after all, is considered (and has been for two centuries) America's most racially diverse and mottled region, and accounts of non-normative, even queer, sex in the West (prostitution, miscegenation, same-sex love and intimacy, bachelor societies, and widow land barons) threaten to outpace tales of pioneer families and straight homes on the ranges. At the same time, journeys West into novel racial and sexual lands help sustain, in productive contrast, the rest of America (the non-West) as racially pure and sexually temperate.

So too, south of the border, simultaneously foreign and erotic, promotes a vision of America as white, or at the very least non-Mexican, and sexually bland. Hence the jolt I always experienced upon seeing the billboard: Mexico and Mexican restaurants proclaimed as a destination for American consumers to enjoy lingual delights, pleasures of the tongue, food and, the ad lewdly suggests, otherwise. As a result, we have a billboard, one of many billboards, in a city not unlike many cities, that so elegantly captures a racial and sexual order that casts Mexico as a product to be consumed and Mexicans, and Mexican women specifically, as receptive, consumable, sexual objects.[1]

But there is a slippage here, an incompleteness in the ad that leaves the owner of the lone (and perhaps lonely) tongue unnamed. We are accustomed to reading such absence of markers, the unmarked, as white and male and straight. But what if the unmarked tongue does not belong to a white, male, straight body? Perhaps the billboard offers something else as well. What if the tongue is of a brown and female body? Or what if the journey south is by a man toward another man or a woman toward another woman? This is the thrill that accompanied the jolt I received from the billboard. What if there was more to the billboard than simply the proclamation of Mexican foreignness and sexual difference?

I take two lessons, then, from the billboard. First, in speaking of sex, the billboard speaks of social order as well, specifically racial and national order. Second, sexualized actions of human bodies, real and imagined, with others and with oneself, can be unpredictable and exorbitant, overflowing even, and can produce unintended and unexpected results. Titillating tongues, even those designed to enforce hierarchies of race and nation, could speak of opposition as well as social and sexual order.

In the history of Western America, talk of sex was no less potent. A century ago, Westerners approached sex from many directions. Social reformers proclaimed the evils of prostitution while medical journals warned of syphilis and masturbation. Men having sex with men were hounded by police and their intimacies harshly condemned by the courts and the press. Intermarriages between those defined as "white," or Anglos, and those portrayed as nonwhite or racially different were similarly policed and reviled.[2] In these sprawling and overlapping accounts of embodied impropriety and deviance, as such sexual discourses certainly were, distinctions of race and nation were rarely far behind.[3]

Actions of human bodies, then as now, were basic to the elaboration of racial and national differences. American race relations and racial hierarchies, in fact, are incomprehensible without a serious examination of sexuality. Think of the image of the "black beast rapist," or the hyperfertile immigrant woman, or the Latin lover, or the demure warbride, or the effeminate Chinese man, and sexuality emerges in each case as integral to understanding race in America. Interracial sex, for example, has proved especially volatile in the country's history. One of the reasons fears of interracial sex were so acute is the capacity of sex between races to blur seemingly solid racial distinctions and hierarchies, suggesting, for instance, that members of one race could find fulfillment, sexual and otherwise, with members of another race, or that individuals themselves, especially the children of these interracial relationships, could be racially mixed. Sex has also played a critical role in deciding who can and who cannot claim American citizenship in both a strictly legal and a more broadly cultural sense. Respectable individuals from politicians and shopkeepers to schoolteachers and suffrage leaders have for centuries had to assert their sexual propriety in order to be seen as responsible and trustworthy citizens. Restrictions on entering the country have similarly targeted sexual "deviants," juxtaposing supposedly normal American citizens with the purportedly "unnatural" sexual customs of foreigners. Women accused of being prostitutes, in fact, were among the first individuals banned from immigrating to the United States.[4]

Just as "taking your tongue south of the border" produced racial differences alongside sexual innuendo, so too did the production of sexual knowledge (the description, evaluation, and categorization of sexual acts) simultaneously enforce a range of social boundaries in the West. Among the most prominent of those boundaries originated with American colonialism in the region.[5] American colonial rule in the West is pronounced: the appropriation and exploitation of Mexican and Native American property and resources, the enduring US military presence, the resettling, with ample government help, of Anglo families into new homes within this newly occupied land, the dependence on easily exploitable labor from subjugated and impoverished colonial subjects. For Mexicans specifically, American settler colonialism was underway in Texas, New Mexico, and California well before the Treaty of Guadalupe Hidalgo in 1848, and Mexican loss of land accelerated throughout the remainder of the nineteenth century, as did the reliance on the labor of Mexican women and men in the expanding agricultural, ranching, and industrial economies of the West. Exploitation and subordination did not cease with increased immigration from Mexico in the early twentieth century. In fact, historians have used terms like "imported colonialism" and "colonized labor" to describe Mexican immigration to the United States over the course of the past century.[6]

The extension of American rule, however—whether as settler colonialism in the West or as imperial power overseas—was two-pronged. Dispossession and the many traumas of occupation were accompanied by a promise, though often deferred, of citizenship and eventual, though distantly imagined, civic inclusion. American colonial order, that is, though committed to vast seizures of land, the overthrow of native economies and cultures, and the supremacy of Anglo America, nonetheless also promoted itself as inclusionary. Turn-of-the-twentieth-century American colonial subjects (Native Americans, Hawaiians, Puerto Ricans, Filipinos, Mexicans) were depicted by a range of colonial elites as potentially achieving citizenship as long as they cultivated an assortment of correctly managed attributes, including civilized demeanor, deference to Anglo American superiority, and proper gender and sexual comportment. Vicious exploitation of people and resources could coexist, if uneasily, with tender promises of eventual incorporation into American society and citizenry.[7]

For ethnic Mexicans, this unsteady balance of racial difference, on the one hand, and potential inclusion, on the other, was especially acute in the early twentieth century. The first three decades of the century was a period of dramatic growth in the West as industries expanded and the population of cities like Los Angeles swelled with newcomers from both inside and outside the US. Mexicans, whether native-born in the United States and with deep roots in the region or more recent immigrants, were central to this economic and demographic boom. Between 1900 and 1930, the ethnic Mexican population of the United States grew from 400,000 to 1.4 million. In 1900, most Mexicans lived in either Texas or New Mexico, comprising populations of 200,000 and 93,000, respectively. Another 50,000 lived in California, with nearly 40,000 in Arizona. Three decades later, the biggest Mexican populations were in Texas and California, and Mexicans were a significant presence in the states of Arizona and New Mexico.[8]

As colonial subjects, Mexicans possessed important advantages within Anglo-dominated racial hierarchies in the West. While notions that only Anglos qualified as "true" Americans were prevalent, Mexicans nonetheless occupied an intermediate, middle-rung position along the region's racial hierarchy, below Anglo Americans certainly, but above African Americans, Native Americans, and at times Asian Americans. Mexican workers, for instance, formed the backbone of several critical industries in the West, like railroad construction and large-scale farming. They were also widely considered a religious people; as practicing Catholics, Mexicans were differentiated from most Asian immigrants and Native Americans, who were denounced as "heathens." Furthermore, US census categories listed Mexicans, tens of thousands of whom were American citizens who had been born in the United States, as "white" in the first three decades of the twentieth century. Valued workers, Christians, and "white" by government decree, Mexicans were largely exempt from laws banning marriages with "whites," and were allowed to own land, to become citizens, to vote, to run for office, and to testify against Anglos in courts of law. The appearance throughout the West of Anglo-run settlement programs that focused specifically on "Americanizing" Mexican women and men is testament to a widely held belief in the capacity of Mexicans to become—eventually, under careful Anglo tutelage—legitimate American citizens.[9]

At the same time, Mexicans faced multiple hardships during the period—political and economic powerlessness, virulent legal and extralegal violence, widespread public denigration as disease-prone, unhygienic, and sexually deviant. In fact, marginalization of Mexicans seemed to accelerate between 1900 and 1930. Broader anti-immigrant legislation, such as the 1924 National Origins Act, and anti-labor crusades targeting "foreigners" converged with specific, often violent anti-Mexican campaigns like the forcible removal of Mexican miners from Bisbee, Arizona, in 1917, the Anglo terror inflicted on South Texas Mexicans in the 1910s, and the repatriation campaigns of the late 1920s and 1930s. Moreover, Mexicans, designated for decades as "white" in the United States, were reclassified racially as "Mexican" in the 1930 US census enumeration. Racial differentiation and exclusion, in other words, appeared on the rise in the early twentieth century, and Mexicans were prominent targets.[10]

As forces of racial exclusion and differentiation seemed to overpower attempts to integrate and Americanize Mexicans, however, a range of ordinary Mexicans struggled to loosen the tightening racial boundaries in the borderlands and continued to press for the recognition and rights promised them as colonial subjects. This struggle to maintain rights appears with special clarity in the legal realm. For Mexicans, the colonial tender of citizenship, proclaimed first in the Treaty of Guadalupe Hidalgo in 1848, promised that Mexicans remaining in the United States and "elect[ing] to become citizens of the United States" would be "incorporated into the Union of the United States, and be admitted at the proper time (to be judged of by the Congress of the United States) to the enjoyment of all the rights of citizens of the United States."[11] In the decades that followed, Mexicans never ceased to press these claims in American courts. Spanish surnames, in fact, consistently appear in legal archives of the second half of the nineteenth century, in Mexican-initiated legal proceedings that ranged from lawsuits over land and voting rights to more ordinary appeals of convictions, writs of habeas corpus, and other sundry petitions and pleadings.[12] The legal system undoubtedly helped enforce racialized difference and, like other American colonial subjects—Native Americans, Hawaiians, and eventually Puerto Ricans and Filipinos—Mexicans suffered greatly under American rule. Mexicans nonetheless often appeared to approach access to the legal system as an important right, one to be both regularly exercised and heartily protected, and in doing so carved out from the law a space of potential inclusion and acceptance.[13]

West of Sex extends this legacy of Mexican legal activism in the United States into the early twentieth century by exploring trial transcripts, some of them hundreds of pages in length, from appeals cases filed to higher courts in the West. During a period in which Mexicans were increasingly targeted as foreigners to American customs and culture and portrayed as unfit for full rights of citizenship, Mexicans appealed over a thousand criminal convictions to appeals courts in California, Arizona, New Mexico, and Texas. Of the 953 criminal appeals heard by the California Supreme Court between 1900 and 1930, for instance, 41 involved Spanish-surnamed appellants, representing 4 percent of the total. In the Court of Appeal of California, between 1905 and 1930, 166 Spanish-surnamed individuals appealed convictions, accounting for 5 percent of the total criminal appeals (2,972) for that period. During the same period in Arizona, there were 78 Spanish-surnamed appellants (of 531 total) whose cases were heard by the Arizona Supreme Court. In New Mexico, 114 of 411 total criminal appeals (27 percent) decided by the New Mexico Supreme Court were initiated by Spanish-surnamed defendants between 1900 and 1930. In Texas, the number of Mexican appeals cases was even higher. Between 1900 and 1930, 677 Mexicans filed appeals before the Texas Court of Criminal Appeals, accounting for 4 percent of the nearly 19,000 total appeals cases heard by the court. While the appeals, taken together, were a small percentage of the tens of thousands of total appeals cases in the West, and percentagewise closely reflect the actual number of Mexicans in the West during the period (Mexicans accounted for between 5 and 10 percent of the total population in states like Texas and California), the cases, and the individual trials that I discuss, are nonetheless remarkable, offering a vivid record of the presence of Mexicans in the West in the early twentieth century.[14]

Historians must approach such records with caution, of course. The trials I examine in this book are to an extent one-sided: as appeals cases, all the defendants, after all, were originally found guilty in their first trials. Most trial participants also have considerable interest in the outcome of a trial. Witnesses testify for the defendant or the prosecution, while lawyers draft arguments and induce testimony in the service of a particular verdict or outcome. The success or effectiveness of individual arguments is also difficult to assess. Case files often do not include the names of jurors, much less present their reasoning for deciding in favor of one verdict over another. A guilty verdict in a rape trial, for instance, could be the result of any number of factors (credibility of victim, persuasiveness of evidence, lack of credibility of defendant, absence of alibi, errors on the part of defense lawyers), and the historical record often offers few clues beyond the trial transcript itself to suggest which factor, or factors, in the end convinced the jury of the guilt of the accused. Moreover, the trials occurred in the midst of a critical period of the professionalization and standardization of the American legal system. The success of certain Mexican appellants in convincing judges of errors committed during their trials may have resulted as much from higher courts' attempts to discipline and control lower courts, and lower court judges, as from Mexicans' ability to present themselves as worthy citizens.[15]

Following the lead of Laura Edwards, who notes in her study of turn-of-the-nineteenth-century Southern legal cultures that "the outcomes of these legal matters were less important than the fact that these cases were brought at all," I focus more on the statements made by and about Mexicans on the witness stand and in the appeals process than on the success or failure of particular arguments. I see trials as public events and testimony from the witness stand as public speaking, and Mexican women and men had precious few such public venues in the early twentieth-century West. Thus, despite the clear limitations of criminal records, when read carefully and interpreted cautiously—as I have attempted to do—trial documents offer compelling evidence that Mexicans considered themselves, under the law, entitled to defend their homes, their families, their work habits, their sexual desires, and even their innocence in American courtrooms.[16]

West of Sex focuses on the involvement of Mexicans in one type of criminal case: sex crimes. Mexicans convicted of sex crimes who appealed their convictions produced an archive of sexual knowledge and sexual practices in Mexican communities that is unmatched by more traditional sources on sex. The cases also offer an especially clear view of both the maintenance of and challenges to American colonial rule. In legal settings where discussions of sexual norms and aberrance were prominent, such as trials for crimes like rape, prostitution, seduction, and sodomy, Anglo trial participants often described Mexicans as different from, and inferior to, Anglos. Mexican trial participants, on the other hand, actively opposed such characterizations, refusing especially to concede to negative depictions of their homes and their families. Ordinary Mexicans (with few exceptions, the appellants were largely manual laborers with few financial resources or influence in the Anglo-dominated worlds of politics or business) often portrayed themselves in trials as respectable, hard-working, sexually temperate members of good families and communities. Mexican women and men thus could use the courts to assert many of the characteristics and comportments associated with American citizenship and American belonging. In doing so, otherwise ordinary Mexicans posed an important challenge to increasingly exclusionary tendencies in American colonial rule in the early twentieth century. At the core of the book, therefore, is this critical tension in talk of sex in the West: sexual discourses could function both to maintain and to challenge Mexican social inequality.

West of Sex emerges from the intersection of two fields: the histories of Mexicans in America and the histories of sex in America. The history of Mexican communities in the United States has emerged with far greater clarity in the past several decades. Award-winning studies have examined immigration patterns, urbanization, gender relations, political mobilization, generational tensions, work, and cultural production. At the same time, corresponding histories of sexuality, though growing, have been relatively rare.[17] Likewise, historians of American sexuality have produced numerous exciting and important works. Nonetheless, most such works have focused almost exclusively on Anglo Americans. Even the handfuls of books that do explicitly address race tend to be limited to discussions of African American sexuality. Rarely do histories of sexuality, especially the history of sexuality before the 1960s, speak of the sex lives of Mexicans in the United States. The period this book focuses on, early twentieth-century America, was a significant period in the American history of sexuality as modern forms of sexuality increasingly rose to prominence. There emerged, among other developments, a growing separation of sexuality from reproduction, expanded forms of commercial sexuality, a legitimizing of female sexual pleasure, a focus on sexual identity over sexual acts, an increasingly rigid division between "normal" heterosexuality and "abnormal" homosexuality, heightened medical knowledge and authority concerning sexuality, and an emphasis on personal fulfillment through erotic intimacy. Modernizing America was in fact fueled by a host of new sexual habits and understandings, and key characteristics of American modernity—the rise of mass consumer culture, the prominence of medicine and science, urbanization and new immigrant populations, emerging American imperialism—were threaded through with transformations in sex and sexuality.[18]

When Mexicans produced accounts of criminal, and criminalized, forms of sexual behavior, like rape, incest, prostitution, sodomy, and adultery, their words shed light on broader trends in Mexican sexuality during this emergence of American sexual modernity. One of the most important findings of this book is the extent to which the Mexican home could be a site of sexual danger. Though wider Anglo society vilified the Mexican home throughout the period as dirty, unhealthy, and dangerous, well-intentioned responses to such attacks—as Chicana historians have consistently pointed out—have too often erred in the opposite direction, toward the romanticization of the Mexican home. Trial transcripts offer a far more nuanced view of domestic life, one in which sexual violence could occur despite the presence of (and to the great horror of) loving and nurturing family members. In this sense, the book attempts a correction of sorts, a recalibration of Mexican domesticity that sees Mexican homes as no less—and certainly no more—dangerous than Anglo households.[19]

Sex was at the center of other tensions in Mexican families, namely concern by Mexican parents about the sexual activity of their teenage and young-adult daughters. Mexican families in this respect often mirrored broader trends in the United States in the early twentieth century where increasing participation of young working-class women in the paid labor force, rapid urban growth, and the expansion of commercial leisure pursuits like dancehalls and movie theaters fueled fears about the sexual behavior of primarily white, working-class young women. While these fears often appeared in generational form (parents' attempts to limit their daughters' sexual involvements and daughters defending their sexual autonomy and sexual activity), race was also an important factor. National anxieties about the seduction and exploitation of young white women focused special attention on interracial relationships involving men of color and white women and crystallized in legislation like the 1910 Mann Act, which targeted prostitution and the sexual traffic of women.[20]

For Mexican communities, as for other communities of color, the effects of such legislation and new judicial structures like juvenile courts were mixed. Mexican parents at times, for instance, used the juvenile courts to attempt to discipline and control unruly daughters. Likewise, narratives of victimized young women could be adopted by Mexican sex workers, who, as described more fully in chapter 4, could on occasion present themselves as innocent women drawn tragically into a life of crime. At the same time, reform efforts tended to ignore sexual dangers facing young women of color in their emphasis on protecting "fallen" white women. Thus, young Mexican women, though modern in many respects, such as working in factories and the service industry and attending movies with their friends, received few of the protections (limited though they may have been) offered young white women in the early twentieth century.[21]

Like sexual danger in the home, generational tensions associated with modernity thus tended to weigh heaviest on Mexican young women, not Mexican young men. Gender inequities within Mexican families, in fact, surface on multiple occasions in court records. For example, Mexican women seemed more likely than Mexican men to testify with the use of translators during trials. Inability to speak English was an important marker of racial difference in the early twentieth century (witness the popularity of English-language classes for immigrant children or the punishments meted out to Native American children who resisted speaking English in Indian boarding schools), and the presence of a translator during testimony often seemed to reflect poorly on a witness's credibility. Seemingly more likely to testify through the use of a translator, Mexican women in this way potentially faced another disadvantage in the courts. In highlighting the role of sex in the lives of Mexican women and men in the West, this book therefore simultaneously underscores gender disparities both within and outside Mexican communities.[22]

This book also supplies detailed accounts of other aspects of Mexican sexuality. Two case files from Texas provide a rare view of same-sex liaisons involving Mexicans. Cross-cultural sex is also profiled, from interracial marriage to courtship and romance. Other chapters focus on the involvement of Mexicans in commercial sex, from brothel operators to prostitutes and their clientele. Sexual desire is also highlighted, from the "normal" and accepted (heterosexual, marital, reproductive) to the transgressive and the "queer." Finally, the book surveys the erotic landscape of Mexican sex in the West, as Mexicans carved intimate space for themselves from garages in Laredo to riverbanks in New Mexico to downtown streets in Southern California.

The capacity of sexual discourses both to maintain and to challenge social order will thus share the spotlight with specific accounts of Mexican sexuality as central players in *West of Sex*. The production of sexual knowledge by Mexican trial participants illuminates other dimensions of Borderlands history as well. During the trials, Mexicans described multiple aspects of their lives in the West. Although the considerable majority of Mexicans convicted of crimes in the West, and those appealing their convictions, were Mexican men, Mexican women appear occasionally as defendants in appeals cases and more frequently as witnesses in the trials. Their testimony covered a wide range of issues from household labor to sleeping arrangements to courtship and romance and going to "picture shows." Mexican women described extensive family networks spanning the US-Mexico border and their own travel to Mexico to visit family or help relatives make their way into the United States. They talked of renting out rooms for lodgers or operating rooming houses and caring for sick neighbors. They spoke of childbirth and raising their own children and the children of others. Mexican men offered similarly detailed descriptions of their work and home lives. Witnesses described lunch breaks from collecting corn husks in central California and the timing of cotton "chopping" season in South Texas. They recounted working as miners in Tuolumne and furniture salesmen in LA, fixing *acequias* in northern New Mexico, and storing their corn harvest in Texas. They spoke of their family and loved ones, nieces and granddaughters they helped raise and parents "across the river in Mexico" they helped support.

Legal activism on the part of such ordinary Mexicans in the early twentieth century forces a reconceptualization of the history of Mexican resistance and civil rights mobilization. This rethinking is twofold. First, we must expand the parameters of resistance to Anglo domination to include seemingly mundane acts like filing an appeal of a criminal conviction. The Mexicans profiled in this book, as well as the many others not mentioned who also appealed convictions, whether sex-related or not, in the early twentieth-century West, devoted significant quantities of time and financial resources to appealing criminal convictions. Marginalized as Mexicans, some of these individuals were also convicted *sex* criminals, found by juries to be guilty of some of the most vilified and deeply denounced of crimes: sodomy, child rape, prostitution. Yet, such Mexicans clearly considered it their right to appeal their convictions to higher courts and thereby challenge increasingly powerful visions of America that sought to exclude Mexicans from the life of the nation. It thus seems not unreasonable to suggest that such Mexicans, even the most unsavory and seemingly despicable among them, be included in a broader discussion of agency, resistance, and political mobilization in early twentieth-century Mexican America.

A second revision would be to see such activism in the courts as broadening our understanding of the Mexican civil rights movement. Though Chicana/o historians and legal scholars have produced recent works on Mexican legal challenges and the civil rights movement, these works rarely cover the period before 1930 and tend to focus on major court cases and groups like LULAC (League of United Latin American Citizens) and the G.I. Forum. The cases discussed in this book were not major cases and did not have grand import beyond their effect on the appellant and his or her family and friends. Taken together, however, the cases point to a legal culture in the Mexican community that was well established and widespread. Laura Edwards has argued that "local law" and legal culture was a powerful force in transforming the early nineteenth-century Southern legal system, and it is worth considering whether ordinary Mexicans could have played a similar leading role in the early twentieth-century West. At the very least, it is clear that Mexican appellants, by the hundreds, refused to abandon their legal rights and give ground to forces of racial exclusion. In an era of anti-Mexican violence, mass deportations, and harsh rhetorical attacks, holding the ground on rights was no small feat. Such ground, and such stoutly defended legal standing, I suggest, may have helped nurture a legal culture of opposition that would, a generation later, blossom into legal victories like *Mendez v. Westminster*, *Perez v. Sharp*, and *Hernandez v. Texas* and eventually generate a fully formed civil rights movement.[23]

Finally, for Borderlands and Chicana/o historians, the enduring reality of colonial rule in the West raises an obvious point of comparison with other American colonial enterprises, especially those elsewhere in Latin America. Historians have often explained Mexicans' relative privileges within Anglo-dominated racial hierarchies in the West (exempt from laws banning marriages with "whites," allowed to own land, allowed to become citizens, allowed to vote, to run for office, to testify against Anglos) by pointing to their relative whiteness. Other scholars, however, have emphasized the role of colonialism in the lives of Latina/o groups in the United States. Frances Aparicio, for instance, describes "analogous colonialism" as a potential bridge between groups as distinct as Central Americans, Puerto Ricans, Cuban Americans, and ethnic Mexicans in the United States. Underscoring Mexicans' status as colonial subjects offers a much-needed point of historical comparison, juxtaposing the colonial experience of Mexicans in the early twentieth century with the more widely understood intensification and formalization of American empire in the aftermath of the Spanish American War of 1898.[24]

The book also seeks to brighten larger corners of American history. In the early twentieth century, political, economic, social, and cultural transformations raced through the country at a blistering pace, leaving widespread anxiety and uncertainty in their wake. Bedrock notions about what was normal and accepted, who was an American, what it was to be a man or a woman, "white" or nonwhite, native or foreigner, were increasingly rendered unstable and rickety. In the West, unprecedented racial heterogeneity, a harbinger of the country's current diversity, further strained such commonplace beliefs. Recent migrants from Latin America, Asia, Europe, and the American Midwest and South converged with a diverse "native" population of Native Americans, Mexicans, Asian Americans, African Americans, and Anglos throughout the region. In Arizona, for instance, in 1900, one-fifth of the population, 26,000 people, was Native American, with a substantial Mexican population as well. In 1920, over 100,000 Asian immigrants and Asian Americans lived in California. In the same year, nearly 750,000 African Americans lived in Texas.[25]

Racial mixing occurred throughout the West from regions along the Pacific Coast and the US-Mexico border to more interior locales, from big cities to small towns. In Oakland's Alameda County, for instance, six of the fifteen men and women charged with murder and attempted murder in 1910 had non-English surnames (Victoriano Barrero, Ow Sing Ock, Wong Yee, Chin Tung, K. Yamakawa, and George Fong). In Los Angeles County, of the twenty-six attempted-murder charges in 1919, nine were men with Spanish surnames, one was a Spanish-surnamed woman, and one, F. Sakimoto, appeared to be of Japanese descent. In one small Texas town, in a case described in detail in chapter 4, Spanish-surnamed Louis Basquez was accused of attacking an Anglo, Henry Schindler, as Schindler exited the home of Mary Chapman, a "Negro" woman. In other cases, prostitution trials from Los Angeles and San Diego as well as sexual assault trials from California, New Mexico, and Texas, the presence of interracial sexual intimacy and violence in the region is no less apparent.[26]

Racial mingling, however, is a far cry from racial equality or shared citizenship rights, and the suffering of non-Anglo communities in the West is well documented. Nonetheless, Mexicans were not alone in turning to the American courts as a form of resistance. During the late nineteenth and early twentieth centuries, a striking number of the most marginalized members of Western America (Mexicans, Native Americans, African Americans, Chinese, Japanese, South Asian, and Filipino immigrants) considered themselves entitled to use the highest courts in the states and territories across the region. Legal victories, of course, are a cornerstone of twentieth-century civil rights and freedom movements, especially legal victories in the post–World War II era. But legal victories are never without precedent, and the existence of a vibrant legal culture among racial minorities in the West not only before World War II, but before World War I, and even before the War of 1898 is worth pondering.[27]

The legal activism of ordinary Mexicans in the early twentieth century stretches American history in other directions as well. As I've mentioned, Mexicans throughout the region inhabited a hazy area between full acceptance and complete exclusion, between judicial rights and jobs, however menial and debased, on the one hand; and the often vicious and violent maintenance of social inequality on the other. Mexican sexual discourses exemplified this contorted civic status. When Mexicans highlighted their sexual propriety in American courts, however, they staked a claim not only on citizenship, but on a particular form of citizenship, one in which marital, reproductive, and heterosexual sex was preeminent. During sex crime trials, courtrooms frequently portrayed Mexicans, even those not accused of crimes, as sexually suspect. In sexual assault trials, for instance, defense lawyers at times attacked both the sexual reputations of Mexican victims and their living situations, seeming to view with special suspicion nonnuclear domestic arrangements like the renting out of rooms to boarders or households composed of extended families like uncles, aunts, and grandparents. During the trials, Anglos tried to associate Mexican sexual deviance (either in general or in the specific actions of the individual on trial) with a range of other aspects of Mexican lives in the West. Households, for instance, not narrowly composed of a husband and a wife and children were often viewed suspiciously by Anglos, and sexual attacks on Mexican children could be blamed, at times subtly, at times more overtly, on negligent parenting, such as the absence of a biological mother or father or the presence of extended kin, like uncles or cousins, in the household.

Mexicans, however, proved remarkably resistant to charges of sexual aberrance and racial difference. Married Mexicans, for instance, were quick to highlight their status to the court, as were those with children and grandchildren. Mexican witnesses also often refused to allow their homes and families to be tarred as sexually deviant. One California *Mexicana*, whose home was subtly criticized by a defense attorney, defended her home as hygienic and properly run and took the opportunity to depict the defendant as not only sexually violent, but a despoiler of a respectable home. Other Mexican witnesses conceded that their home lives differed from Anglo norms, particularly in terms of the presence of extended family members, but refused to apologize for such homes, highlighting affectionate and durable family bonds, some stretching across regions and into Mexico. Mexicans answered charges of sexual impropriety on the part of daughters and nieces with similar aplomb. Witnesses, for instance, acknowledged alternative family structures while at the same time upholding young women's sexual reputation by describing the careful supervision of chaperones during outings to dances and movie theaters.[28]

In *The Straight State*, Margot Canaday argues that the dramatic growth of the American state in the mid-twentieth century depended on a certain set of exclusions from citizenry, namely exclusions based on homosexual practices or status. *West of Sex* extends this critical observation both back in time, into the early twentieth century, and into a different realm of state formation, the American colonial state. When Mexicans spoke approvingly of their own marital, reproductive, heterosexual lives, they were speaking about, and for, and in the service of, a great many things. They undoubtedly recognized the premium placed on sexual respectability in the courts and understandably sought to depict themselves and their loved ones in the best possible light in the Anglo-dominated courtroom. Still, the courts were exemplary sites of American state formation, locales where the state molded, as much as it revealed, proper citizens. In this respect, the early twentieth-century testimony of Mexicans in sex crime cases may offer an early example of what in the coming decades would become a dominant feature of the American state: the drive to create married, reproductive, and ultimately heterosexual "straight" citizens.[29]

Viewing Mexicans as colonial subjects adds a further wrinkle to the history of American state formation, especially when we see Mexicans' demands and expectations as colonial demands and expectations, born from conquest and settlement and promises of incorporation in which sexual propriety was a central feature of any and all hopes of eventual inclusion in the American nation. Mexicans in this way followed a familiar colonial pattern. According to this strategy, when sexual norms were assiduously maintained and performed, sex could become an avenue to racial inclusion. This deeply colonial process may be worth considering alongside more traditional approaches to the emergence of the American state over the course of the twentieth century. Mexicans, of course, were not the only subjects of American rule in the twentieth century. But their position was nonetheless exceptional, poised in a typically ambiguous space between more widely acknowledged colonized people (Puerto Ricans, Filipinos) and racialized groups within the US mainland, like African Americans. In this respect, this study offers a view of the American state at one of its principal joints, the point where imperial America is hinged to its mainland partner.

In conclusion, the Mexican women and men who appealed their convictions for sex crimes like seduction, prostitution, sodomy, and rape to higher courts have left historians of sexuality with a wealth of information. Witnesses described sex with a level of detail and complexity rarely found outside either the memoirs of the rich and famous or reports on the infirm and the institutionalized. This is especially true when the case files include the transcripts of trials, which can often extend over a hundred pages of witness testimony. In light of such sources, this book is organized thematically rather than chronologically. Each chapter focuses on a different site of contestation: colonialism, home, prostitution, queer sex, and courtship. Since talk of sex and the effects of talk of sex (the creation by Mexicans and others of sexual knowledge) are central to the book, and because trial transcripts offer such rich sources of sex talk, I will devote considerable attention to individual trials involving Mexicans and sex. I also hope to provide a narrative that does justice to the complexity of Mexican lives, including their sexual lives. Close readings of the transcripts of these sex trials will highlight competing, even contradicting, accounts of events and seek to balance local particulars with broader regional and national trends. Individual chapters will also at times present selected data on sex crimes collected from three major Western cities: Los Angeles, Oakland, and San Antonio. Local criminal records often contain little more than dates, names of individuals, and class of crime, which could range from more serious crimes like murder, rape, and assault to petty offenses such as gambling violations and motor vehicle infractions. Age, place of birth, occupation, marital status, and racial designation tend not to appear, nor do more specific details about the crime or the arrest. Nonetheless, such records offer an important general view of crime and punishment, including charges of sex crimes, in the West.

A core concern of this book is the proliferation of sexual knowledge: how individuals described, categorized, and evaluated sexual behavior. The book explores the processes by which the circulation of sexual knowledge contributed to the policing of personal conduct and the enforcement of critical social boundaries. At the same time, and perhaps more importantly, *West of Sex* attends to the dissolution of social boundaries, to the production of sexual knowledge by ordinary Mexicans and the resulting oppositional claims to civic inclusion. In highlighting the central place of sexual knowledge in the constitution of American citizenship and colonial order, this book thus speaks directly to the contribution race and sexuality, intertwined, have made to the structuring and contestation of social inequality in American history.

TWO

Colonial Convictions

It must have been horrific, the scene that Altagracia Enriquez encountered when she pushed open the door of her small cabin in Merced, California, in October 1905. Altagracia had left her eight-year-old niece Stefana Grenada alone in the cabin playing with a doll while she and her husband pulled a nearby tree stump out of the ground. When she returned to the cabin, she noticed that the front door was partly open. Altagracia walked to the door and opened it further. She was shocked to see a man inside the small home, standing with his back to the door.[1]

"Then I found the little girl," Altagracia recalled, "with her legs opened and his parts exposed."

"Pardon, pardon, don't tell your husband," the man stammered, as he hurriedly pulled on his pants.

Altagracia turned and called to her husband, "Come, come right away, come quick, there is a man here." The intruder pushed past Altagracia and out the door, but not before her husband, rushing to the home, saw his face. Altagracia turned back to her niece and demanded to know what had happened. Stefana Grenada described a man coming to the cabin. He offered her a cup of wine, she told her aunt, and held an axe to her head, warning her not to scream. Then he attacked her.[2]

Altagracia Enriquez, who at first had not recognized the man in her home, soon identified him. He was Álvaro Fernández, she said, a farm laborer who had visited the Enriquez family with his brother and a friend days earlier. Altagracia's husband, Eduardo Enriquez, promptly reported the crime to his employer, George Barfield, who summoned the sheriff. Three days later, Eduardo Enriquez positively identified Álvaro Fernández as the man he had seen running from his house, and Fernández was placed under arrest.[3]

On November 28, 1905, Álvaro Fernández's first trial for attempted rape opened in the Merced County courthouse. The trial lasted a little over a week, but the jury was unable to reach a verdict and the judge declared a mistrial. A second trial was promptly scheduled for early the next year. Colonialism's unruly blend of inequality and inclusion is evident throughout the subsequent trial. In California, a half century of American settler colonialism had by 1900 stripped Mexicans of land and other material resources and rendered the vast majority economically vulnerable and politically subordinate. Anglo settlers also relentlessly promoted themselves as California's "true" pioneers, erasing or minimizing Mexican claims to the land and its history. Accompanying such figurative and literal subordination was an emphasis, also colonial despite its apparent inclusivity and magnanimity, on the incorporation and eventual assimilation of Mexicans into American culture and society. Immigration restriction had yet to turn to Mexican immigrants, as it had targeted Chinese and Japanese immigrants, and reform efforts sought to transform Mexican homes and families into proper American households. Anti-intermarriage laws, moreover, did not cover Mexicans, who were often legally defined as "white."[4]

Still, Mexicans were marginal members of Merced in the early twentieth century. In 1900, most of Merced County's 9,200 inhabitants lived outside the town in smaller villages or on isolated farmhouses and ranches. Less than 2,000 people lived in the city of Merced that year, a slight population *decrease* from ten years earlier. A decade later, in 1910, the county had grown only slightly, to 15,000. While Anglo Americans represented the clear majority of the population, the county was far from homogenous. More than one in five individuals in 1900 was foreign-born, with nearly four hundred Italians, three hundred Chinese and Portuguese a piece, and two hundred each from England and Ireland.[5]

While the United States census listed only ninety-three Mexicans living in Merced County in 1900, closer examination of the census reveals a much larger Mexican population. Based on surnames, over three hundred ethnic Mexicans lived in the small county in 1900 and more than five hundred in 1910. Mexicans in Merced nonetheless had little economic or political power. Like Altagracia and Eduardo Enríquez, most rented their homes and worked on the land of Anglo property owners. They were wage laborers and, like Álvaro Fernández, often newly arrived in the region, part of a large, mobile workforce, vulnerable to unscrupulous employers and fickle business cycles.[6]

At the same time, Mexicans involved in *California v. Álvaro Fernández* asserted certain rights associated with citizenship. Under American colonial rule, recall, colonial subjects were promised eventual, though often deferred and conditional, acceptance as citizens. Proper forms of land use, employment, political allegiance, gender norms, marriage patterns, sexual activity, and religious practices were some of the more important attributes of American citizenship and were emphasized by both leaders of Americanization efforts and ordinary Mexicans across the region.[7] During *California v. Fernández*, participants highlighted several such citizenly characteristics, namely their own diligence in the workplace, their properly constituted homes, and their commitment to family and marriage. While sex and sexual violence understandably stood at the center of the trial, a related set of issues also emerged, most notably a sharp racial boundary separating Anglos from Mexicans, employers from laborers, and longtime residents from more transient members of the community. The sexual setting also provided space for Mexicans, such as the defendant Álvaro Fernández, as well as Stefana Grenada's aunt and guardian, Altagracia Enriquez, whose testimony was by far the trial's most lengthy, to contest their social marginalization and make claims on American citizenship.

On February 14, 1906, Álvaro Fernández's second trial began in Merced. Fernández was represented by attorneys Ben Berry and Frederick Ostrander, while E. H. Hoar argued the case for the prosecution. The judge and the lead attorneys were all prominent Anglo figures in Merced. Judge Elbridge Rector was born in California into a recognized Merced family. His father was a Southerner, born in Tennessee, who arrived in California in 1849 after serving as a soldier in the Mexican American War. Like many in Merced, the elder Rector was also a farmer, with land along the Merced River. After helping to found Merced County in 1855, he became its first county clerk and later its sheriff.[8]

Álvaro Fernández's lawyer, Frederick G. Ostrander, was a native Californian, and the name Ostrander had a rich history in the region around Merced. His father was Harvey Ostrander, named in one account as a "very early pioneer of the county." Ostrander had also arrived in California in 1849 and tried his hand at a range of businesses, including mining, cattle sales, and running a steam-powered flour mill. He settled eventually on farming and led the movement to bring irrigation to the region. One of his sons, Frank Ostrander, "the first white child born in Merced County," had been a district attorney in Merced and secretary of the Merced board of trade, but had committed suicide in 1890 after his own son's death. The obituary noted that the thirty-seven-year-old had been found dead in the cemetery "on the grave of his child." Frederick Ostrander followed in his brother's footsteps in the legal profession and became a well-respected member of the legal community. He eventually served as a district attorney in Merced and as a superior court judge. When his father died in 1913, the *Merced Express* reported that "the Superior Court adjourned immediately after convening last Tuesday out of respect to the memory of the late Harvey J. Ostrander, father of F. G. Ostrander, a leading member of the local bar." Twenty years after the Fernández trial, Ostrander was still practicing law in Merced, with the son of his late brother Frank in the firm Ostrander and Ostrander.[9]

Though less prominent than the attorneys and judge in the trial, all twelve male jurors were also Anglos and many were farmers who hailed from outside California.[10] Eglin Evans, for instance, was nearly forty, a married grain farmer from Wisconsin. In 1893, at the age of twenty-six he had married a Swedish immigrant woman, also twenty-six, and the couple had four children. In 1910, Elgin and Minnie Evans presided over a family of two daughters and two sons, as well as two hired men, both "white," single, twenty-year-olds from Georgia. Juror George Vetterle was also from the Midwest. Born in Michigan of German parents, he too was a prosperous farmer. His wife, Elizabeth, twelve years younger than he, had been born in California, and by 1910 they had two daughters and lived with a farm hand. Finally, fifty-six-year-old Carl Clausen and his thirty-three-year-old wife, Petra, were natives of Denmark. By 1910, the sprawling Clausen family (Petra Clausen was the mother of thirteen children) lived with two Danish farmhands and a Japanese cook.[11]

Racial divides would thus likely have been hard to miss as the trial opened. Prosecuting attorney E. H. Hoar in fact mentioned race almost immediately upon delivering his opening statement. He recounted for the jury the events of October 17, 1905, when, according to Hoar, Altagracia Enriquez burst in on Álvaro Fernández as he attempted to rape eight-year-old Stefana Grenada. The attack, Hoar said, occurred while "one Eduardo Enriquez, a Mexican employed by George H. Barfield, [was] chopping wood, on George H. Barfield's ranch, on the north bank of the Merced River." Hoar went on to describe the day of Fernández's arrest. "The Sheriff," he said, "drove down to the bottom at the Schafer ranch and arrested this defendant [Fernández], his brother, and his two partners." The sheriff, however, did not know "which of the four was guilty of the offense," and took all four men to a nearby railroad station, where Eduardo Enriquez was waiting. Hoar added that there was "some conversation" between the men, but "they were speaking in Spanish and the Sheriff, not understanding that language, cannot state what they were talking about." At the railroad station, Enriquez identified Álvaro Fernández as the man who had attacked his niece. The sheriff immediately placed Fernández under arrest and released the other three men from his custody. After identifying the man who had attacked his niece, Hoar added, Eduardo Enriquez returned to his home, "back across the railroad bridge to the place where he was living at that time."[12]

After the opening statements, the first witness to testify in the trial was Altagracia Enriquez, whose testimony in Spanish was translated for the jury. Months earlier, and only a week after the attack had occurred, Enriquez had provided a lengthy eyewitness account in a preliminary examination and the defense clearly hoped to expose inconsistencies in her story during their cross-examination. Defense attorney Frederick Ostrander doggedly pressed Enriquez to repeat long sections of her testimony. During Ostrander's cross-examination, Enriquez described her arrival in California from Mexico in 1899 and said that she had recently returned to Mexico "at which time [she] brought all of the family with me from Mexico," including the parents of Stefana Grenada, who were relatives of her husband, and Stefana herself. The extended family lived together for several months, until Stefana's parents decided to leave their daughter with Enriquez. They did so for "company's sake," Enriquez added. "I lost my little boy about three years ago," she explained. Enriquez went on to clarify her relationship with Stefana. The girl had been born in Gaujillo, Mexico, around 1898, she said. Enriquez estimated her birth date at 1898 because she herself had arrived in California in 1899 and remembered visiting family in Mexico, including Stefana's mother, the same year that she recalled seeing the infant girl.[13]

The brief appearance of the trial's next witness, George Barfield, accentuated the distance between Mexican witnesses like Eduardo and Altagracia Enriquez and Merced's Anglo community. Barfield was a wealthy forty-nine-year-old native of California who owned the land on which the Enriquez family lived and worked. His father had moved to California from Georgia in midcentury and had helped found Merced County in 1855. Described in 1925 as a "pioneer of the county," William Barfield was one of the original three members of the board of county supervisors. The same account says of his son, "George Barfield is also a pioneer of the county; he was born at his father's place on the Merced River in January 1855." George Barfield and his Anglo wife, Flora, had lived together in Merced for over twenty-five years at the time of the trial.[14]

Married to an Anglo woman, a landowner, and born to a prosperous family with an extended lineage in the county, Barfield had much in common with both the judge and lawyers in the case and with members of the jury, especially when compared to the trial's Spanish-speaking Mexican witnesses. Barfield strengthened this distinction when he described his relationship with the Enriquez family and Álvaro Fernández. "I had in my employ a man by the name of Eduardo Enriquez," he told the court, and also stated that he knew "where these Spaniards, the defendant and his brother and two partners lived." Barfield confirmed the prosecution account that Eduardo Enriquez had promptly reported the attack on his niece and, unlike Altagracia Enriquez, was quickly excused from the stand with little in the way of pointed questioning from defense attorneys. Following as it did the lengthy testimony of Altagracia Enriquez, the brevity and noncombative tone of Barfield's testimony further sharpened racial differences. While Barfield certainly was less directly involved in the events at the Enriquez home than Altagracia Enriquez, he was treated with far more deference and respect than she was by attorneys from both sides. Though a subtler reminder of social hierarchies than phrases like "the Mexican" or "the Spaniards," the respect afforded Barfield highlighted his credibility, both as an Anglo and as a man, in direct contrast to the numerous challenges Altagracia Enriquez faced in trying to persuade the court of the accuracy of her account.[15]

Medical evidence was the next topic of the trial. Dr. F. E. Twining, a self-described "bacteriologist," had traveled sixty miles from Fresno to address the court. "I was called upon to make an examination of the little dress and a pair of drawers of the child for seminal stains," he said. Twining testified that he twice discovered evidence of semen on the clothes of Stefana Grenada, once upon the original examination, and a second time after being asked by the court to reexamine the clothes. But semen on the clothes of Stefana Grenada did not turn out to be the main subject of the doctor's testimony. In fact, both sides agreed, for the record, that his tests were accurate. Instead, the bulk of Twining's testimony concerned alcohol and the effects of wine on a young child. Besides clothing, Twining had also been asked to test a sample of the wine reportedly given to Grenada by Álvaro Fernández. After reporting that the wine "contained eight per cent alcohol," Twining answered a series of questions put to him by the prosecution, all designed to demonstrate one point: while the girl may have consumed alcohol, her ability to "actually remember and state what had occurred on a given occasion" would not have been impaired.[16]

Defense attorney Ostrander, for one, was not convinced. He pressed Twining to describe his own experience in the matter. "I have never made an experiment," the doctor conceded, "of what the effect of a cup full of wine of dago red would be on a child seven years old." Nonetheless, he contended, he had seen examples of the effect of "intoxicating liquors of various kinds" on children. He agreed that two cups of wine would have a significantly greater effect on a child than a single cup, but added that in his view, such an amount would "be pretty hard for her to get down." If a child, he said, "drank two cups full [it] would be more apt to make them sick than the alcoholic effect." "It would make them vomit," he added.[17]

The medical testimony is notable in two respects. Dr. Twining reinforced for the jury some of the racial distinctions coursing through the trial. His reference to the effects of "dago" wine on Grenada magnified the divide between respectable Merced, which likely included members of the jury and witnesses like George Barfield, and more marginal members like the Enriquez family and Álvaro Fernández. "Dago," of course, is a slur against Italian immigrants, a group widely denigrated in early twentieth-century America, and "dago wine" suggests a cheap, inferior alcohol, suitable for poor, immigrant communities, not successful, native-born Americans. The medical testimony also revealed the troubling presence of semen on at least some of the clothes of Stefana Grenada. While such evidence was not proof of Fernández's guilt, it seems likely that someone sexually assaulted Stefana Grenada, if not Álvaro Fernández then her uncle or another male family member or neighbor. Despite the efforts of family members like Altagracia Enriquez who tried to protect and defend Mexican children from sexual assault, the Mexican home, like all domestic spaces, including Anglo homes, was not always a place of safety and security.[18]

When Stefana Grenada was next called to the witness stand by the prosecution, she first faced questions from the defense, as the judge allowed Fernández's attorneys to "examine the witness to determine whether the witness was competent to testify." After directing Stefana to state her name, Frederick Ostrander asked her a set of questions, including whether she had heard of God or hell, whether she knew what heaven was, and whether she knew "where good little girls go when they die." "Where do they go," he asked, "do they go to some big city, some nice place?" Stefana repeatedly answered no to such questions, all of which had been in English, leading Ostrander to ask for and receive a translator for the girl. He immediately returned to the same line of questioning, and received, for him, similarly unconvincing answers. Although Stefana stated that she knew that "it was wrong to tell a lie" and that she would be punished if she lied, Ostrander formally objected to her testimony. The judge overruled the objection, however, and Stefana began her testimony, in Spanish like her aunt Altagracia Enriquez, for the prosecution.[19]

Stefana identified Álvaro Fernández as the man who first offered her wine from a small cup at the home of her aunt and uncle, and then "he threw [her] on the bed." Apparently pointing at her genitals, Fernández asked her "what I had there and I told him I had a pison" and he told her "to show it to him." Fernández then told her, "I have a pison too," unbuttoned his pants, and promised Stefana that in the future "when he would meet [her] he would give [her] five cents," before Altagracia Enriquez burst into the room and Fernández fled the house. The term *pison* drew the attention of the court. Asked for his translation of the word, the interpreter M. Molera (the court record did not include Molera's first name) answered, "I understand from my own knowledge and from what I have learned since the last trial, I understand it is the private." "It is not a Spanish word, really," he added, "it is a California word." Though he conceded that he had only heard the word recently, Molera claimed to have learned that "among Californians" the word was commonly known to "mean 'privates.'" One of Fernández's lawyers asked whether *pison* was "confined to the Mexican people," and Molera replied, "to the California people here, the Spanish speaking people in this state." In this sense, *pison* exposed an important tension in the trial between the recognition of internal variety within the Spanish-speaking community and the collapsing of ethnic and regional differences into a uniform Mexican identity: nonwhite and non-American. Where Molera and others saw variations by nationality and region, Anglos tended to see only "Mexicans."[20]

At the trial's halfway point, Álvaro Fernández had some reason for optimism. His lawyer, Frederick Ostrander, had been a vigorous advocate from the trial's beginning, dueling with witnesses and prosecution lawyers alike. He had exposed what seemed to be serious inconsistencies in the testimony of Altagracia Enriquez and Stefana Grenada, the prosecution's two star witnesses, and had skillfully cross-examined medical experts, another linchpin of the prosecution's argument. The defense's next strategy was straightforward: to prove that Álvaro Fernández had neither the opportunity nor the temperament to commit the brutal attack on Stefana Grenada.

The first step was to establish an alibi. Ostrander called three men to the stand, each of whom testified that on the day in question Álvaro Fernández had been working alongside them gathering corn husks on a nearby ranch along the Merced River. Pete Rodriguez, the first witness, said, "the four of us were gathering corn husks and were all partners in that business." The day of the attack, October 17, was, according to Rodriguez, no different than any other day. The men worked until around noon, took a lunch break, and then returned to the fields. "It was our custom to eat dinner at twelve o'clock and we would go back to work at about half past one or a quarter of two." Fernández, Rodriguez told the court, "was with us at that time as well as every other day."[21]

Álvaro Fernández's brother, T. A. Fernández, and another fellow worker, Melchior Mendez, told essentially the same story. On the 17th of October, Fernández testified that he and his brother and two other men were "all occupied in gathering corn husks." He described the daily routine of the four men, "all partners," in his words, "in the same business" of collecting corn husks. "We usually ate dinner about twelve o'clock," he stated, "and would return to work about half past one or two." Asked if he was "sure that [his] brother was there all day on the 17th of October," Fernández replied that he was sure, "because we were always working together."[22]

Hoping that the initial witnesses had been enough to convince the jury that Fernández did not have the opportunity to attack Grenada, Ostrander next turned to the second prong of his strategy: establishing the good reputation of his client. A string of witnesses, all Anglo men, swore to the good reputation that Álvaro Fernández had for chastity and for telling the truth. In what was likely a further attempt by the defense team to bolster Álvaro's reputation in the eyes of the Anglo jury, the interpreter testified that while Álvaro spoke Spanish, "the language that he speaks is entirely different to the language of the Mexican or Greaser which he is sometimes called in California." "I do not know whether he came from Spain or Cuba," the interpreter said, "but from the conversation I have had with him I firmly believe that he is Spanish."[23]

Álvaro Fernández himself was the final major witness of the trial and he made a point of repeating that he was not of Mexican descent. He began his testimony by stating, "my nationality is Spanish." He also gave the court a brief account of his last few months in the region. Before arriving in Merced, he had worked in two mines in Tuolumne for several months. In the Rawhide mine, he said, "my work consisted of pushing a little car loaded with minerals to the chutes." "I came down from Tuolumne about the beginning of September," he said, and began working at the Shafer ranch around the middle of that month. Fernández confirmed that he had been working with his partners gathering corn husks on the ranch on October 17 and stated that he "did not leave the ranch upon that day at all." He claimed only to have seen Enriquez's cabin from a distance and never to have been inside the cabin.[24]

Moreover, he was unequivocal regarding the attack on Stefana Grenada: "I never assaulted that little girl in any shape, manner or form, and I never saw her but once in my life prior to the time that I was arrested." He and his brother, he continued, visited the Enriquez home about a week before the attack, with the "intention of getting the job cutting wood" on George Barfield's ranch. They brought wine, he said, and shared it with the family. "The husband," he said, "drank first when I arrived there then afterwards the woman and girl came and they drank a little out of the cup." They stayed for less than an hour and then returned home. "I never was on that ranch again," he concluded. Unfortunately for Álvaro Fernández, the jury was unconvinced by his testimony and found him guilty of attacking Stefana Grenada. He was sentenced to six years in the California state penitentiary.[25]

Defeated in the courtroom, his subsequent request for a new trial turned down by Judge Rector, Álvaro Fernández nonetheless refused simply to accept his fate and serve his six years in the state prison. Fernández, once again represented by Ben Berry and Frederick Ostrander, filed an appeal in California's third appellate district in June 1906. The appeal listed a half dozen major errors supposedly committed during the trial. Altagracia Enriquez, they claimed, should not have been allowed to describe to the jury what Stefana Grenada told her about the attack, including the identity of the man who attacked her. They also argued that the judge had improperly limited the closing arguments in the trial to one hour and forty-five minutes, "render[ing] it impossible for the counsel for the defendant to submit a full and fair argument of the cause to the jury in that time."[26]

When the higher court's decision was announced in September, the three-judge panel revealed deep skepticism about the evidence presented in the case. Judge Chipman described Altagracia Enriquez's identification of Fernández as the man who attacked her niece as "one of the strongly contested facts in the case, as to which evidence is by no means clear." Elsewhere, the court's suspicion about Fernández's guilt was made even more obvious. While attempting to avoid "indicating [their] impression of the sufficiency or insufficiency of the evidence to justify the verdict," Chipman nonetheless listed, in one sentence, eight different "considerations which might be suggested lead us to the belief" that Fernández had been wrongfully convicted. The "considerations" included "the tender age of the child and the importance of her testimony," the fact that "the medical experts did not agree as to the results of a microscopical examination to discover spermatozoa on the child's clothing; [and] that much of the testimony was given by witnesses who could not speak or understand the English language and testified by an interpreter." Although none of the eight examples proved decisive in the court's final decision, it is notable that the inability to speak English, especially in the case of Altagracia Enriquez and Stefana Grenafa, casts doubt, in the court's opinion, on the credibility and trustworthiness of Spanish-speaking witnesses. Like many colonial regimes, facility with the language of the colonizer was a fundamental step in the process of Mexican civic inclusion and acceptance.[27]

Distrust of the evidence led the court to what they considered the most egregious error in the trial: the trial judge had improperly limited the defense team's final argument. Given the string of seemingly dubious forms of evidence, Chipman wrote, "we must conclude, under the authorities cited, that there was prejudicial error in [the judge] making the error complained of." So critical was this point that one of the judges, Judge McLaughlin, added a brief note to the decision. "I concur," he wrote, "but base my decision wholly on *People v. Keenan* and *People v. Green*, which I deem as binding on this court." The two cases he cited were the principal cases relating to time limitations placed on defense lawyers arguing their clients' cases. Chipman concluded his decision with a simple pronouncement: "The judgment and order are reversed and the cause remanded for a new trial." Álvaro Fernández, Spanish speaker, itinerant laborer, and newcomer to the region, had won his appeal.[28]

The verdict overturned, the case returned to Merced. Then, it essentially disappeared from the historical record. In all likelihood, Merced County prosecutors, gun-shy after their case was defeated on appeal, chose against retrying Fernández on the rape charges. It would have been the third attempt to convict Fernández after a hung jury on the first trial and the successful appeal of the second, and officials probably preferred to drop the charges rather than risk a third setback. The major participants in the trial also largely disappeared from the record. Four years later, in 1910, Altagracia Enriquez, Eduardo Enriquez, Stefana Grenada, and Álvaro Fernández were no longer listed in the US census as living in Merced County. Those remaining in public view were those who had been there in the first place: George Barfield, the owner of extensive property, Frederick Ostrander, the prominent attorney, and Elbridge Rector, the trial judge.[29]

While Anglos like Barfield and Ostrander remained in Merced, Mexicans like the Enriquez family moved on, perhaps relocating to elsewhere in California, perhaps returning to their native country, perhaps continuing to migrate back and forth across the border. As mobile members of marginalized Mexican communities, their experiences reflect broader, at times, colonial patterns in the region. The exploitation of resources at the heart of colonial rule included human resources as well, specifically human labor, and the Western economy depended increasingly on Mexican workers in the early twentieth century. American territorial expansion, in fact, would have foundered badly without precisely the type of labor (clearing fields, collecting corn husks, pushing mining carts) men and women like the Enriquez family, the Fernández brothers, and their coworkers provided.[30]

The trial in one sense reinforced colonial distinctions between Anglo employers and Mexican laborers. Altagracia Enriquez's identity as a Mexican, for instance, was established early in the trial and consistently reinforced, especially in the repeated questions about her birth in Mexico and enduring family links in the country. The description of her husband as "the Mexican" sustained this association with Mexico and Mexican identity. Similarly, the attempt by Álvaro Fernández and his supporters to distance him from Mexico and Mexicans seemed to bear little fruit. Subtle distinctions between Spaniards and Cubans on the one hand and Mexicans on the other were likely lost in the face of a much more imposing binary: American versus foreigner. While the Enriquez family, the Fernández brothers, M. Molera, and their compatriots may have been keenly aware of ethnic and national differences dividing their communities, the larger Anglo society tended to consider all those of Latin American descent, even actual citizens born in the United States, as foreigners.[31] Anglos, by contrast, consistently identified themselves as "Americans" and in doing so positioned themselves as those most deserving the rights of full citizenship. Those unable, or unwilling, to identity as Americans were thus relegated to a more ambiguous citizenship status; in America, but not fully American.

While the trial highlighted the foreignness of Spanish speakers, and their distance from America and American citizenship, other aspects of the case offered a different perspective on citizenship. When Altagracia Enriquez stumbled upon Álvaro Fernández sexually assaulting her niece, she behaved as did many other women and men, Mexican or otherwise, when they discovered evidence of sexual violence: she promptly reported the assault to police officers. Throughout the West, Mexican victims of sexual assault found that other family members would jump to their defense when news of the attack was reported. When Juanita Flores, for instance, told her mother in Texas in 1917 that the blood on her clothes was the result of a rape by her stepfather, Pablo Villafranco, Flores's mother, Pilar Flores, immediately confronted her husband and sought to have him arrested. "My mother said something to Pablo," Juanita Flores testified. "My mother did not continue to live with Pablo," she added, "Pablo has never lived with my mother since." Like Enriquez—and other Mexican women and men throughout the region—Pilar Flores did not hesitate to contact American legal authorities to defend and protect vulnerable family members.[32]

Altagracia Enriquez also appeared in the Anglo-dominated courtroom as a skilled ally of her niece in the effort to convict Álvaro Fernández for assaulting the girl. She was the trial's first and by far longest witness. In the four-hundred-page trial transcript, her testimony ran well over one hundred pages. Only Stefana Grenada's testimony was close in length, and it covered only seventy pages. Although the California appeals court appeared unimpressed, even suspicious of her testimony, twelve Anglo, male Merced jurors apparently had fewer concerns and convicted Fernández largely on her testimony. Lawyers for the defense had clearly hoped to discredit her eyewitness account, but found in Enriquez a capable and determined opponent. She fended off repeated defense maneuvers, including suggestions that she had been too overwhelmed by anger to accurately identify Álvaro Fernández and that she had whipped Stefana into confessing that he was her assailant. Near the end of her testimony, a diagram of the area around her home was produced and she was asked to point out the location of the tree stump, water pump, and stable. "This is the stable on this side, and on this side, the bandit passed," she answered, slyly taking the opportunity to discredit the character ("the bandit") of Fernández. Next, asked the distance between a nearby tree and her house, she shot back, "I am not a surveyor."[33] Such assertive, even confrontational behavior by ordinary Mexican women in the courtroom, in fact, occurred throughout the region, on both sides of the US-Mexico border.[34]

Altagracia Enriquez's husband, Eduardo, also wasted little time before summoning legal authorities after his niece was attacked. Nor was he ignored nor summarily dismissed by local law enforcement agents, but instead found his complaint against Álvaro Fernández readily accepted. When Enriquez pointed out Fernández as the man he had seen rushing from his home, the sheriff promptly arrested Fernández. For his part, though originally convicted, Álvaro Fernández clearly felt entitled to some rights in the American legal system. He appealed the conviction, after all—hardly the action of an individual stripped of all rights and left to the mercy of the law. Of course, in granting his appeal and reversing his conviction, the California court was not ruling directly on his citizenship or his capacity for colonial inclusion. The court based its decision instead on the trial judge's erroneous decision to limit the closing statement of Fernández's lawyer. As I mentioned in the previous chapter, the early twentieth century was an important period of professionalization and standardization in American law, and the higher court's reversal of Fernández's conviction may have reflected in part broader efforts to correct and standardize local legal processes. Nonetheless, Fernández initiated the appeal, and its ultimate success points to his commitment to a model of American citizenship spacious enough to include ordinary, Spanish-speaking workers like himself.[35]

This Mexican capacity for hard work, in fact, was a theme emphasized by several Mexicans on the witness stand. In many respects, for instance, Altagracia Enriquez was a typical Mexican immigrant woman. Like so many Mexicans in the West, she was a worker, both inside and outside the home. That she had been helping her husband pull a tree stump from the ground when her niece was attacked testifies to the daily range of tasks required of her. Hundreds of thousands of hardworking women like her arrived in the United States from Mexico and elsewhere in Latin America in the early decades of the twentieth century. Historian Vicki Ruiz says of these women, "[they] worked at home taking in laundry, boarders, and sewing while others worked in the fields, in restaurants and hotels, and in canneries and laundries."[36] Alvaro Fernández, for his part, testified at length about his recent work history as a miner and farm laborer. Such testimony contrasted sharply with anti-Mexican political rhetoric that increasingly in the early twentieth century described Mexicans as poor workers with inferior skills and unreliable habits.[37]

Critiques of Mexican work habits were often linked to depictions of Mexicans as unrooted and excessively mobile. As newcomers to Merced, Mexicans in *California v. Fernández* could not claim long residence and stability in the region. They could, however, reframe their mobility in positive terms. Altagracia Enriquez testified that she traveled north from Mexico not as an individual, but as a part of a family. Strong family connections, she suggested, did not dissolve in the United States, but were reinforced. In her story of how her niece Stefana Grenada came to the United States, for example, Enriquez straightforwardly described her trip from California to Mexico. "In January of last year [1904]," she stated, "I went to Mexico and I brought all of my family here." Like so many women across the country, Enriquez had also endured the loss of a child. "I lost my little boy about three years ago," she told the court, explaining why Stefana Grenada's parents would leave their daughter with the Enriquez family. They decided "to leave her in my care for company's sake," she said. Enriquez was thus a critical link in a kin network stretching hundreds of miles from Mexico deep into California's Central Valley. At one point, when she was asked about the birthplace of Stefana Grenada, Enriquez made clear that her connections with family, whether nearby in the Central Valley or in faraway Mexico, remained strong. "I naturally know where the child was born and when she was born," she said "because we are all of the same family." Mobility here appears in a far more positive light, as an attempt to re-form family as opposed to a sign of pathology and dysfunction.[38]

Mexicans similarly challenged negative accounts of their home lives and families. Altagracia Enriquez, for instance, resisted efforts to portray her home as dirty and disrespectable. Defense attorney Ostrander at one point asked her about the bed in the family's home. "Your bed there in the cabin," he said, "do you use sheets on it or is it just quilts or blankets, or do you use sheets on your bed?"

Enriquez answered flatly, "We have two sheets and two pillows and a quilt on top." "This man," she added, referring disdainfully to Fernández, "didn't even consider or respect the fact that it was the couch of a married couple." As in many, if not all, colonial regimes, the home was a particularly contentious site in Mexican America. Enriquez seemed well aware of negative characterizations of Mexican homes as unkempt and dirty and responded defiantly to the lawyer's questions. Defending her home, Enriquez also asserted her own respectable status as a married woman. Though she was clearly a marginalized member of Merced's wider community, Enriquez took the opportunity of her testimony to claim several of the basic prerogatives of American citizenship, namely a home life that was heterosexual, marital, and clean.[39]

California v. Fernández thus reflected dual aspects of American colonial rule. Testimony that highlighted Anglo land ownership and civic leadership, on the one hand, and Mexican labor dependence, transience, and foreignness, on the other, reinforced racial differentiation and exclusion. At the same time, ordinary Mexicans staked important claims of inclusion—the right to call the police when a family member was attacked, the right to appeal convictions, recognition as hardworking men and women, commitment to family and sexual respectability ("the couch of a married couple").

Across the West, other sex crime trials involving Mexicans provided similar spaces for claims of citizenship within colonial America. During the 1920 rape trial of Alexander Avila in Los Angeles, thirteen-year-old Daisy Atencio described being attacked by a man in an American military uniform and identified Avila as the attacker. Avila denied the charges and argued that another man, also in uniform, had actually committed the crime. According to Avila, the real culprit was "Albert," who had come to Avila's apartment shortly after the time of the attack on Atencio and shared several glasses of whiskey with him. Soon after Albert departed, a neighbor stormed into Avila's apartment and accused him of raping Atencio. Mrs. Foster, Avila recalled, said to him, "'I know you done it, because you have got uniform on, and I know you are dirty enough to do that.'" "I denied it," Avila testified, "and I answered back to her that I was not dirty." That night, however, he was arrested and charged with raping Daisy Atencio.[40]

Defending himself against the rape charge, Alexander Avila tried to accentuate his honorable service in the US military. While a member of the US army in WWI, he was subject to a poison gas attack in Europe and had been treated in various hospitals in Europe and the United States in the past year. After describing his medical care, Avila and his lawyer reminded the court of his military experience. "You saw overseas service?" his lawyer asked.

"Yes sir," Avila answered. Avila also told the court that when he met the other soldier, "Albert," the man noticed a military coat he was wearing. Albert, Avila testified, asked him, "You were in the war?" "And I says I was," Avila answered. Like a range of other Mexican trial participants, Alexander Avila portrayed himself as a worthy citizen. In his case, he framed himself as a man who had risked his life and good health in service of the United States.[41]

Avila and his lawyer also repeatedly referred to his "wife" in establishing his alibi. Noting that the couple had lived together for several years, but were in fact not married, the prosecution objected to the use of "wife," but the term appears throughout Avila's testimony and he even describes her as "Camille Avila," substituting his last name for her own. When a neighbor came to his apartment looking for him, "my wife," he said, "opened the door" to their home. Later, he recalled, "my wife" told him that police officers had been to the apartment asking to speak to him. Careful to note his US military service, Avila and his defense team were no less mindful of the importance of highlighting his adherence to sexual norms.[42]

Although the court did not comment directly upon his standing as a citizen or as a veteran of the American armed forces, Alexander Avila ultimately won his appeal to the Court of Appeal of California. The higher court ruled that the trial judge had erroneously not allowed the victim's Spanish-speaking aunt to testify through the use of an interpreter until well into her cross-examination by the defense. "Not only did the witness repeatedly state that she did not understand the language in which the questions were asked," the court noted, "but an examination of the answers made by her to questions propounded shows that as to many of them she did not understand or comprehend their meaning." The woman's testimony, the court continued, "should have been clear in meaning and to no extent left to the conjecture of the jury." Avila's conviction was subsequently reversed and his case returned to the local court. Beyond the ultimate success of his appeal, and his depiction of himself as a US soldier and married man, Avila's determination to appeal his conviction in the first place speaks to his sense of rights and inclusion within American society.[43]

Appeals cases involving sex could also generate legal opinions in which the rights of ordinary Mexicans were clearly affirmed by Anglo legal authorities. In 1927, Ignacio Muñoz, who was convicted of raping the twelve-year-old daughter of his employer, appealed his conviction to Texas higher courts. The decision, on the one hand, reinforced Mexicans' racial difference by repeatedly marking Muñoz ("the young Mexican," "Mexican boy," "the Mexican") as racially distinct. At the same time, the court viewed with great suspicion the testimony of the victim, who is never identified in the decision and, given the powerful tendency across the region to mark racially all non-Anglos (as, for instance, "Negro," "Indian," "Chinese," or "Mexican"), may in fact have been Anglo. "There was serious doubt," the court noted, "as to whether there is sufficient proof that prosecutrix understood the nature and character of an oath" and little corroborating evidence to support her charge. As a result, the court overturned Muñoz's conviction. "We deem it far too serious a matter to take away," the court stated, "the liberty of a citizen, even though he be an ignorant and unknown Mexican, and incarcerate him in the penitentiary upon the testimony of a child who seems to display an entire ignorance concerning the moral responsibility involved in giving testimony." "Ignorant," "unknown," and "Mexican," Ignacio Muñoz nonetheless managed to persuade the highest court in Texas of his essential rights as a citizen.[44]

Cases in which sex was not a prominent topic could also at times highlight Mexican challenges to exclusions from American citizenship. Ordinary Mexicans convicted of a variety of crimes, ranging in severity from murder, assault, and rape to minor theft and possession of liquor, initiated appeals cases across the region in the early twentieth century. Many of the cases involved crimes against other Mexicans, however a significant number of appeals, even successful appeals, involved Anglo victims. In 1904, for instance, Aniceto Guerrero, who was originally convicted of stealing a hog from an Anglo neighbor, appealed his conviction on theft charges to the Texas Court of Criminal Appeals and won his case. In a 1909 case from Taos, New Mexico, Malaquias Cortez and Gregorio García were originally convicted of killing a steer belonging to C. L. Craig. On appeal, however, the New Mexico Supreme Court reversed the decision and returned the case to the lower court.[45]

Pedro Barstado, Saturnina Garza, and Blazeo Pedro were similarly successful in appealing assault convictions in Texas in 1905. According to the court record, after Tom Gallamore hired several men, including Barstado, Garza, and Pedro, to pick cotton on his land, an argument erupted outside a local store over the wages owed the men. As the argument escalated, Barstado reportedly called Gallamore "the damned sorriest white man in Taylor County." Gallamore entered the store, found a gun, and proceeded to shoot at Barstado. Garza and Pedro jumped to Barstado's defense, disarmed Gallamore, and the three men then beat him severely. Barstado was subsequently convicted of assault with intent to murder and sentenced to three years in the state penitentiary. Garza was sentenced to two years in prison, also for assault with intent to murder, while Pedro received a fine of $1,000 and a two-year sentence for aggravated assault.[46]

All three men appealed their convictions, and in all three cases the Texas higher court ruled in their favor, reversing their convictions and sending their cases back to the local court. The cases are exceptional, of course. Most Mexicans did not win their appeals, though many did, and even those successes largely involved crimes committed against other Mexicans. Still, it is notable that a trio of Mexican manual laborers in Texas in the first decade of the twentieth century managed to convince a higher court to award them a new trial after clearly being involved in the violent beating of an Anglo employer.[47]

On occasion, Anglo judges not only ruled in favor of Mexicans, but commented positively on the rights of ordinary Mexicans appearing before the court. In 1920, for instance, Tomás Gutiérrez filed a petition in a San Diego court asking that his two daughters, aged one and three, be returned to him. According to the higher court's opinion, "the mother is dead, and the children had for some time been in the immediate care of the maternal grandmother, with the father's consent, and under an arrangement whereby he paid for their upkeep." After a dispute between Tomás Gutiérrez and the girls' grandmother, Gutiérrez assumed custody of his daughters: "He at first kept them at his home, with the help of a woman he employed, but later sent for and paid the transportation of a brother and his family, who lived in New Mexico, to come to San Diego and live with him and make a home for himself and the children." The juvenile court in San Diego, however, ordered that the children be taken from Gutiérrez and declared wards of the state. The court "place[d] them in the custody of the probation officer under the immediate care of the grandmother." Gutiérrez subsequently appealed the order to California's Court of Appeal.[48]

In its decision in favor of Gutiérrez, and reversing the lower court, the higher court lauded Gutiérrez as "an industrious man, earning good wages, affectionate with the children, spending his money freely to provide for them, and able and willing to care for them." While the court agreed with the judge in the lower court that the grandmother provided the children "better attention and more wholesome surroundings" than the newly constituted household of their father—suggesting that nonnuclear families were frowned upon by the courts—there was nothing in the case, according to the judge in the higher court, to "justify depriving the father of the custody of his children." The court added a sharp note in conclusion: "The juvenile court law certainly does not contemplate the taking of children from their parents and breaking up family ties merely because, in the estimation of probation officers and courts, the children can be better provided for and more wisely trained as wards of the state. Probably from the mere consideration of healthful and hygienic living and systemic education and training this would be true in the cases of thousands of families of wealth and respectability." Though clearly differentiated from "families of wealth and respectability," members of the Gutiérrez family were nonetheless portrayed by the California higher court as similar to a broader group of Americans and deserving of the right to raise their own children.[49]

In 1929, Beneficio Tendia's appeal of a conviction for transporting intoxicating liquor elicited a similar statement by a Texas court in support of Mexicans' rights. During a car drive with his wife and children, Tienda had stopped their car when they noticed acquaintances in a nearby sheriff's car. While Tienda spoke with the men in the car, the sheriff walked to Tienda's car and, noticing a "grass or 'tow' sack in the back seat," removed the bag from the car and discovered "a jug containing intoxicating liquor." Tienda was subsequently arrested, convicted, and sentenced to jail. In his appeal, Tienda argued that the search of his car was illegal and that the closed bag was not suspicious enough to warrant the search and eventual discovery of liquor. The court agreed, noting "the absence of proof that the appearance and shape of the sack was such that it led the officer as a prudent man to believe it concealed articles which offended against the law." Although one judge dissented in the reversal, Tienda nonetheless won his appeal. "Appellant appears to be only an humble citizen of the state," the court stated, "but he is entitled to the protection of the law in the preservation of his constitutional rights from invasion." Tienda's determination to challenge his conviction thus engineered a remarkable, legally empowered statement asserting the rights of "humble citizens" to "the preservation of his constitutional rights."[50]

The year this occurred, 1929, is not insignificant. The previous decade had witnessed steady erosion in the sense of Mexicans as legitimate Americans, not to mention a disturbing level of Anglo-led violence. *Tienda v. Texas* thus represented a powerful challenge to the accelerating national tendency to alienate Mexicans from the rights of citizenship and inclusion in the nation. Much had changed in the two decades after Altagracia Enriquez took the witness stand in 1906 and testified that Álvaro Fernández had attempted to rape her niece, Stefana Grenada. During that time, hundreds of thousands of Mexicans had found new homes in the Western United States, and their labor had help catapult the region into national and international prominence. The border had also changed, from a fluid boundary, easily crossed and recrossed, as Enriquez herself observed, to a terrain increasingly guarded and policed, especially after the formation of the Border Patrol in 1924. Mexicans themselves were increasingly policed as well, as a growing anti-immigrant fervor targeted Mexicans and Mexican communities.[51]

As this chapter has suggested, however, ordinary Mexicans, as well as the occasional "Spaniard" like Álvaro Fernández, refused to concede their claim on American citizenship during this difficult period. Like Altagracia Enriquez, trial participants asserted their qualifications for citizenship from the witness stand, citing such citizenly attributes as hard work, respectable homes, and commitment to family and marriage. Colonial rule in the Southwest had offered the promise of eventual inclusion and membership in the nation, and such assertions and the legal activism of Fernández and other Spanish-surnamed appellants across the region sought to force the nation to comply with its commitments to its colonial subjects.

THREE

Home Fires and Domesticity

The future must have seemed bleak for Tanis Cabana. On trial for rap-ing and impregnating his thirteen-year-old neighbor in Live Oak County, Texas, in 1927, Cabana faced a convincing accuser as well as compelling circumstantial evidence of his guilt.

The victim, Luisa Estraca, was the prosecution's star witness, appearing on the witness stand cradling a child in her arms. The child's father, she claimed, was Tanis Cabana. Estraca testified that Tanis had first attacked her while she was shucking corn alone in her grandparents' barn. "Tanis Cabana," she said, "threw me down and got on top of me . . . and said he would kill me if I wouldn't let him." "When he threw me down," she con-tinued, "it hurt me." Cabana raped her at subsequent points as well, "wher-ever he would meet me." "When I would go to take water [in the cotton fields] to my grandfather or my uncle," she said, "he would catch ahold of me and have intercourse with me." Estraca further testified that she "never told anybody about Tanis Cabana having intercourse" with her because she feared that he would kill her. Finally, she claimed never to have had sex with anyone other than Tanis Cabana, specifically denying that she had sex with her grandfather or her uncle. "I am telling you the truth," she asserted, "I need not be ashamed to do it."[1]

Like Stefana Grenada in the previous chapter, the home and its imme-diate surroundings were clearly not places of safety and security for Luisa Estraca. This chapter will focus on the home as a site of danger and contes-
tation in the early twentieth-century West. Assessing families and domes-ticity, determining proper sexual behavior, gender roles, reproduction, and parenting was at the heart of colonial rule. The racial taxonomies that sus-tained colonial projects depended on highlighting the proper families of colonial elites and disparaging the home lives of colonial subjects. Colonial

reports from a range of settings were filled with colonizers' accounts of the improperly, even dangerously constituted living arrangements and family relations of colonial subjects. And yet the proper families of particular colonial subjects—most frequently defined as controlled by men and based on church- or government-sanctioned marriage—could be described by colonial elites in positive terms and at times celebrated as examples of the civilizing potential of colonial rule. In the early twentieth-century West, competing portrayals of Mexican families (whether denigrating accounts by Anglos or the occasional spirited defense of one's home by a Mexican witness) emerged within a similar colonial context. Mexican homes, that is, could be sites of both racial difference and exclusion, on the one hand, and Mexican claims of inclusion and citizenship on the other.[2]

Across the region, depictions of homes reflected broader tensions between forces of racial exclusion and inclusion in the West. During Alma Carrillo's trial for murdering her husband in rural California in 1929, for instance, an Anglo witness was asked to describe the home of the Carrillo family. "Kind of a shack of a house?" the prosecutor asked Mrs. E. W. Leininger, a neighbor of the Carrillos.

"Well, yes," she answered.

"Dilapidated in places?" the prosecutor asked.

"Yes, quite dilapidated now," Mrs. Leininger answered.

"These people had all the resemblance of being very poor people?" the prosecutor continued.

"Well, yes," she answered. Similarly, in turning down Alvino Méndez's appeal of a murder conviction in the beating death of Mike Farnesaro in California's Imperial Valley in 1923, the court noted that at the time of the attack, "sixteen Mexicans were occupying a shack upon the Farnesaro ranch a quarter mile north of the place where the decedent (Farnesaro) was living and were employed upon the Sample ranch." In a pattern often repeated in the region, the opinion filed by the California Supreme Court repeatedly differentiated the "ranch" of the unfortunate Farnesaro family, as well as the nearby "ranch house" of the Sample family, from the "shacks" occupied by Mexican workers.[3]

Criticisms of Mexican homes could extend to entire neighborhoods as well. Samuel Ginsberg, a merchant testifying in defense of Cruz Vicuña during his trial for murder in Los Angeles in 1930, described Vicuña in a positive light, as a "law-abiding citizen," yet at the same time sustained a common image of Mexican neighborhoods as overcrowded and unfamiliar. Asked if he knew any of Vicuña's neighbors, Ginsberg answered, "I know several of them" and identified one man, a "Mr. Espinoza."

"Anybody else?" the prosecutor asked.

"Well," Ginsberg paused, "a lot of Mexicans live together down there." "I know a few," he continued, "I don't know them all." Acquainted to a certain extent with Mexican communities ("I understand Spanish," he told the court), Ginsberg nonetheless accentuated racial difference in his testimony, portraying large numbers of anonymous Mexicans clustered together in congested living quarters.[4]

Anglo trial participants also tended to dwell on the nonnuclear domestic arrangements of Mexican families, highlighting the presence and residence of stepbrothers and stepsisters, stepfathers, cousins, aunts and uncles, and grandparents in the home. During the 1911 trial of Frank Ramírez for raping the fourteen-year-old sister of his wife in Stockton, California, witnesses were repeatedly asked to enumerate the occupants of the house, which included Ramírez, his wife, their two children, and her sister (Carmelita Salazar, the victim of the attack), as well as several other members of the extended family. Ramírez's wife described the household as consisting of her "three brothers, and my sister, my mother and my stepmother and me and my husband." The defense, anxious to suggest that another man besides Ramírez had raped Carmelita Salazar, further imputed the reputation of the home by asking Ramírez's wife if she had ever seen "a prostitute at [the home] associating with Carmelita?" It is not surprising, of course, that sex crime trials, especially those involving attacks in the home, would tend to focus on members of the household and, from the perspective of the defense, other possible attackers besides the defendant. Nonetheless such depictions of Mexican homes as ramshackle abodes filled with extended kin reflected a broader Anglo current of thought about the inferior state of Mexican domesticity in the region.[5]

Prominent among such Anglo critiques of Mexican homes were those of Progressive-era reformers, largely Anglo women, who sought to remake Mexican homes in Anglo images through numerous settlement-house-style programs across the region. Historian María Cristina García has described the establishment of the Rusk Settlement House in Houston, which began in 1907 to offer "cooking classes, sewing classes, recreational activities for children and teenagers, and a social club for young women" to an increasingly ethnic Mexican population in the city. Though acknowledging that the exclusively Anglo staff ("Mexican Americans," she notes, "did not join the staff until the 1950s") provided much-needed services to the impoverished Mexican community, García is clear that a main, and persistent, goal of the program was to transform—and, in the eyes of Anglos, improve—the homes of Mexican families. Other historians have noted similar sets of initiatives targeting Mexican domesticity throughout the region during the period.[6]

Critiques of Mexican families, however, did not go unchallenged in courtrooms. Proponents of inclusion and Mexican fitness for citizenship, including ordinary Mexicans involved in criminal appeals cases, often defended Mexican homes as loving, nurturing, and properly constituted. Mexican witnesses, for instance, described multiple occasions on which extended kin networks provided important sources of sustenance and support during times of special need. During the trial of Eulogio Castro, who was accused of raping his stepdaughter Elvira Salazar in San Bernadino, California, in 1899, the accuser's aunt described how different family members helped raise her niece after the death of the girl's mother seven years earlier. "I was present at her birth," Manuela Quintana, who was the sister of the girl's dead mother, told the court, "she was born at Yucaipa." According to Quintana, after her mother's death, the girl "went to live at Castro's because Mrs. Castro is her godmother and when Mrs. Salazar died they took her to raise." Elvira Salazar lived with her godmother and her husband for seven years, until she became pregnant, allegedly after being forced to have sex with her stepfather, Eulogio Castro, and fled the home. After leaving the Castro home, Elvira Salazar took up residence at the home of her aunt, Manuela Quintana. As detailed in the preceding chapter, in which Altagracia Enriquez described strong familial bonds stretching across the US-Mexico border, and in the case of Tanis Cabana in this chapter, in which the victim, Luisa Estraca, is raised by her grandparents after the death of her mother, Mexican women and men throughout the West could at times testify to the warmth and love radiating from extended, not nuclear, family arrangements.[7]

In another case, from Texas in 1922, a Mexican witness, defending her brother against a charge of attempted rape, described their home as more American than Mexican. Celia Castañeda testified that her brother, Domingo Brown, had been at the family home the entire evening of December 19, 1919, the night he was accused of sneaking into the bedroom of a neighbor and attacking her in her bed. That night, according to Castañeda, "we were making some cakes and fixing things for Christmas time." "My brother was there too," she said, "he went to bed at 11 o'clock and then me and my sister, my young[er] sister, went to bed at one o'clock." "My family always cooked up things to celebrate Christmas," she added, "we celebrate like you all do here, we do not celebrate like they do in Mexico." In her testimony, Castañeda did more than simply provide an alibi for her brother. She presented herself and her sister as properly domestic in cooking for the family in preparation for a holiday. Significantly, she placed this domesticity in national terms. Rather than following Mexican traditions and practices, she affiliates herself and her family with American customs. For Celia Castañeda, and many other Mexicans, their well-managed homes and orderly home lives underscored their qualities as good citizens and proper Americans.[8]

Texas v. Tanis Cabana, the case at the center of this chapter, similarly speaks to the tensions between racial differentiation and inclusion embedded in American colonial rule. As in *California v. Fernández* from the previous chapter, Mexicans in *Texas v. Cabana* were clearly subjects of Anglo rule. Anti-Mexican hostility in fact was pervasive in 1920s Texas. "The dominant white society," according to historian Cynthia Orozco, "enacted the physical, geographical, social, and psychological 'otherness' of 'Mexicans' and institutionalized La Raza's colonized position in the new racialized order." In the legal realm, Mexicans faced similar barriers. According to Clare Sheridan, Mexicans in Texas were effectively barred from serving on juries until the 1950s. "While not prohibited by law from serving," she writes, "they were almost universally excluded on the grounds that they were not qualified to serve." In the Cabana case, lawyers and judges during the trial proceedings and subsequent appeal were exclusively Anglo, and, while the jury list from the trial is unavailable, it is likely that all twelve of the jury members were also Anglo. Anglo witnesses moreover consistently highlighted the racial differences separating Anglos from Mexicans and made clear that Mexicans were inferior members of Anglo-ruled Texas.[9]

At the same time, the trial record from *Texas v. Cabana* suggests that Mexicans were not entirely powerless within the American legal system and could on occasion turn the law to their own advantage. Luisa Estraca and her family, namely the grandparents who were her guardians, clearly considered it well within their rights to bring criminal charges against Tanis Cabana. Luisa was a prominent witness during the trial and showed few signs of being intimidated or cowed by the Anglo-dominated court atmosphere. The same was true of her uncle and grandparents, all of whom appeared confident and composed when they took the witness stand during the trial. For his part, Tanis Cabana, who was convicted of the crime, maintained his innocence throughout the trial and refused to accept the jury's guilty verdict. As the trial transcript and his appeals brief make evident, he was adamant in declaring his innocence and, though a man of clearly limited means, managed to cobble together enough money to finance the appeals process. Thus, while *Texas v. Tanis Cabana* speaks to significant aspects of Mexican sexuality, including sexual danger in the home, the case also illuminates the role of ordinary Mexicans in challenging their increasingly marginal position in both Texas and the region.

When *Texas v. Cabana* opened on a Saturday afternoon in January 1928, the first witness for the prosecution was Fermín Estraca, the grandfather of Luisa Estraca. He began his testimony by telling the court that he had been born in 1850, seventy-seven years before the trial, and had lived "here in this county most of [his] life." He married his wife in Live Oak County and "all of my family was born here," he said. Estraca recounted the past several years when he lived and worked on the property of Demory Miller with his wife and son Florentine and granddaughter Luisa, who joined the family "when she was very small," after her mother died.[10]

While the family lived at the Miller farm, Estraca's son Florentine "cut cane on that ranch, gathered cattle there, and did any kind of work that came up; and also farmed there." One of their neighbors was the defendant Tanis Cabana, who lived "about two hundred yards away" and at first "visited us a great deal." In the past year, however, "since August of last year," Cabana began to visit less often, and where once the families stored corn in adjacent pens in a nearby barn, "this past year our corn was kept separate and apart from the corn of Tanis Cabana." Estraca had also noticed a change in his granddaughter in the past year. He could not remember the exact date that he became aware of, in his words, "her condition," but he described going to the town of Lagarto and "asking advice from the justice of the peace about it." With "Mr. Bud Goodwin" and the Lagarto justice of the peace, Estraca returned to his home and "they talked to Luisa Estraca." In December 1926, his granddaughter gave birth to twins.[11]

During cross-examination, the defense returned to Estraca's description of his household, focusing special attention on his son, Florentine. "My son lived with us during the entire two years that we were on that place," Estraca testified. He was asked if his son was married and how old he was. "My son is an unmarried man, never has been married, and says that he won't get married until we die," he replied, "I think he is about thirty-seven years old." The defense asked Estraca to describe Florentine's social life, and if he ever attended dances or "picture shows" with his niece Luisa. "Florentine goes to dances," he answered, "but the little girl doesn't go." Luisa had attended movies in the town of Mathis several miles away with the family of a neighbor, Faustino Ramirez, and once, he said, "the little girl went with my son Florentine to the picture show." Asked later if he would allow his son to move elsewhere and live alone with his granddaughter, Estraca's answer was emphatically no. "As long as I am alive," he stated, "if my son Florentine wanted to take that little girl off by himself and live with her, I certainly would not let him do it." "Florentine," he repeated, "has told me that he is not going to get married until both my wife and I die." Though expressing clear reservations about his son's capacity as a caregiver (and even a hint of anxiety about sexual abuse occurring between his son and granddaughter), Fermín Estraca nonetheless presented himself as a respectable member of the community: he was a dependable worker, native to the region, a long-term resident, as were his children, and could reliably turn to the authorities in times of need.[12]

Estraca's wife, seventy-six-year-old Luisa Estraca, was the trial's second witness. In English, apparently without the use of a translator, she described in even greater detail than her husband had the arrival of their granddaughter Luisa (their son Santiago Estraca's daughter) into the family. "She was a year and two months and a half old when she came to me," she said, "and was very little and nursing at the time." "Her mother died," she continued, "and when her mother died, why, they gave her to me." "She is my daughter by raising," she added. Her son Florentine was the sole breadwinner for the family, she testified, and had been supporting his parents "ever since he was fourteen years old."[13]

Tanis Cabana was the next topic of Estraca's direct testimony. She confirmed that he shared use of a corn crib and a barn with her family. Cabana, according to Estraca, "visited my house all the time year before last." Luisa Estraca's granddaughter would also "visit the wife of Tanis Cabana sometimes" at the Cabana home. During her daily chores, the girl would draw water from a well that was closer to Cabana's house than the Estraca home, and she would pass by the field worked by Cabana on her way to the Estraca field to deliver coffee and tea to her uncle and grandfather. At the same time, Estraca said, her granddaughter seldom strayed far from family and home. "My granddaughter," she said, "never visited anybody but the neighbors there close." "She did not attend dances," she testified, "sometimes she would go with her father when he would go to town." "By her father," she clarified, "I mean Fermín, my husband." Pressed by the prosecutor to be more specific about the dates of the pregnancy, Estraca also mistakenly identified her granddaughter. "I know that my daughter went to see a justice of the peace," she said, "but I can't know how long it was before that time that I knew my granddaughter was in a family way, because I don't even know the days that I have." "I can't read or nothing," she added.[14]

During cross-examination, Estraca returned to matters of genealogy. "The little girl's mother was named Luisa," she said, "she was the wife of my son Santiago Estraca." "I gave birth to Santiago," she added, "I am actually his mother." Estraca was asked first about the age of her son Florentine and then of her son Santiago. "I don't know how old my son Florentine is," she replied, "I can't tell you how old Santiago is, but he is still older than Florentine." "I also had another son, named Leonardo, but I can't tell you his age," she continued, "I cannot give you an estimate of the ages of any of my other children."[15]

The defense team's emphasis on age is worth examining more closely. By returning repeatedly to the ages of members of the Estraca family, the defense perhaps hoped that a witness's uncertainty about the age of a member of one's own family would suggest to the jury that other, more central claims by that witness were also less than reliable. At the same time, emphasizing Estraca's uncertainty about the age of her children served to accentuate the racial divide between Mexicans and Anglos. Unable to recall the age, or even the whereabouts, of all her children, Estraca was presented as an unfit, or at best inattentive, mother, an association that drew upon common images of Mexican mothers in the early twentieth century.[16]

Florentine Estraca was the next witness called to the stand. Like his parents, he recalled his niece's arrival into the family when she was an infant, as well as his own years of supporting the family. A portion of Estraca's cross-examination focused on Cabana's initial grand jury examination in Lagarto. At one point during grand jury testimony, defense attorney Sid Malone had apparently asked that the clothes that Luisa Estraca was wearing be entered into evidence, even going so far as to ask that she, who was in attendance at the proceedings, allow the literal clothes on her back to be presented to the court. During the trial, Florentine Estraca was asked why he had refused to allow his niece's clothes to be used as evidence, despite the fact that, in Estraca's words, Malone offered to "buy new ones for the girl if I would be willing for the girl to turn the clothing over to Judge Hobbs." Estraca explained that he was concerned that she would be left standing naked in the courtroom.[17]

Bizarre as the notion may have been on the surface, Estraca's caution was perhaps not entirely unwarranted. Estraca was undoubtedly well versed in the racial inequities in Texas and seemed to consider the possibility quite real that his niece would be forced to disrobe in open court. While he may have been unaware of the recent Rhinelander trial from New York, given the expansive network of newspapers and periodicals spreading through the nation in the 1920s, it is also possible that Estraca may have known that during that marriage annulment trial, Alice Jones Rhinelander had been forced to undress in front of the judge and the jury in order to demonstrate the color of her skin. Portrayed by the defense as excessively, even suspiciously, protective of his niece, Estraca was at the same time attempting to steer himself and his family through racially troubled waters, and it is perhaps to his credit that Luisa Estraca seems never to have in fact taken her clothes to the court and its officials.[18]

Luisa Estraca herself followed her uncle on the witness stand, testifying, recall, with one of her two children, supposedly fathered by Tanis Cabana, sitting on her lap.[19] On cross-examination, she was first asked to identify the doctor that she had seen during her pregnancy. "Doctor Thompson, of Mathis, attended me at the time I was confined," she answered. Her testimony next returned to the matter of the clothes that she wore during grand jury proceedings and her uncle's refusal to allow her clothes to be entered into evidence. She was asked if the clothes that she was wearing were the same clothes that she had worn during the previous trial. "All of them [are] the same," she answered, "except the undergarments." At the time, she added, her stockings, shoes, and dress all "were newer and in better shape." Like many *Mexicanas* in the West, Estraca appeared undaunted by her appearance on the witness stand and seemed to answer her lawyer's questions with confidence and composure.[20]

Luisa Estraca's testimony is significant also in what she was *not* asked to describe. Considering the centrality of her testimony to the prosecution's case, the defense attorney Malone spent a relatively short amount of time examining her and limited his questions to the clothes she wore in court, the doctor who attended her pregnancy, and the fellow moviegoers who accompanied her to the Mathis movie theater. Missing is any mention of Tanis Cabana or attention to her own account of the attack. The defense thus chose not to challenge Estraca's accusation of rape or her social life (aside from a handful of questions about picture shows), or even the possibility that another man besides Tanis Cabana could have been the father of her twins. The defense may have concluded that Estraca was a compelling and sympathetic witness and judged an attack on her sexual reputation and intimacies, even in an Anglo-dominated courtroom, to be less than judicious. The defense strategy of course is hard to fully discern, however, there was clearly a reluctance to challenge the sexual propriety of Luisa Estraca. Such reluctance speaks once again to the uneasy balance in the trial between denunciations of Mexicans on the one hand and their limited civic acceptance on the other.

The final witness for the prosecution was W. L. Hobbs, the Lagarto justice of the peace. According to Hobbs, Fermín Estraca "came in to see me about the fourteenth day of November this past year." Hobbs agreed to accompany Fermín to his house to speak with his granddaughter. "Mr. Bud Goodwin accompanied me out there," Hobbs continued, "me and the old man and Bud Goodwin got in Mr. Goodwin's car and went over to Fermín's house and talked to Luisa Estraca." Hobbs testified that during his visit to the Estraca home, he noticed the proximity of the house to both the barn and corn crib and the Cabana family home. "The Estracas lived in a small house in an easterly direction from the barn," he said, "and Tanis Cabana's house is on the back side, on the north side of it." Though the trial offered opportunities for positive portrayals of Mexican homes and families (the Estraca family as loving, protective, and hardworking, Luisa Estraca as chaste and obedient), the prosecution, perhaps cannily, given the likelihood of an male, all-Anglo jury, concluded their case with Anglo male authority and knowledge: W. L. Hobbs, justice of the peace, provided the court with the precise size and location of Mexican homes.[21]

After the prosecution rested its case, Tanis Cabana's defense team took the stage, turning first to the possibility that another man, not Cabana, had assaulted and impregnated Luisa Estraca. The first witness for the defense was Eusebio Zapata, who worked for Florentine Estraca and had occasionally stayed overnight with the family. "I slept in the kitchen during the time I worked for him," Zapata recalled when asked to describe the sleeping arrangements in the two-room house. "The old man and the old lady slept in a bed," he continued, "and Florentine and the girl slept" in the same room, with Florentine and Luisa "both on the floor close together." Zapata's otherwise unremarkable direct examination ended on an odd note. Asked if he remembered speaking with Sid Malone, Cabana's defense attorney, Zapata replied that he had spoken with Malone, as well as Dean Miller and Tanis Cabana, earlier that day in a small room in the courthouse.[22]

The prosecution opened its cross-examination by immediately returning to the topic of Zapata's conversation with Cabana, Malone, and Miller. "They told me what to say and do," Zapata testified to the court, "Tanis Cabana has talked to me several times about this case and told me that he would pay me to come up here as a witness for him." According to Zapata, Cabana asked him to testify that he "had seen the old man [presumably Fermín Estraca] with the child." Zapata, however, stated that "it wasn't true what that man there [Tanis Cabana] wanted me to tell." Florentine Estraca had also never behaved inappropriately with Luisa. "Their conduct towards each other has always been all right," he said, "I have never seen any improper relations between Florentine and Luisa during my visits to their home." Zapata explained that he had originally agreed to help Cabana and lie on the witness stand because, he stated, "I was afraid of him." While Zapata's testimony was relatively brief, his conversation with Tanis Cabana and his lawyers would become a major issue in Cabana's later argument for a new trial. Also notable is the defense's emphasis on the sleeping arrangements in the Estraca home. The sleeping arrangements of immigrants and poor families in turn-of-the-century America were often linked with sexual impropriety, a strategy Cabana's defense team seemed, if subtly, to pursue.[23]

Sleeping arrangements and hints of sexual misconduct by family members aside, Tanis Cabana faced a seemingly persuasive accuser and was likely staring into the abyss of a long prison term. Perhaps out of desperation, Cabana and his defense team embarked on a curious path. When Cabana took the witness stand in his own defense, he stated that he knew the Estraca family but had never had sexual intercourse with Luisa Estraca. "I never did at any time have carnal knowledge of Luisa Estraca," he claimed. Under cross-examination, he repeated his denial. "I will swear to this jury and to God and to these here lawyers," he said, "that that's just a story that this girl is telling." "If I had done anything wrong to this little girl," he testified, "I would tell it now, even if they should hang me." In fact, Cabana told the court that for nearly twenty years he had been incapable of sexual intercourse with anyone, including his wife of several decades.[24]

According to Cabana, eighteen years earlier, in 1909, he had injured "his privates." "A horse was pitching me," Cabana testified, "and broke and run and fell down and caught me under him and fell on my privates." As a result, he said, "I have hardly any emission at all when I do have intercourse." In the past ten years, he added, the condition had worsened, and his wife, who he described as "in normal health, like the average woman," had not become pregnant since his accident. The prosecution challenged Cabana repeatedly about his assertions of impotence, and expressed great skepticism about the fact that this important detail had only come to light at this point in the trial, not at an earlier point, when, the prosecution implied, Cabana may have been more confident that he would be acquitted. Cabana, however, did not waver from his claim of sexual incapacity.[25]

After Cabana left the stand, a string of witnesses, all of them Anglo men, testified for the defense. Arthur Coffin told the jury that he considered Tanis Cabana to be "truthful" and to have a "good reputation." Cabana also reportedly "raised more corn than any other tenant on the place last year." "He gathered about 350 bushels of corn," Coffin continued. Though he was a witness for the defense, Coffin had similar praise for the Estraca family. "I never went over there that I didn't find Fermín either plowing or chopping cotton," Coffin stated. On the Miller ranch in 1927, Coffin calculated, Fermín Estraca farmed "about forty acres," while Tanis Cabana and his son "farmed about sixty acres."[26]

Dean Miller and W. V. Wright followed Coffin on the witness stand. "I am a man of family," Miller said, "and so is Mr. Coffin." "We both have little girls in our family," he continued, before describing his relationship with Tanis Cabana. "I have known this defendant since 1890," he said, "I have known him ever since I was about eight years old." "I know his reputation for truth and veracity in the community in which he resides," he added, "and that reputation is good." W. V. Wright, a butcher and part-time farmer, next testified that he had known Cabana for nearly three decades and considered him to be a man of good reputation. Under cross-examination by the defense, Wright described knowing Fermín Estraca as well. "I have known old man Fermín Estraca ever since 1911 or 1912, maybe 1913, somewhere along there," he said. Estraca's reputation was also good, according to Wright. "I think he is a pretty good old man," he added. In calling respectable Anglo men to the stand to testify to the good reputation of Tanis Cabana, Cabana's defense team followed an oft-repeated pattern in trials involving Mexicans in the West. While Mexicans could, on occasion, appear as character witnesses, defense attorneys leaned heavily on Anglo men to establish the credibility of their clients. A related theme, the fraternal bonding between Mexican and Anglo men in the workplace—and the implied, if not overt subordination of Mexican women—similarly appeared during the trial proceedings. Whether attesting to the character of Tanis Cabana or Fermín Estraca, the testimony of prominent Anglo men evoked an interracial setting of jointly laboring Anglo and Mexican men, a setting that served to bolster the reputation of Mexican men.[27]

Dean Miller's seemingly offhand comment about himself and Arthur Coffin, "we both have little girls in our family," follows a similar pattern. The suggestion, of course, is that as fathers of daughters, the men were especially attuned to the vulnerabilities of girls to sexual assault and to matters of sexual protection. By testifying in support of Tanis Cabana, the Anglo men demonstrate a shared (by themselves, as well as Cabana) patriarchal duty to oversee and protect girls and women. Missing from the historical record is Luisa Estraca's reaction to such posturing about the protection of girls. Despite her family's attempts at protection, in fact, Estraca suffered the greatest trauma of any of those involved in the trial, first in the reported sexual assaults by Tanis Cabana and second in the public description of the assaults she was compelled to provide on the witness stand.

A final proposed witness for the defense never actually appeared on the stand. Tanis Cabana's wife of many years would presumably have been able to confirm that her husband was sexually incapacitated and that he had been so for some time. She apparently contracted chickenpox, however, and was unable to make the thirty-mile journey to the Live Oak County courthouse to testify on her husband's behalf. Hoping to convince the judge to delay the trial until Cabana's wife was physically able to testify, defense attorney Malone had asked Dr. H. LaForge to visit the Cabana home and report on her condition. Told that she might be suffering from smallpox, LaForge discovered instead that she had "broken out with a severe case of chickenpox." LaForge stated that, in his opinion, a trip to the courthouse was not in her best interests.[28]

The bulk of the doctor's remaining testimony focused on the sexual and reproductive health of Tanis Cabana and his wife. LaForge, who described himself as a practicing physician with over a dozen years of experience, was asked by prosecutor W. G. Gayle whether a medical examination could determine if a man was, in Gayle's words, "desexualized or sterile." Provided that such a man "was in such condition sexually as to have emissions," LaForge answered, "his sterility or non-sterility could be ascertained." Follow-up questions from both sets of attorneys prompted LaForge to describe the various methods used to obtain semen samples from a man, including the massaging of the prostate in order to induce ejaculation.[29]

Perhaps in an attempt to distract the jury from the fact that no doctors had testified in support of Tanis Cabana's contention that he was physically incapable of either raping Luisa Estraca or fathering her children, his attorney tried to redirect the testimony. Malone proposed to LaForge that the absence of children from a couple who continued to have sexual intercourse might suggest a problem. "If a man and his wife have had seven children during their lifetime," La Forge agreed, "and the wife never became pregnant after the birth of the last child, which was some nineteen years ago, and she had had intercourse with her husband after that time, that would absolutely indicate to my mind that there was something wrong with one of them."[30]

Prosecutor Gayle, in turn, shifted the attention back away from Tanis Cabana and toward his wife. Gayle asked LaForge if there was therefore something unusual about a woman "who never becomes pregnant after the birth of her seventh child." LaForge answered that his opinion would depend on a woman's age and the number of children born to her. "After they have had a number of children," he said, "it seems they do not conceive as easily as they did in their younger days." LaForge added that some women who have multiple children, which he defined as "four or five or six," may become "sterile and less apt to become pregnant" despite not yet reaching the age of menopause or "change of life."[31]

Malone, trying once again to draw the jury back to the sexual inadequacies of his client, asked LaForge to speculate as to the age of Cabana's wife. "I would judge that this woman that I examined night before last was somewhere in the neighborhood of between forty-five and fifty," he said, "just judging from her looks." "You can't tell a thing on earth about a Mexican's age just from looking at one of them," he added, "but I would judge her to have been between forty-five and fifty." LaForge went on to estimate that the couple's subsequent childlessness convinced him that "there was something wrong somewhere." After LaForge left the stand, the judge turned the case over to the jury. When the jury returned to the courtroom with its verdict, Tanis Cabana was found guilty.[32]

Tanis Cabana did not wait long to appeal his conviction to the Texas Court of Criminal Appeals. According to the appellant brief, just as Cabana was beginning his testimony, the prosecution walked Luisa Estraca into the courtroom and positioned her "standing between appellant and the jury looking right straight at the defendant." The prosecutor then "directed the prosecutrix to a seat on State's counsel side of the table, which she took, during which time appellant was in the witness chair under the surveillance of the jury." The higher court, clearly displeased, admonished the prosecution: "we have many times condemned theatrical exhibitions before the jury." The incident, they added, "is not to be commended." Nonetheless, the court did not consider that "enough prejudicial facts [were] shown . . . to justify a reversal" and to award Cabana a new trial.[33]

The most significant issue for the court was the testimony of Eusebio Zapata. According to the appeals decision, Zapata "testified to certain facts showing opportunity that other male persons [namely Fermín Estraca and Florentine Estraca] had to have intercourse with prosecutrix." Under cross-examination, however, Zapata revealed that Tanis Cabana and Cabana's lawyers had pressured him to accuse Fermín Estraca of having intercourse with his granddaughter. A flurry of questions and legal maneuvers followed, including Tanis Cabana's attempt, while on the witness stand, to refute Zapata's accusation. Of central concern to the appeals court was the prosecution's objection, upheld by the trial judge, to Cabana's statement that Zapata had lied, when Cabana stated that he "had not made any such suggestion to Zapata and had not offered to pay him." The prosecution argued that Cabana's testimony was in effect an attempt to impeach the defense's own witness (Zapata, after all, had been called to the stand ostensibly in order to help defend, not further implicate Tanis Cabana). The appeals court was unconvinced. "We confess our inability," the court wrote, "to follow the District Attorney's logic." More importantly, the court disagreed with the decision by Judge Cox not to allow Cabana to testify that Zapata had lied about their conversation. The prosecution, the appeals court argued, had introduced new evidence into the trial when Zapata claimed during cross-examination that he had been offered money by the defendant to accuse Fermín Estraca of rape. The defense had the right to "contradict or discredit such newly developed evidence," the court concluded, even if in the process the defense would be forced to impeach its own witness and in effect call its own witness a liar.[34]

In the end, the Texas higher court ruled in favor of Tanis Cabana. He emerged victorious from the appeals court and was awarded a new trial. The court's written decision encapsulated the vexed position of Mexicans in the Southwest. Judge Martin, the author of the decision, was clearly persuaded that Tanis Cabana had been treated unfairly by the trial court and deserved a new trial. At the same time, Martin and his colleagues seemed keen to point out the salience of race and racial difference in the case. Martin's written decision began with a brief summary of the case. "The interested parties are Mexicans," he wrote, and the victim was "shown to be a Mexican girl from thirteen to fifteen years old." By describing the "interested parties" in the case in the first sentence as Mexican, Martin installed a dividing line between Mexicans, on the one side, and Anglos, whose racial and ethnic identity is not explicitly mentioned, on the other.[35]

This border was reinforced by explicit references to the sexual improprieties involved in the case. Martin's rhetoric was restrained at first, recounting the sexual aspects of the trial in more distant, clinical terms ("several acts of intercourse," "impotence," "act of copulation"). Halfway into the decision, however, his language changed dramatically. Cabana, he said, "gave testimony showing his physical inability to copulate, the repulsive details of which are not necessary to set out fully." "Repulsive" is notably strong language for a judge on Texas's highest court of appeals. Paired with the use of "Mexican" to identify the trial's "interested parties," Martin's decision created a clear racial and sexual boundary, even as he was defending Cabana's right for a new trial.[36]

This tension between inclusion on the one hand and Mexican racial difference on the other was evident throughout the trial of Tanis Cabana. Recall doctor LaForge's testimony ("You can't tell a thing on earth about a

Mexican's age just from looking at one of them, but I would judge her to have been between forty-five and fifty"), which framed racial difference in terms of age and appearance. Another witness, Arthur Coffin, described his impression of Tanis Cabana under cross-examination. "I consider him to be an honest, truthful Mexican," he reported. Coffin also recalled meeting Florentine Estraca, Luisa's uncle. "Florentine Estraca worked over at Demory Miller's place across the river sometimes this past year," he remembered, "and there were also some twelve or fifteen other Mexicans." Coffin recalled a conversation with Florentine and Eusebio Zapata in the previous April. "Florentine and Eusebio and two other Mexican boys were there," he said. Mexicans themselves at times reinforced the border separating the two groups. During his testimony, Tanis Cabana described his duties at Demory Miller's farm. "When Mr. Demory is not there, I am in charge of all the work on the place," he stated, "insofar as the Mexicans are concerned."[37]

W. L. Hobbs's testimony for the prosecution revealed a similar dividing line between Anglos and Mexicans. Hobbs recounted his interview of Luisa Estraca when "me and the old man and Bud Goodwin got in Mr. Goodwin's car and went over to Fermín's house." Hobbs identifies Fermín Estraca, on the one hand, as "the old man" and by his first name Fermín, while he uses Bud Goodwin's full name and "Mr. Bud Goodwin" when referring to Goodwin. It is possible, of course, even likely, that many Texans, regardless of their own race, addressed elite men like Bud Goodwin with deference. Non-elite Anglos, especially those involved in sexual improprieties, may have also been referred to at times by their first names or as "old men." But the fact remains that throughout the trial of Tanis Cabana, no Anglo is described, either by Anglos or Mexicans, as an "old man" or with simply a first name (such as "Bud" rather than "Mr. Bud Goodwin" or "Demory" rather than "Mr. Miller"). Mexicans, in contrast, are consistently referred to by their first names or as "the old man" or "the old woman" or "the Mexicans."[38]

For Tanis Cabana and the Estraca family, other government documents reinforced their marginal role in broader American society. None of the four Estraca family members, for instance, appear in the 1930 census; that is, none of the four with the last name "Estraca." The Karnes County, Texas, census from 1930 includes the four-person "Estrigo" family—Florentine, the head of household, Fermín and Luisa, listed as father and mother respectively, and Luisa, who is listed as a sister. Unlike the Estraca family, who were mistakenly recorded as "Estrigo," Tanis Cabana appears to have been overlooked entirely by census takers in Texas. Cabana, who described himself in the trial as fifty-one in 1927, makes no appearance in the 1910,

1920, or 1930 Texas census (nor does a Tanis Cabana of the correct age appear anywhere in a census in the Southwest in the early twentieth century).[39]

At the same time that Mexicans were rendered socially marginal in *Texas v. Cabana*, the trial provided a venue for more positive depictions of Mexicans. Lawyers on both sides of the aisle made clear to the court that both the Cabana and Estraca families were longtime residents in Live Oak County and were well-known members of the community. Cabana's defense team made a special point of establishing their client's ties to the region. Arthur Coffin, when asked how long he had known Cabana, answered, "It's hard to say just how long I have known him, but I have known him the biggest part of my life and he worked for my father when I was a boy." "That's something like twenty-five or thirty years," he added. The next witness, Dean Miller, stated, "I have known the defendant personally for about thirty-seven years . . . so I have known him ever since I was about eight years old." Another witness, W. V. Wright, a local butcher, had also known Cabana for several decades. "I have known the defendant about twenty-eight or thirty years," he said.[40]

Anglo witnesses were also asked to describe their relationship with Fermín Estraca, Luisa's grandfather. During a brief cross-examination, W. V. Wright was asked how long he had known Fermín. "I think I have known old man Fermín Estraca ever since 1911 or 1912, maybe 1913," he answered, "I think he is a pretty good old man." "I have also known old Fermín for a good many years," Arthur Coffin reported, "I have known him since he farmed for Vivian Miller along about 1916." Dean Miller told the court, "I have known this old man Fermín for a long time, and he is a man of good reputation." While Mexicans were clearly treated as racially different and to a significant extent inferior during the trial, such praise for non-elite Mexicans in 1920s Texas in a public setting like a courtroom suggests that the possibility of Mexican acceptance, and perhaps even citizenship, could emerge in the midst of virulent anti-Mexican crusades.[41]

As with the case discussed in the previous chapter, the space offered by sexual discourses in *Texas v. Cabana* for competing visions of Mexican inclusion and exclusion also presented details about sexual danger in the home.[42] Such cases bolster historian Lynn Sacco's account of child rape and incest in turn-of-the-twentieth-century America. While such accusations, of incest especially, were rarely extended to middle-class families (as Sacco argues, gonorrheal infections in the daughters of middle-class families elicited fantastic and medically unsupported explanations ranging from shared sleeping arrangements with other girls and women to unclean toilet seats), the fact remains that young girls and boys throughout America were subject to sexual violence in domestic settings. In turn-of-the-century New York City, for instance, historian Stephen Robertson notes that the home similarly offered few more protections to young children than did the streets or the public parks. "When approached by their assailants," Robertson points out, "just as many girls were close to home, in hallways, bathrooms, and yards, and within apartments, as girls were playing or walking in the street." Of forty cases in which the location of the assaults was recorded, more than half (twenty-two) occurred around the home of the child. In New York, doctors and court officials could also use the opportunity of the trial to criticize the condition of the victim's home, critiques that paralleled many of the charges of domestic disarray leveled against Mexican families in the West. Finally, like many Mexican families, many parents and family members in New York who discovered injuries on a child seemed not to hesitate to summon the police and report the assault.[43]

Sexual violence in the home appeared to inflict disproportionate harm on Mexican girls and women, reflecting seemingly widespread gender disparities in the West, in Mexican as well as non-Mexican communities. Acknowledging the determination by certain Mexican defendants to challenge their convictions on criminal charges should not obscure some of the original charges brought against many of the men profiled in this book, charges that could often involve horrifying sexual violence. Early twentieth-century efforts across the nation to protect young women, even young Mexican women and other women of color, contained—in a most generous assessment—significant gaps, where reformers, such as age of consent activists, reinforced rather than undermined prevailing social inequities.[44] In this respect, sex crime trials reveal the uneven terrain of Mexican citizenship claims: while Mexican men, and significant numbers of Mexican women, used the courts with purpose and aplomb, trial records also contain evidence of ongoing sexual violence committed against vulnerable Mexican women and girls.

A final example from the West—like the Cabana trial, also from 1920s Texas—highlights both sexual violence committed against young Mexican women in and around the home and the tension between racial exclusion and inclusion in the West. In 1923, eight-year-old Mercedes Pérez from Fort Worth, Texas, described a series of attacks by a family friend, Santiago Martínez. "The first time that I was with him," she said, "he taken [sic] me to a garage back of the home." "The last time he did it before his arrest was under the tree by the side of the house," she continued, adding that "the time in the automobile was in the day time and the last time under the tree was at night." At first she told no one of the attack, including her mother, because, she said, "Martínez told me he would whip me if I told." Martínez was only arrested when the girl developed an infection with gonorrhea. A different doctor testified that he had made a physical examination of Martínez while he was being held in jail on the rape charges and that Martínez too had gonorrhea. Most incriminating was a statement signed by Martínez admitting that he had "stayed with Mrs. Mercedes Pérez's daughter on two occasions and had intercourse with her both times." Moreover, he attested to having gonorrhea when he had intercourse with the Pérez girl. "I did not think I would give it to her," he said, "she being a little girl and me being a grown man."[45]

Santiago Martínez told a much different story during his trial. He described, through an interpreter, arriving in the United States from Mexico six years earlier and how he and his brother had "paid their way" for his mother and sister-in-law and a friend to come to the country in 1917. He had known the Pérez family, owners of a grocery store and themselves immigrants from Spain, for several years, he said, and Francisco Pérez had even loaned him seventy-five dollars to pay for his mother's trip to the United States. Though he was acquainted with Mercedes Pérez, he was adamant about the attacks. "I have never harmed that little girl since I have known her," he swore. Nor, he said, had he ever had gonorrhea. As for the confession that he signed, Martínez claimed that it had been coerced. The interpreter, he said, took out a gun and "showed it to me and told me that if I did not sign that he would blow my brains out." Fearing for his life, Martínez signed the statement.[46]

Martínez, however, also revealed that he had been engaged in a long-term sexual affair with Mercedes Pérez's mother. "[I] have known her pretty good," he said, "and have had intercourse with her many times out there in the store where she lives." "We have been sweethearts since 1919," he added, but explained that the affair ended a year earlier when, according to Martínez, "my money played out . . . and I did not have any more to give her." Pressed under cross-examination, Martínez admitted to a series of unflattering facts, while at the same time maintaining his innocence of the rape charges: "It is a fact that I have had intercourse with the little girl's mother, that I have been with her; I have been staying with the wife of this man that loaned me the $75.00 to get my mother and sister and bring them to the United States; yes I make that claim before this jury and I also bought groceries at that man's store and they treated me alright and I was trading there at the time I was arrested." Martínez was convicted and sentenced to fifty years in the Texas state penitentiary. He successfully appealed the conviction, however, after convincing the Texas appeals court that the interpreter's actions cast enough suspicion on the verdict to warrant a new trial. Deeply unsympathetic an individual as he was, Santiago Martínez, a recent migrant to the United States from Mexico with seemingly few financial resources, nonetheless managed to conduct a successful appeal of his rape conviction in 1920s Texas.[47]

While sex—and sexual violence—was the primary focus of *Texas v. Martínez*, the trial also served as a site for racial differentiation. Dr. Alden Coffey, for instance, described examining "this little Mexican girl, Mercedes Pérez," while another doctor testified, "I know this little Spanish girl Mercedes." Martínez's defense team called several character witnesses, all Anglo men, who testified to his good character and reputation for honesty. Chester Jenkins, a supervisor at the George W. Armstrong & Company Rolling Mill, said that Martínez's "reputation is good among Mexicans" and that "his reputation is good in the plant so far as a workman and getting along with other Mexicans is concerned." R. L. Sanders, a foreman for the Texas and Pacific Railroad, told the court that he had known Martínez for over a year. "I have on an average thirty-two or thirty-three Mexicans working on my gang and the defendant worked twelve or thirteen months," he testified. Cal Estill, the district attorney who solicited Martínez's statement, similarly told the court, "I have worked with Mexicans a little three or four months and I was with them constantly and understand some Spanish." Asked to describe whether Martínez appeared frightened during questioning Estill answered, "I cannot testify as to his race not showing emotions or feeling, [but] he did not have the appearance of being scared." Estill thus imposed a formidable racial barrier between "Americans" and Mexicans, the latter constituting a separate race that, in Estill's estimation, may be so different from Anglos that they do not even share the expression of a basic human emotion like fear.[48]

At the same time that racial differences were accentuated, other testimony during the trial offered examples of racial intermingling and complexity. Following Estill on the stand, Harry Tepfer, the interpreter and police officer accused of threatening to kill Martínez if he did not sign a confession, recounted his childhood in El Paso, where "there are many Mexicans." "I have talked Spanish ever since my childhood days," he testified, "when I was in school there were about twenty Mexicans to one white boy and they all attended the same school." "I do not read the Mexican language perfectly," he added, "but I speak it, although I am able to take a

Mexican letter written in Mexican language and translate it into English a little at a time." Though reinforcing certain racial divisions ("twenty Mexicans to one white boy," "the Mexican language"), Tepfer also described, if not exactly charitably, spaces of shared Mexican-Anglo schooling and a childhood filled with the Spanish language and, one would assume, Mexican culture.[49]

The trial also highlighted another important form of boundary crossing as Mexican witnesses spoke of their histories of migration to the United States. Santiago Martínez testified that he had lived in Texas for six years before the trial began. "I have lived in Texas," he said, "ever since I crossed over from Mexico." He also recalled helping to pay for his mother and sister-in-law to move to the United States. The Pérez family had similarly migrated to Texas. As "Mrs. Pérez" noted, "I am Spanish, having been born in Spain; my husband was born in Spain [in] the same town I was." James Anderson, who served as an interpreter during the trial, identified himself to the court as a native of Mexico who had lived in the United States since he was a year old. "I am a Mexican," he said, "but was raised in this country but was born in Old Mexico."[50] The above witnesses thus emphasized internal differences within their own communities, as well as important transnational family ties, elements of the lives of Mexicans, and Spaniards, in the United States that tended to receive little attention in the increasingly polarized racial climate of the West.

This chapter has highlighted two themes in particular: (1) the sexual dangers faced by young Mexicans, mostly girls, in and near the home; and (2) the colonial tension between Mexican racial difference and Mexican inclusion. As the chapter suggests, such colonial tensions emerged with special clarity in matters of domesticity and the home. As the Cabana case and several other trials make clear, however, the home was not alone in showcasing shifting notions of Mexican citizenship. Discussions of modern medicine and popular culture, for instance, could also speak to Mexicans' vexed position in the early twentieth century and the challenges ordinary Mexicans posed to sharp racial divisions and inequalities.

Historians of medicine along the US-Mexico borderlands have made clear that medicine and medical interventions (both in the creation of medical knowledge *about* Mexicans and in the medical treatment *of* Mexicans) helped sustain racial hierarchies across the region. Criminal trials involving Mexicans during the period echo these observations. During a rape trial, Dr. McDuff, for instance, testified that he was familiar with a range of patients, including those from both "northern" and "southern" climates, suggesting that many of the doctor's patients were Mexicans, and that medical knowledge, for the doctor, helped differentiate and categorize his patients. Trial records also contain accounts of Mexicans turning to the medical profession in a range of contexts. Pablo Villafranco, testifying on his own behalf as a defendant during the aforementioned Texas rape trial, attempted to establish his whereabouts, and an alibi, during the alleged attack. He was at home with his wife, he remembered, "during that time my wife was sick." "She had a pain right here on her right side, on her shoulder blade and back," he continued, "I took her to Dr. Charlie Reagan."[51]

In the Cabana case, recall, Tanis Cabana's ability to achieve and maintain an erection and to ejaculate became a point of medical speculation. Describing how he was rendered impotent by a kicking horse, Cabana testified to the following: "My privates haven't been like they used to be: I haven't had the pleasure I used to have with them. The way I am affected when I try to have pleasure, it goes back on me. The way it goes back on me, about the time I go to put it in, why, it just falls down. Sometimes the erection lasts long enough for me to get it in, and sometimes it don't. When the erection does last long enough for me to get it in, why, then it just falls down." Asked whether or not he was able to "complete the act of intercourse with emission," Cabana answered, "when I feel that I am going to enjoy it, why, it falls down." Given the evidence presented against him, Cabana's claim of impotence as legal strategy certainly had its advantages, and in fact was not unprecedented. Other men in the West turned to their supposed sexual incapacities as proof of their inability to commit the terrible crimes facing them. What is notable is the extent to which Tanis Cabana, a Mexican tenant farmer in rural Texas, turned toward the language of medicine in an attempt to clear himself of rape charges.[52]

Mexicans could also prove adept at navigating other modern realms. The trial's first witness, Fermín Estraca, was asked during cross-examination by the defense to describe his granddaughter's social habits, particularly whether she frequented local dances or attended movies. "Last year," he recalled, "she went down to a picture show with the family of Faustino Ramirez." In fact, he continued, "she did not go to the picture show just once, but went two or three times" to movies in nearby Mathis, Texas, with the Ramirez family. Luisa Estraca, asked similar questions, answered, "I sometimes went to the picture shows with Faustino and his family." As noted in chapter 1, in the early twentieth century, places of commercial leisure (movie theaters, amusement parks, dancehalls) were widely understood as troubling modern arenas, provoking anxiety and consternation among a range of social actors from Progressive-era reformers and public officials to immigrant parents. Concerns about gender improprieties and transgressions, especially the behavior of young women, were at the forefront of such disquietude. As the work of historians like Vicki Ruiz makes clear, courtship, romance, and intimate liaisons all blossomed in these commercial public spaces, and *Mexicanas* like Luisa Estraca were among the independent women and girls who dared to lay claim to such deeply modern spaces.[53]

FOUR

Uncommon Women and Prostitution

In February 1923, sixteen-year-old Dorothy Hall ran away from her home in Los Angeles. Several months earlier, Dorothy—who was described in trial records as a "white American girl"—had told her father that she wanted to marry a young man named Miguel Mayo. Her father flatly refused his daughter's request. "When she wanted to marry him," David Hall later said, "I told her no."[1]

Soon afterward, Dorothy ran away from home with Mayo. Over the next six weeks, Dorothy Hall and Miguel Mayo lived as wife and husband, residing in hotel room after hotel room throughout central Los Angeles before finally arriving at 1217 Temple Street, a business owned and operated by Marina Torres. With Miguel Mayo translating (Torres did not speak English and Hall did not speak Spanish), a lodging agreement was reached, and two days later Hall and Mayo moved into a first-floor room in Torres's building. For the next week, Hall had sex with, in her estimation, at least a half dozen men, receiving "from two to three to five dollars" in each case. A portion of that money (fifty cents) she gave to Marina Torres.[2]

On April 28, 1923, the Los Angeles city police raided 1217 Temple Street. Soon after the raid, Marina Torres was charged with several crimes associated with Dorothy Hall's arrival and lodging. The first count of the indictment charged Torres with the crime of "pandering": "procuring, persuading, and encouraging a female to become an inmate of a house of prostitution." Torres was also accused of two counts of rape and accessory to rape. According to the prosecution, by encouraging and persuading Dorothy Hall to remain at Temple Street and to work as a prostitute, Torres was a party to Dorothy's rape by male visitors to her establishment.[3]

During the 1920s, Los Angeles was one of the West's biggest and most racially heterogeneous cities, and racial divides in the city were pronounced.

Between 1900 and 1930, Los Angeles's population grew from 102,000 to 1.2 million and the city vaulted from thirty-sixth place among American cities to fifth. The Mexican population of Los Angeles is estimated to have been 100,000 in 1930, about 10 percent of the city's total population. Like other non-Anglos, Mexicans were consistently rendered politically and economically marginal in the city. As historian Natalia Molina notes, the 1920s were a period of important transformation in the lives of Mexicans in LA. New public health measures and rhetoric produced racial dividing lines that increasingly separated Mexicans from "whites" in the city and the region. This chapter uses Marina Torres's trial in Los Angeles to explore how sexual discourses, such as determinations of sexual deviance and propriety, could serve as spaces for racial ordering. Talk of sex, the chapter suggests, could be a site for distinctions between Anglos or "Americans," on the one hand, and "Mexicans," on the other. The chapter also examines how marginalized Mexicans, such as commercial sex workers like Torres, as well as other Mexican women in the West, used the American judicial system to contest their own subordinate status in the region. Finally, I'd like to suggest that commercial sex involving Mexicans in places like 1920s Los Angeles might be understood within a colonial context, with resemblances to settings that are more traditionally understood as colonial, such as Puerto Rico, Hawaii, and the British Empire.[4]

The trial's first witness was David Hall, Dorothy Hall's father, a plumber who in the spring of 1923 had lived alone with his daughter. Her mother had died, he told the court, and Dorothy was his charge and responsibility. In the early months of 1923, he said, Dorothy began her relationship with Miguel Mayo. "And he was of the Mexican race, was he?" the prosecutor, John J. Hill, asked, reminding the jury that Dorothy Hall had run away from home and defied her father's wishes in order to marry a "Mexican." During David Hall's testimony, and the subsequent testimony of his daughter, Dorothy, the prosecutor also emphasized Dorothy's age and innocence. As Dorothy approached the stand, Hill asked the judge if "under the law she is entitled to a woman companion, or some woman attendant in the room." "Isn't the matron here," the judge asked, at which point Dorothy's government chaperone announced, "Yes, your Honor," and the trial proceeded. Hill began his direct examination by encouraging Dorothy to "face the jury and speak loudly." "I don't want to have any embarrassment," he continued, "I want you to talk just like you were talking to your own mother or your own father."[5]

The next witness, Ordinata Delfin, was asked to "speak as distinctly and plainly in English as you can." Delfin's foreignness was further emphasized when he was asked, "You are a Filipino, are you not?" "Yes, sir," Delfin replied and proceeded to describe how J. E. Davis of the Los Angeles Police Department and A. J. Ortega, "another Filipino who is working for the department," gave him marked money and instructed him to go to 1217 Temple Street. Delfin identified Marina Torres as the woman who opened the door, introduced him to other women in the house, and assigned him a room. While waiting, Delfin recalled, Torres also offered him whiskey. Another man, "another Filipino boy," also an agent of the LAPD, was similarly given marked money and directed to enter Torres's establishment.[6]

During Delfin's testimony, he explained that he had come to the city two years earlier from the Philippines. "Did you go under the name you gave here?" he was asked, and "What business have you been in during that two years?" Both questions suggested Delfin's disreputable, even illegal passage to the United States and an inability, or unwillingness, to support himself in his new home. Delfin, however, resisted such attempts to discredit him. He had entered the country under the same name, he said, and studied auto mechanics for the first ten months at the National Automotive School. In March, he continued, he opened a garage of his own. Delfin was also asked to describe the people sitting in the front room of 1217 Temple Street prior to the raid. "Some women and some men and some Mexicans," Delfin answered, as well as "a tall fellow . . . an American boy." With witnesses like Ordinata Delfin, and David and Dorothy Hall, the prosecution, in describing Dorothy Hall's arrival at Marina Torres's building and the subsequent police raid, accentuated, rather than blurred, racial distinctions.[7]

A final prosecution witness was J. E. Davis, an eleven-year veteran of the LAPD. On April 28, he testified, he and two other police officers as well as "three Filipinos" approached the house. Davis gave marked money to the men and waited while they entered the building. Twenty minutes later, Davis led the raid on the house, kicking in the front door while Ortega and another officer went to the back of the building. Davis recalled finding "one of the Filipino boys that [he] had sent into the house with a girl." "The Filipino boy," he recalled, "his pants were open and his privates were exposed." Davis continued searching the first floor, discovering "a large number of men" in another room down the hall, "trying to get out of the window." Davis directed that the several women detained during the raid be placed in the front bedroom. Among the women were Dorothy Hall and Josephine Verdugo, as well as two other women identified by Davis as Mary

Gomez and Carmen Rubio. Davis next described finding a trunk hidden in the house filled with bottles of liquor. In total, he estimated, there were seventy quart bottles and thirty-five to forty pints of liquor in the trunk.[8]

For the defense, Marina Torres and her legal team called several witnesses who testified that they were unaware that prostitution occurred at 1217 Temple Street. Torres also took the stand to testify in her own defense. "I am a widow," she told the court through an interpreter, adding that she had no children and had lived in Los Angeles for the past sixteen years. Her occupation, she said, was "sewing, washing and ironing." She had also owned and operated four different rooming houses in LA in the past three years, including her last rooming house at 1217 Temple Street. Torres went on to describe Dorothy Hall's arrival at the house. According to Torres, Miguel Mayo had asked, in Spanish, if Torres had a room to rent to them. Torres emphatically denied ever being given money from Dorothy Hall (Mayo, she said, paid her the $4.00 rent) or witnessing the couple "using her room for an immoral purpose." Torres was also asked to explain the discovery by police of bottles of liquor in her room. "It was very little," Torres explained, "I had it there in case of sickness I should use or could use it when I was ill." Her attorney turned then to the night of April 28.

"Did you show any dark complected young man, either a Filipino or Mexican, to your knowledge," she was asked, "into any room with any girl in your house the Saturday night you were arrested?"

"No sir," Torres replied. Torres also stated that she had been in a rear building behind the house when she heard the noise of the police breaking down her front door. "I had been called to see a child of one of the tenants," she said, "when I heard some noise." Torres thus used her direct testimony to emphasize her respectable marital status (a widow), her domestic labor, and her maternal concern for her tenants and their children. She also denied knowledge of "immoral" acts committed at the rooming house.[9]

Torres's cross-examination began by returning briefly to her marital status. "You say you are a widow?" the district attorney asked her confrontationally.

"Yes sir," Marina replied.

"Husband dead?" he asked.

"Yes sir," she answered again, and the lawyer changed the subject to the night of the raid. Torres once again denied that she had even been present when police officers burst into the house. The family in the back room had a baby that "had been sick for three days," she repeated, and she had been helping to care for the child for at least an hour when the raid commenced.[10]

When Torres left the stand, the outcome of the trial was left in the hands of the jury. After extensive deliberation, the jury finally found Torres guilty of enticing Hall into prostitution, but innocent of the two rape charges. Nonetheless, Torres, who had proclaimed her innocence of all charges throughout the trial, retained H. M. Dalton as her attorney and filed an appeal brief to the Supreme Court of California. Her brief made two main arguments. First, she argued that she could not have lured Dorothy Hall into a brothel because she (Torres) only spoke Spanish and Hall only spoke English. Thus, the two women could not have communicated with each other and Torres could not have "persuaded" Hall to become a prostitute. Torres also argued that the judge had improperly instructed the jury as to the law governing pandering. In the end, however, the appeals court ruled against Torres and affirmed her conviction on the charge of pandering.[11]

Despite losing her appeals case, Marina Torres managed to escape the two most serious charges against her. Though guilty of pandering, she was found innocent of two counts of assisting in the rape of Dorothy Hall. This was no small accomplishment. Marina Torres was a *Mexicana* with apparently limited English skills who was accused of running a liquor-serving brothel in Los Angeles, a city that did not have a reputation for either racial tolerance or the ready acceptance of non-Anglos.[12] Distanced from proper domesticity, femininity, and Americanness, she appeared undaunted either by the raid or the subsequent legal actions. Like other trials involving sex throughout the region, her case presents a critical tension: sexual discourses offered spaces for both (1) the elaboration and sustenance of racial differences and (2) the opposition to such racial hierarchies and order.

Accused of ensnaring Dorothy Hall into prostitution and facilitating her rape, Marina Torres was consistently portrayed by court officials as foreign and non-American. Comparisons, even by Torres's defense team, between Torres and Dorothy Hall, the "white American girl," magnified this distance between Torres and both whiteness and Americanness. From the trial's outset, the prosecution went to considerable lengths to emphasize Dorothy's youth and vulnerability. During his opening statement, the prosecutor described Hall as a "young girl" who was lured into prostitution. When the police raided 1217 Temple Street, he continued, "this girl, Dorothy Hall, was found there together with three other young women." David Hall, the first witness, was asked if he was "the father of a young lady by the name of Dorothy Hall." Recall also that when Dorothy herself was called to testify,

Hill quickly stepped in to ensure that Dorothy's "matron" was present in order to provide further protection to his witness. Even Marina Torres's defense attorney seemed concerned to safeguard the apparently delicate sensibilities of Dorothy Hall. During Miguel Mayo's testimony, just as Mayo began recounting his initial conversation with Marina Torres regarding Hall working as a prostitute at Temple Street, Dalton interjected, "I will ask that Dorothy Hall be allowed to go into the other room." Hill readily agreed, offering to hold his apparently overly sensitive questions until she had exited the room.[13]

Dorothy Hall was also consistently portrayed in prosecution accounts, with little objection from the defense, as a member of a respectable family. Although both prosecution and defense acknowledged that Hall ran away from home, neither side depicted the home itself in a critical or derogatory manner. Hall ran away from home, according to her father, because she wanted to marry Miguel Mayo and her father prevented her from doing so. The white home materializes here as a place of patriarchal authority and racial purity. Despite the fact that Hall runs away, her father does not capitulate to her demands to marry a "Mexican" such as Miguel Mayo.[14]

Such descriptions of the Hall home stand in stark contrast to the racial heterogeneity and domestic fluidity portrayed in accounts of life within Marina Torres's female-led establishment. While it seems clear that one of the main uses of the building was for commercial sex, the building also served as a rooming house for several other lodgers, none of whom seemed directly involved in prostitution. A handful of these lodgers testified in Marina Torres's defense during the trial, such as Eduardo Heredia, a furniture salesman who lived on the second floor and had known Marina Torres for several years. Like Heredia, Louis Castano, a waiter, offered no direct evidence of prostitution at Temple Street. "Sometimes I would go in and take a glass of water," he testified in Spanish, "greet the lady [presumably Torres] and some other things." He had even seen Dorothy Hall on occasion, but denied ever entering her room or even speaking with her. "We couldn't understand [each other]," he said. Castano also could not recall ever being offered alcohol by Torres. "I never had the good fortune to see that," he quipped.[15]

Miguel Miranda was Eduardo Heredia's neighbor on the third floor. Miranda described in Spanish his job in a grocery store on Sunset Boulevard. Like Heredia, Miranda was single and had known Torres for "two or three years." Miranda was similarly unable to recall "lewd or immoral acts" committed at the house, though he remembered seeing Dorothy Hall on a handful of occasions. Under cross-examination, Miranda further described the spatial arrangements at Temple Street. In the half dozen rooms on the second floor, he said, lived "two single men and, to my knowledge, two families," including children. During her testimony, Dorothy Hall had similarly recounted the living quarters at the house. She noted that while the "living room was used for people who came there for prostitution," lodgers from second- and third-floor rooms would occasionally sit in the living room. Dorothy took care, however, to point out that only "some of the roomers" congregated downstairs. "The roomers and their wives," she observed, "didn't have any use of that living room downstairs."[16]

Marina Torres was unsurprisingly the best source of information on the domestic arrangements at Temple Street. Single men, a "young fellow by the name of Teswall" and a man she knew only as "Juan," and a family ("a man, a lady, and some children") lived on the second floor. While Dorothy Hall occupied one of the first-floor rooms, the other rooms were "my room, the kitchen, another room that I rented to a family," and the room where Josephine Verdugo lived. In a final room in the back corner of the house lived five people, a "lady," in Marina's words, her husband, who was a cement worker, and their three small children.[17]

In contrast to the fluid use of domestic space at 1217 Temple Street and the racial mixing of both the building's inhabitants and its visitors, Anglo witnesses and court officials nevertheless seemed keen to separate "American" trial participants from their "Mexican" and "Filipino" counterparts. During his account of the raid, for instance, J. E. Davis recalled seeing a back room of the building, where "a Mexican and his wife seemed to have been awakened by Marina Torres and she directed them to take care of the house during her absence." Under cross-examination, Davis described accompanying Torres to the upper floors of the building. A couple lived in a front room on the second floor, he remembered, "and there were possibly two or three Mexicans living in the room directly behind."[18]

Such a commitment on the part of Anglo officials to racial separation and difference suggests an enduring colonial presence in the American West. The creation of social divisions around sexual customs and practices has come to be seen as a foundation of colonial rule. Recent histories of American colonialism in Hawaii and Puerto Rico and prostitution in European colonial settings, for instance, have highlighted the creation and maintenance of overlapping sexual and racial distinctions. As Laura Briggs points out in her study of the colonial relationship between the United States and Puerto Rico in the twentieth century, discourses on sexuality, including prostitution, have the power to create colonial subjects, to differentiate colonizer from colonized. In Puerto Rico after 1917 (when Puerto

Ricans received US citizenship), debates over prostitution policy, Briggs argues, offered a forum for the expression of contending understandings of citizenship and the proper place of Puerto Ricans within the American polity. Efforts, for instance, to control prostitution, and the sexuality of working-class Puerto Rican women in general, reflected a broader colonial struggle between American government officials and Puerto Rican elites over the direction and leadership of the island.[19]

California v. Torres provided a similar public narration of sex and prostitution, and also, following the lead of Briggs, offered a forum for discourses on racial, and colonial, difference, most notably constructing a divide between Americans and Mexicans. Briggs also notes the prominent role in 1920s Puerto Rico of the Women's Christian Temperance Union in simultaneously opposing prostitution and advocating for the establishment of "racially homogenous nuclear families." A like concern with domesticity appears in the Torres case in the racially inflected opposition between Dorothy Hall's "white" home (reinforced by Hall's father, who forbids his daughter's marriage to a "Mexican") and the racial heterogeneity of 1217 Temple Street. [20]

As evidence of the commitment by ordinary Mexicans to use the courts to press their claims of civic inclusion, Marina Torres's decision to appeal her conviction bears a further resemblance to Sally Engle Merry's exploration of the role of sexuality in structuring American colonial rule in Hawaii, especially in native Hawaiians' increasing ability to maneuver successfully within the American judicial system. Merry also notes that Chinese immigrants to Hawaii in the later nineteenth century similarly managed to assert certain legal rights. "Over the long run," she writes, "the law provided a discourse of rights and entitlement that provided the opportunity for at least some of the immigrant and colonized groups to assert more powerful positions in the emerging social order of the twentieth century."[21] Like Merry, Philippa Levine describes the use of the legal system by colonial subjects, in Levine's case by colonial prostitutes within the British empire. Levine notes that "the Superintendent of the Calcutta lock hospital spoke of women who 'employ counsel to defend them,'" adding that "there were similar reports from northwest India." In southern India, Levine continues, "one woman successfully appealed her registration [as a prostitute] to the High Court."[22]

Obviously, there are many dissimilarities between colonial locations like Puerto Rico, Hawaii, and the British colonies, and the early twentieth-century American West. Still, the resemblances are worth noting and, I suggest, worth exploring. Sexual discourses, like those produced in the trial of

Marina Torres, could clearly be sites of racial differentiation and ordering. At the same time, talk of sex could also open spaces for opposing such racial, and sexual, boundaries. During both her testimony on the witness stand and her determined legal maneuvers, Marina Torres, though consistently portrayed by court officials as foreign, non-American, and possessing a disordered and aberrant home life, produced an important alternative narrative of her life and the lives of her neighbors.

After being detained by the police, Torres was described by Officer Davis (who had little reason to lie about her even-tempered demeanor) as calm and composed when he questioned her. She was similarly unflustered during courtroom testimony and showed little hesitation, despite the financial cost, in petitioning a higher court to overturn her conviction on the last of the three felony charges leveled against her. Besides appealing her conviction (itself an important indicator of her claim to American rights and status), Torres stated unequivocally to the prosecutor that she was a respectable, once-married widow—not, she suggested, a single woman. Torres also offered a positive view of domestic life at her rooming house, one that highlighted her nurturing qualities (she had been nursing a sick child when the raid commenced) and the properly familial aspects of the house (the presence of married couples and families lodging in upstairs rooms).

Other Mexican trial participants similarly highlighted their own sexual respectability. Also testifying in the Torres trial was Josephine Verdugo, whose main language was also Spanish, and who was twenty-three that spring in Los Angeles. Like Dorothy Hall, Verdugo had been drawn to the house by the recommendation of a young man. According to trial testimony, Verdugo and Enrico (she did not know his last name) had worked together elsewhere, and Enrico invited her to rent a room from Marina Torres. He introduced her to Torres, and Verdugo began renting a room at a rate of four dollars a week. Enrico stayed at Temple Street for a few days, but then departed. "He went away to Oakland," Josephine said. Asked later if she immediately began to "have sexual intercourse with men," she replied, "not at first because I was working." Soon, however, she too began having sexual relations with men. While Verdugo's testimony was far less detailed than that of Marina Torres, and Verdugo was far more deferential to the prosecution, her testimony offers an intriguing, if brief, narrative of her fall from respectability into sex work. Such a narrative was most commonly applied to young middle-class white women (like Dorothy Hall) to explain their descent into prostitution. Yet Verdugo frames herself in a similar light as a victim of unfortunate circumstances. More hesitant on the witness stand than Marina Torres, Verdugo nonetheless portrayed herself—

like white, American Dorothy Hall—as an innocent young woman rather than as a hardened sex criminal.[23]

Other witnesses similarly challenged racial dividing lines. While most of the non-Anglo witnesses in the trial were Mexican women or men, a handful of the witnesses were Filipino men. Cities like Los Angeles, of course, were notable for a racial heterogeneity that far exceeded simple black-white or even brown-white dichotomies. Racial barriers in Los Angeles that differentiated Mexicans from Anglos functioned similarly to divide Filipinos in the city from their Anglo counterparts. Anglo witnesses and attorneys, for example, consistently used the term "Filipino" (and not, for instance, "American") to describe men like the police interpreter A. J. Ortega. J. E. Davis, the LA police officer, identified Ortega as "the young Filipino boy who testified here in this case." Davis was also asked about "two Filipinos whom [he] sent to the house" as part of the police raid. At the same time, A. J. Ortega confounded Anglo attempts to portray Filipinos as intractably foreign and un-American. Ortega, when asked to describe his previous employment, answered, "I used to be in the navy."

"What navy?" Hill asked.

"American Navy," Ortega replied, stating that he had served four years in the US Navy as well as ten years in the US Army. As A. J. Ortega's assertions of American military service suggest, courtroom discussions of sex could be the site of multiple, and at times competing, narratives of both racial difference and national belonging.[24]

While Marina Torres was exceptional in challenging her conviction to a higher court, she was not the only Mexican woman in California to follow such a path. In the first three decades of the twentieth century, seventy-three criminal cases involving prostitution were appealed to higher courts in California. Four directly involved Mexican women, including *California v. Marina Torres* and *California v. Juanita Casanova*. Like Marina Torres, Juanita Casanova was charged with a crime associated with running a brothel. While both women probably had the option of accepting guilty pleas and foregoing a trial, both (presumably) chose to plead not guilty and contest their charge in a trial. Both also initiated, and likely financed, their own appeals cases.[25]

In *California v. Juanita Casanova*, Juanita Casanova was accused of operating the New Mexico Hotel, a San Diego rooming house notorious for prostitution and "immoral" acts. Casanova denied the claims and maintained her innocence throughout the trial, swearing on the witness stand that she "did not know of any room in her hotel ever being rented for immoral purposes or for purposes of assignation or immoral conduct." Jurors were apparently convinced and acquitted her of the charges. San Diego officials nonetheless almost immediately charged her with a different crime. She had lied and committed perjury, they argued, when she claimed to have known nothing about prostitution occurring in the rooms of her hotel. This time, Casanova was found guilty. A year later, she appealed the perjury conviction to the state court of appeals.[26]

The three-judge panel that heard the case turned down Casanova's appeal and upheld the perjury verdict. The opinion written by judge P. J. Finlayson summarized the case, including a description of the testimony of two critical witnesses for the prosecution. Juan and Jennie Garcia, a married couple, apparently had rented a room for a week in the New Mexico Hotel in the middle of December of 1920. They claimed not only to have witnessed multiple instances of prostitution (numerous different men visiting a nearby room, room number nine, occupied by "Lucille Roderiquez" and a woman described only as "the Rogers woman"), but to have spoken with Casanova herself about what transpired in the room. Jennie Garcia testified that Casanova had told her that the room was "for the girls to do business in" and that "the charge for the men doing business with the women there was two dollars, and that she was to have fifty cents out of the two dollars." Garcia also described the diverse group of men who visited Roderiquez in her room. "I saw different men go into room nine with Lucille Roderiquez," she testified, "I don't remember how many, but different men, colored people, Mexicans, Americans, and Indians." She added that she saw "as many men visit the Rogers woman as [she] saw visit Mrs. Roderiquez." Juan Garcia described overhearing conversations between Casanova and men at the hotel. "Men," he said, "would sometimes come and ask Mrs. Casanova for girls and she sent them to room nine."[27]

Casanova's case suggests, in part, the involvement of Mexicans in multiple aspects of commercial sex in the Southwest. Recall that witnesses testified that in the New Mexico Hotel run by Casanova, a *Mexicana* (Lucille Roderiquez) was a prostitute while Mexican men were among the many "different men" routinely paying for sex in the establishment. If Casanova's example is any indication, Marina Torres was not the only Mexican woman to assume a leadership position in the sex trade. Like Torres, Casanova purportedly received fifty cents for every two dollars Roderiquez collected from customers. The Casanova case, also like *California v. Torres*, calls attention to a fluid quality in Mexican social relations. Where Anglos and Mexicans regularly passed each other in the halls of 1217 Temple Street in LA, in San

Diego there mingled a similarly diverse set of racial and ethnic groups. As one witness put it, visitors included "colored people, Mexicans, Americans, and Indians." In addition to Roderiquez, one of the other prostitutes at the hotel was the apparently Anglo "Rogers woman." This social fluidity extended beyond racial mixing to include marital status and family composition. The main witnesses in Casanova's trial were a married couple who lived in the hotel long enough to be intimately aware of the comings and goings of hotel residents and their guests. As in the LA rooming house run by Marina Torres, supposedly respectable married couples like Juan and Jennie Garcia lived side by side with Mexican madams and prostitutes.[28]

Such accounts of commercial sex work as the Torres and Casanova cases provide are indebted ultimately to the determination of non-elite Mexican women to challenge criminal convictions in American courts. Few other traces of the two women's lives appear in historical records. Marina Torres does not appear in the US census enumerations for either 1920 or 1930, though there is a possible listing for Juanita Casanova in the 1920 San Diego census schedule. A Juanita Casanova, age twenty-nine, appears in a household with a husband who is a carpenter, a ten-year-old daughter, and a mother-in-law and sister-in-law. Casanova's court case does not mention a husband or family, but the census enumeration intriguingly includes several lodgers in the Casanova household. One, twenty-four-year-old Bonita San Juan, is described as an "Actress, Vaudeville." Women in the theater were often associated with commercial sex, suggesting that the Juanita Casanova listed in the 1920 census may have been the same woman in the 1920 San Diego appeals case.[29]

Newspaper records for both women are similarly scarce. In fact, the only appearance of either woman in newspaper records from the period stems from the appeals process itself. In June 1924, the *Los Angeles Times* reported the following under the headline "Court Sustains Conviction of Marina Torres":

> The case of Marina Torres, whose residence was raided by police on April 28, 1923, as a disorderly house, reached its conclusion yesterday in the State Supreme Court, when a final decision, written by Justice Lawlor, was handed down affirming the original conviction in superior court on a statutory charge.
>
> The Torres woman temporarily won a reversal of the verdict in the Second District Court of Appeal recently because of alleged technical errors committed by the trial court.
>
> The Supreme Court has now held, however, that no prejudicial error was

committed during the woman's trial or that certain evidence was not sufficient to support the verdict of guilty.

The language and tone of the newspaper is notably restrained. Though Torres is identified with prostitution ("disorderly house"), she is not vilified or ridiculed in the piece. Nor does the article describe Torres as "Mexican," a common practice with Spanish-surnamed individuals appearing in the press, or highlight her apparent inability to speak English. The article, of course, hardly celebrates "that Torres woman," however, her relatively measured and respectful treatment was not the usual treatment meted out to Mexicans in 1920s LA. As in the trial and her appeals process, which prompted the newspaper article (the police raid was apparently not reported), Torres appears surefooted and capable before the law, a stance in sharp distinction to developing visions of Mexicans as unfit for and incapable of citizenship.[30]

Though exceptional in many ways, Marina Torres and Juanita Casanova were not the only women involved in commercial sex to appeal criminal convictions to higher courts in the West. In 1920, Ida Ott filed an appeal with the Texas Court of Criminal Appeals to overturn her manslaughter conviction in the shooting death of her husband, Andrew, in a Dallas street in December 1918. Ott, who claimed during the trial that her husband had frequently pressured her into prostitution ("he suggested to me to sell my body to men for his profit") and often attacked her viciously, at one point shooting her in the stomach and nearly killing her, argued that she shot him in self-defense. "I shot my husband," she told the court, recalling their confrontation in the middle of a Dallas street, "because I thought he was going to the car to get a gun to kill me with." Appealing her conviction of manslaughter and her three-year sentence in the state penitentiary, Ott argued that the trial judge had erred in not allowing testimony regarding Andrew Ott's conversation with a lawyer in which Ott "asked his attorney for legal advice as to what punishment he would have received if he had killed defendant [Ida Ott]." The higher court sided with Ott and granted her a new trial. The next year, however, presumably after Ott had received a new trial and been once again convicted of manslaughter (receiving a two-year sentence, rather than three years imprisonment after the first conviction), Ott again appealed to the Texas higher court. This time her appeal was unsuccessful and the higher court affirmed her manslaughter conviction.[31]

Three years later, another Anglo woman, Pearl Snyder, appealed two prostitution convictions to the New Mexico Supreme Court. Snyder, the manager of a rooming house in Raton, New Mexico, and several other women were arrested in a police raid on the establishment. During the subsequent trial, a main witness for the prosecution was Jerry Levans, who testified that she worked as a prostitute at the rooming house and gave Snyder one dollar for every three dollars she earned from sex with men. During the defense, Snyder disputed Levans's account and claimed that she had no knowledge of prostitution at her establishment. Snyder admitted running several dancehalls in New Mexico and Texas, but denied that prostitution occurred in her establishments. Snyder's appeal on one count of the conviction was denied, but her other appeal was successful and the conviction on that count was reversed. Despite her claims to have operated dancehalls and not brothels, it seems clear from the trial transcript that Pearl Snyder, like Ida Ott, engaged in some form of commercial sex. It also seems clear that pervasive denigration of prostitution and prostitutes notwithstanding, women like Ida Ott and Pearl Snyder—and Marina Torres and Juanita Casanova—believed that they had the right to appeal criminal convictions to higher courts in the West.[32]

Other trial transcripts, though not directly involving prostitution, could also address commercial sex in the West. Another example of commercial sex appears in the 1929 case of *Texas v. Louis Basquez*. In the small town of Victoria, Texas, located between Houston and Corpus Christi, Louis Basquez was accused of severely beating Henry Schindler. The first witness in the trial was Henry Schindler, described elsewhere as an "old man," who testified that on the evening in question that he had spent most of the night at the home of Mary Chapman, in his words, a "negro woman." "I paid her for her services," he said, "I gave her five dollars." Schindler claimed that he left Mary Chapman's house at about four in the morning and that almost immediately upon stepping out the door was attacked by Louis Basquez, who threw a bottle at him, beat him with his hands, and stabbed him with a knife. Schindler testified that during the attack, Basquez exclaimed that Chapman was "my woman, you son of a bitch, I will kill you." Mary Chapman supported this version of the events, testifying further that she had "been going with [Basquez] and having intercourse with him for four months," but had recently ended the relationship. "I told [him] that I wasn't going to have intercourse with him anymore," Chapman testified, "He asked me why and I said because I don't want to." "He said, 'I guess you don't want to because you're going to fool with white men,'" Chapman continued, "I told him that was none of his business what I do." That night, Chapman did not recall Basquez saying anything about "my woman," but she did say that she had clearly heard Basquez say, "you god damn son of a bitch I will cut your god dam throat."[33]

Basquez, for his part, did not deny that a fight had occurred but claimed that Schindler had initiated the brawl. Schindler, he said, had run into him in the alley outside Mary Chapman's house and asked him what he was doing there. "I told him I was going to my room to sleep," Basquez testified, at which point, according to Basquez, Schindler said, "you are a liar, you mother fucking Mexican," and attacked Basquez. Basquez also denied that he was jealous of Schindler or that he had been enraged at Mary Chapman's rejection of him in favor of Schindler. "She is not a woman of mine," Basquez testified, "it is none of my business who she goes with because she is a prostitute." Basquez's appeal was eventually turned down and his attempted murder conviction was affirmed.[34]

Like the cases of Marina Torres and Juanita Casanova, this trial reveals a world of substantial cultural mixing, with the intimate proximity of Mexicans, African Americans, and Anglos. Turn-of-the-twentieth-century sexual interminglings across race, ethnicity, and class are of course familiar phenomena for historians of the urban East and Midwest. The same is true for large Western cities like San Francisco, Los Angeles, and Denver in the early twentieth century and in boomtowns like cattle centers or mining towns. But Victoria was neither a major urban center nor a boomtown. Victoria, Texas, in 1930, one year after the trial, had a population of 7,421. Three decades earlier, in 1900, the population was 4,000 people. Yet, even in small towns in the West, sexual commerce could serve as a space of significant cross-cultural interaction.[35]

At the same time, the case points to the potential assertiveness of women, even non-elite African American women, in the courts. Mary Chapman, recall, testified to the court that she had told Basquez that her sexual life was "none of his business." Like Chapman, female commercial sex workers, Anglo, Mexican, and African American, could on occasion speak with confidence and conviction from the witness stand, and some could go so far as to challenge guilty verdicts to higher courts.[36] That Anglo women, especially non-elite women associated with prostitution, initiated legal claims in the courts is also notable. Historians have observed that ordinary Anglo women turned to the courts in multiple contexts in the early twentieth century, using the courts to help discipline and manage their wayward daughters, to punish and protect themselves from abusive and negligent husbands, and to defend loved ones from dangers in and around the homes. Women also increasingly served on juries across the West and the nation. Despite jury service, the right to vote, and increased participation in the legal system, inequities based on gender nonetheless persisted throughout the early twentieth century.[37]

Racial and class differences aggravated these inequities, and poor Mexican women, even the vast majority of whom were not involved in commercial sex, faced exceptional and deepening challenges in the century's early decades. Still, like Anglo women, Mexican women appealed convictions for a variety of crimes across the West.[38] In 1917, Petra Lerma was convicted of selling whiskey in the town of Wilson, Texas, and was sentenced to a year in the state penitentiary. Lerma appealed the conviction on three grounds: (1) the trial judge should not have allowed the jury "to handle and smell the bottle of liquid which was introduced as evidence"; (2) the judge had erroneously permitted testimony about her supposed adultery; and (3) the trial record failed to state specifically that the sale of intoxicating liquor was illegal in the district where Lerma's crime had supposedly occurred. The court dispensed with the first two arguments, but agreed with the third. The judgment must be reversed, the court decided, and Lerma's case should be returned to the lower court. Trixie Gonzales was less successful in her case stemming from a conviction for illegally possessing alcohol in San Bernadino, California, in 1928. Gonzales, who had pleaded guilty to the possession of alcohol, was sentenced to one year in prison and a fine of five hundred dollars. Gonzales asked the higher court in California to reduce what she and her lawyers considered an excessive punishment. The court disagreed, however, and affirmed Gonzales's sentence. In another case involving alcohol possession, Julia Fernández successfully appealed a liquor-related conviction and sentence of a year in prison in Texas in 1917. Fernández argued that two jurors had been improperly placed on the jury after both men stated during initial questioning, and before the trial began, that regardless of the evidence they would not vote for a lesser, suspended sentence for Fernández. The higher court agreed with Fernández and awarded her a new trial. Like women across the nation, Mexican women faced considerable barriers to full citizenship, barriers that were magnified by the increasing hostility to Mexican peoples in the early twentieth century. Nonetheless, seemingly ordinary Mexican women like Petra Lerma, Trixie Gonzales, and Julia Fernández (aside from their appearance in the legal record, there is no evidence that the women were politically influential or members of an elite class) refused to accept guilty verdicts, even for relatively minor offenses like alcohol possession, and seemed determined to exercise their rights in the American legal system. Two, Lerma and Fernández, even found success in their courts and managed to have their convictions reversed and new trials ordered.[39]

Mexican women also appealed convictions on more serious charges. In 1905, Carmen Fonseca appealed a murder conviction from El Paso, Texas. Fonseca had been involved in an argument with an Anglo man, Alexander Mitchell, in El Paso's Favorite Theatre. According to one witness, after Fonseca and Mitchell argued about beer, Mitchell staggered out of the theater and collapsed to the ground. "Whetta cut me," Mitchell told the witness just before his death. "Said witness," according to the appeals case, "furthermore testified that defendant [Carmen Fonseca] was called 'Whetta,' which was a term applied to a girl of light complexion." "Whetta" was likely in fact the word *guera*, a Spanish term that indeed often referred to a person of light skin or complexion. That the witness, an Anglo man, would use the term suggests once again the substantial level of cross-cultural mingling that occurred in the West, including in places like saloons and theaters. Fonseca's appeal, however, proved unpersuasive to the court, and her murder conviction was affirmed.[40]

Two decades later, Maud Peña similarly appealed a murder charge from Valencia County, New Mexico. Peña and George Burkhold had lived together for several months and had been romantically involved ("He often asked me to marry him," Peña testified during the trial). The relationship soured, however, and Peña asked Burkhold to move out of the house that he shared with Peña and another lodger, Guadalupe Quintana. Soon afterward, Burkhold returned to the home and asked to be let in. Peña refused and Burkhold broke down the door. Peña called to Quintana for help and a gunfight ensued between the men. After several shots, Burkhold fell dead with a bullet to the forehead. Quintana and Peña were both charged with murder.[41]

During the trial, Peña denied being sexually involved with Quintana and testified that when Burkhold broke into the house he told Quintana and Peña, "I am going to kill a Mexican and that woman." Her lawyer argued for a mistrial on the grounds that Peña had not in fact shot Burkhold or been responsible for his death. The prosecution, he told the court, believed that "there is an eternal triangle," a love triangle between Peña, Quintana, and Burkhold. "Probably there is," he continued, "probably this woman was implicated in it, in some way connected with it, but that doesn't make her responsible for the killing." The jury, composed of twelve Spanish-surnamed men, was not persuaded and convicted Peña of murder, sentencing her to fifty years in the state penitentiary.[42] Peña appealed her conviction, at first unsuccessfully, to the New Mexico Supreme Court. In 1924, the court ruled that the trial court had acted properly and affirmed Peña's conviction. In 1925, however, Peña asked the court to rehear her appeal. This time the court found in her favor. "We have carefully re-examined the record," Judge C. J. Parker wrote for the unanimous court, "and are compelled to say that it is extremely doubtful whether the state has shown any facts pointing directly to the guilt of the defendant Peña." "She was in her own house when the deceased broke in the door," Parker continued, "and entered over her express protest, and she called upon the other defendant, Quintana, to help and protect her against the impending assault of the deceased." Peña was awarded a new trial.[43]

While Carmen Fonseca's conviction was affirmed, and Maud Peña's reversed, the women shared a determination reflected by many women in Mexican America. During an exceptionally difficult period for Mexicans in the United States, as forces of racial exclusion broadened their attacks, the Mexican women profiled in this chapter insisted on using the courts and forcing the American legal system to recognize their rights as citizens and members of the nation. None of the women, moreover, seem to be especially wealthy or politically powerful, suggesting that other women not ensnared in the courts may have shared the sense of entitlement and rights in the American legal system that the women in this chapter, and the book, seem to exhibit.

Talk of sex by and about Mexicans in the West spoke to multiple forms of inequality, including colonial hierarchies. Female colonial subjects in fact turned to the courts in a variety of colonial settings during the early twentieth century.[44] Colonial rule was always unstable, especially at the points where promises of inclusion intersected with racial differentiation and inequality. This chapter, especially in its exploration of the colonial and countercolonial dynamics in the trial of Marina Torres, has suggested that Mexican women proved themselves quite capable of navigating such unruly and perilous colonial waters. The following chapter will proceed along a similar course, turning from the involvement of Mexicans in prostitution and commercial sex work to other nonnormative sexual practices, and desires, across the region.

FIVE

Sexual Borderlands

cross-cultural sexual intimacy in the south west (handwritten)

Little remains of the sex that two men by the names of Gomez and Heller had together on July 3, 1915, in Austin County, Texas. Lost is the time of day, whether it was an afternoon tryst or a late-night encounter, and the location, whether they met at one of their homes or in a hotel room or in a more public place like a park or an alley. Missing from the historical record is whether the men knew each other previously or whether they had just met, how long they spent together, how happily or unhappily they departed from their encounter. Legal documents, our only tangible evidence of their sexual liaison, do not even include Gomez's first name; he is identified only as "the defendant A. Gomez."[1]

What *is* known is that six months later, an Austin grand jury indicted Gomez and William Heller on the charge of "together with each other commit[ting] against the order of nature the abominable and detestable crime of sodomy." Though indicted together, Heller and Gomez were apparently tried separately. While no record exists of William Heller's trial, Gomez was tried and convicted of sodomy and sentenced to five years in the Texas state penitentiary. It was Gomez's decision to appeal his conviction to the Texas Court of Criminal Appeals that led to the creation of a transcript of his trial and the uncommon trace that his transcript leaves of Mexican same-sex sexual desire in the history of the American West.[2]

Like the trial of A. Gomez, *Texas vs. Juan Muñoz*, which originated in Laredo, Texas, in 1926, also involved sexual relations between two men, thirty-five-year-old Juan Muñoz and fifteen-year-old Carlos Myers. Taken together, these two trials offer valuable evidence of same-sex sexual activity involving Mexicans in the early twentieth-century West. Historians of sexuality rarely mention Mexicans in their accounts of sex in American history, and Mexican same-sex desire is no less absent from historical accounts of the period. Evidence of sexual relations between Mexican men nonetheless exists in the historical record, especially in legal records like local criminal charges and appellate court cases. In particular, Mexicans charged with sodomy offenses and committing what was known as "the infamous crime against nature" can offer evidence, albeit fragmentary and incomplete, of Mexican same-sex sexual activity in the West.[3]

This chapter explores a range of Mexican desires in the West, as well as the relationship between sex, citizenship, and colonialism in the region. The legal arena provided Mexican men and women in the early twentieth-century West with a public space for the articulation of alternative, nonnormative forms of sexual desire, practices, understandings, and social arrangements. In each of the criminal cases that I will discuss here, Mexicans spoke publicly from the witness stand of sex and sexuality, and in each case, those articulations expanded that which was sexually possible. Their testimony, I argue, challenged, if at times only briefly and fleetingly, the notion that the erotic, whether Mexican or otherwise, could exist only in the context of the heterosexual, the marital, and the reproductive.

The chapter will thus follow Roderick Ferguson's provocative call for theorists of racial and class formation to follow "sexuality's many extensive routes" for insight into enduring forms of social inequality.[4] One such route leads to colonialism. Colonial regimes often insisted that aberrant sex (sex between men, for instance, or between women, or across racial boundaries, or between family members, or with oneself) was largely the domain of colonial subjects, not colonial rulers.[5] Following sexuality's many routes leads to another set of developing social boundaries. Just as racial dividing lines hardened in the early twentieth century, so too emerged increasingly solid divisions between normative sex (marital, reproductive, heterosexual) and "queer" sex (same-sex sexual intimacy; sex outside a marital, reproductive setting; interracial sex).[6] Mexicans engaged in nonnormative sex were thus the targets of multiple, overlapping, and accelerating forms of exclusion. The challenges posed by otherwise ordinary Mexicans to these new sexual and racial categories and divisions—the expressions of nonnormative desire that occurred during a period of increasing marginalization and violence directed at Mexicans in the United States—point to instabilities in colonial rule, gaps where Mexicans could present their sex lives as the opposite of aberrant: as normal, healthy, and fulfilling.

On January 6, 1916, three days after being sworn in and beginning its term, an Austin County grand jury heard testimony from three men (J. D. Palm,

William Palm, and T. A. Sproles) in the case of A. Gomez and William Heller. Two of the three witnesses, William Palm and J. D. Palm, both Anglos, were related. William was a German immigrant in his mid-fifties and J. D. was his twenty-seven-year-old son. In 1910, six years earlier, they had lived in the same house in Austin County with forty-two-year-old Emma, the mother of the family and also an immigrant from Germany, and three other children ranging in age from thirteen to twenty-one. The third witness, T. A. Sproles, was also an Anglo. He was thirty-six when the trial began and in 1910 had lived in Wallis, Texas, with his wife and four young children. In Wallis, Sproles owned his home and was employed, according to the census, in "hauling" and "public work."[7]

While the testimony of the three men has disappeared, as have many of the documents related to the case, their words must have been persuasive. The grand jury voted to charge A. Gomez with the crime of sodomy. Although the names of the members of the grand jury have disappeared, the case files include the name of the foreman of that grand jury: Louis Machemehl. Machemehl was born in Texas of German descent on his father's side, his mother was a Texas native, and he was in his mid-thirties when he was called upon to serve on the Austin County grand jury. In 1910, the census had identified him as married for five years, with two small children. His wife, also a native Texan, had listed herself as the mother of three children in total, one of whom had apparently died. Louis Machemehl was a rancher, a "stockman," according to the census, and the Machemehl family owned its own home in a relatively well-to-do neighborhood. Their neighbors, several of whom had been born in Germany like Machemehl's father, were largely Anglos, with one exception. The Mosley family was of mixed background, with mother Alice listed as "Mexican," father John as "Black," and sons Henry and George, both in their teens, like their mother also listed as "Mexican." Despite the presence of a non-Anglo family in the Machemehl's neighborhood, it is clear that Anglos (witnesses, foreman of the jury) dominated the courtroom during Gomez's grand jury inquiry.[8]

The sodomy indictment that Machemehl's grand jury would draw up against Gomez would later become an issue in Gomez's appeal. The indictment accused both Gomez and William Heller of engaging in "a venereal affair with each other and carnally [knowing] each other" and "together with each other commit[ing]" sodomy. As Gomez's appeals brief would point out, nowhere in the indictment was there specific language about the particular sexual acts that Gomez himself, as an individual, had committed. The indictment stated only that Gomez and Heller *together* had been guilty of sodomy.[9]

Five days after being indicted by the grand jury, Gomez, who had managed to obtain legal representation, appeared in court with his legal team to plead not guilty to the charge. On the same day, his lawyers, from the firm of Johnson, Mathaei and Thompson, filed a motion asking the court to suspend Gomez's sentence in the event that he should be convicted of the crime. The motion to suspend the charges informed the court that Gomez was "a boy of about seventeen years of age and that he has never heretofore been convicted of a felony in this state or in any other state." The motion, however, was denied, and Gomez's trial began.[10]

Charles Kaechele was the only juror identified in Gomez's court records. Kaechele, white, thirty-six, and a Texas native, was the foreman of the jury and signed the guilty verdict sentencing Gomez to five years in the state penitentiary. The last census, from 1910, listed Kaechele living in Wallis, a small town in southeastern Austin County, with Clara, his wife of ten years, and their nine-year-old daughter, Edna. He was a farmer like his neighbors, many of whom were either European immigrants or African Americans, but Kaechele stood out as one of the few to own his land, rather than rent it. A decade later, Kaechele still lived in Austin County with his wife, daughter, and an eight-year-old son. Like the grand jury proceedings, Anglos thus seem to have held exclusive positions of authority during Gomez's trial.[11]

During the trial itself, the prosecution apparently called only one witness, whose name is not recorded in the court records. One possibility, unverifiable without further evidence, is that the witness was William Heller, who may have testified against Gomez in exchange for a lesser sentence or immunity from prosecution. Regardless of his or her identity, the prosecution's lone witness must have been convincing indeed, for not only did the jury convict Gomez, but his motion for a new trial did not directly refute any of the charges against him.[12]

Two months later, on March 21, 1916, Gomez filed an appeal of his conviction before the Texas Court of Criminal Appeals. Gomez and his lawyers argued that the trial court's first error had been to accept the wording of charges brought against Gomez by the original grand jury indictment. "The indictment," they argued, "[did] not charge any offense against the laws of this State with such particularity as is necessary." Like the indictment, the verdict provided few details about the particular criminal sex acts that Gomez had supposedly committed. The verdict read simply: "We, the jury, find the defendant guilty, as charged in the indictment and assess his punishment at confinement in the penitentiary for a term of five years." Unfortunately for Gomez, his legal team seems to have neglected to include a trial transcript or a statement of facts with the documents submitted to the higher court. Noting the omission, the court ruled against Gomez and affirmed his conviction.[13]

Close reading of the documents, bolstered by the work of other historians of sexuality, can help peel back some of the mystery surrounding the event in question and the individuals involved. It is notable, for instance, that the two men were charged with the crime of sodomy and not one of the many other crimes that have historically been used to police same-sex intimacy. Legal officials throughout the country had, and continue to have, at their disposal a wide array of criminal offenses that they could level at men having sex with men. Charges could range from the less severe, like loitering or disturbing the peace, to those crimes carrying the harshest sentences, like sodomy. Any number of reasons could lead to lesser charges being filed against men arrested in compromising sexual situations, including the protection of "respectable" citizens from undue exposure and humiliation as well as a lack of strong evidence of same-sex sexual contact. That both A. Gomez and William Heller were charged with sodomy suggests that there was fairly compelling evidence available against them, most likely an eyewitness who actually saw the men having sex.[14]

Mexicans' thin purchase on citizenship is also evident in *Texas v. Gomez*. Gomez's response to both his indictment and his conviction reflects on the one hand a certain sense of entitlement under the law. Gomez could have pleaded guilty to the original charges and accepted his sentence without going to trial. Likewise, he could have decided either not to request a new trial or not to appeal his conviction to a higher court. Instead, he obtained legal counsel and seemed determined to exercise his full range of legal options. At the same time, Gomez clearly faced several barriers in claiming full citizenship. While he may have been able to claim legal equality (or at least the ability to navigate the criminal justice system and defend himself through legal briefs and court filings), broader cultural citizenship proved more elusive. For instance, while the full list of jury members was not included in the case file, neither the foreman of the grand jury nor the foreman of the trial jury had Spanish surnames, and all three witnesses testifying in the case were Anglo. Mexicans in the West were largely excluded from jury membership, and so it is unlikely that any Mexicans served on either the grand jury or the trial proceedings. Gomez was also invisible in census documents from the period. While other, Anglo trial participants like J. D. Palm, William Palm, T. A. Sproles, Charles Kaechele, and Louis Machemehl appear in the decennial census, some persisting in the census over several decades, A. Gomez is far harder to track. No "A. Gomez" appears in either the 1910 or the 1920 US census living in Austin County, Texas. In fact, in 1910 and 1920, there were no individuals with the Gomez surname living in the entire county. The court's repeated decision to omit his first name renders such archival tracing especially difficult; such omission seems to point further to Gomez's marginal civic status.[15]

A decade later and two hundred miles to the southwest, Juan Muñoz was charged with sodomy in Laredo, Texas. Muñoz, thirty-five years old, was accused of engaging in oral sex with fifteen-year-old Carlos Myers in a garage behind a house in late October 1925. A month later, Muñoz's criminal trial began in the Webb County courthouse in Laredo with John Valls, the district attorney in Webb County representing the prosecution, and two Anglos, Gordon Gibson and John S. Morris, representing Muñoz. The first witness called by the district attorney was none other than the district attorney himself. Valls testified that he had conducted the preliminary examination of Muñoz on the morning after his arrest. "I explained the nature of the case against him," he said, "that he was not obliged to make any statement whatever." Muñoz, he said, nonetheless chose to make a statement to Valls, who was joined in the room by several police officers, including the justice of the peace and the deputy sheriff. "He spoke in the Spanish language," Valls recalled, "and the statement was written in the Spanish language." Valls, who described himself as "able to read and write Spanish," then read the statement back to Muñoz, who signed it. The statement read, in full: "No tengo mas que decirle a Usted que es verdad que yo le mame a Carlos Myers." "I have nothing more to say to you," Valls translated for the jury, "than that it is true that I sucked Carlos Myers."[16]

Carlos Myers was the second, and final, witness for the prosecution. Myers said that he was fifteen years old and lived at 917 Victoria Street in Laredo. He also stated that his father's name was Enrique Myers.[17] After identifying himself, Myers recounted what had occurred a month earlier, on October 21, 1925. "What happened was this," he said:

> When I got there at the garage back of the house, there was also a room and in the room there is a bed, and I went in and sat down on the bed and he knelt down in that position and he opened or unbuttoned my pants and he would take my member into his mouth, that I use to urinate with. He put that member into his mouth, and when I told him I was going to throw off what comes to him, he would tell me no, that he would eat it. That happened at the garage back of Alexander's house, one block from the Junior High School, on the right hand side.

Muñoz's lawyers declined to cross-examine Myers, and the prosecution rested its case.[18]

Juan Muñoz was the only witness for the defense. He testified in Spanish that he had "never been convicted of a felony" and "never been in Court before for any trouble." "I am not married," the thirty-five-year-old said, "I have a mother and a father who are dependent on me, but they are not here." "They are across the River," he added, in Mexico. Under cross-examination, Muñoz readily admitted that he and Carlos Myers had engaged in sexual acts together. "I sucked Carlos Myers," Muñoz testified. "He did not put his male member into my mouth—I did it," he said, "I took into my mouth his male member, here in Laredo, Webb County, Texas."[19]

Muñoz was subsequently convicted of sodomy and sentenced to five years in the Texas state penitentiary. Like A. Gomez, however, he appealed his conviction to the Court of Criminal Appeals of Texas. Muñoz and his attorneys argued that the statute governing sodomy did not include oral copulation and that oral sex was not legally a crime according to the Texas legal code. A clearly vexed court agreed, noting that "however vile and detestable the act may have been, it does not come within the definition of 'sodomy' as known to the common law and adopted by legislative enactment in our State." Muñoz's conviction was subsequently reversed and his case returned to the lower court. Local authorities, in light of the higher court's clear statement that Muñoz did not commit sodomy, may have opted to try him on a lesser charge. It is also possible that no new charges were filed and Muñoz was released, a free man once again.[20]

Juan Muñoz and A. Gomez were both tried and convicted of sodomy in early twentieth-century Texas and both men appealed their cases, one successfully, to the state's highest court. While their appeals cases are exceptional in many ways, Muñoz and Gomez were not the only Spanish-surnamed men charged with same-sex sexual crimes in the West. In Los Angeles County, for instance, six non-Spanish surnamed men and one Mexican man were charged with "the infamous crime against nature" between 1917 and 1920. To the north, in Oakland, California, records from Alameda County indicate that one man was charged with sodomy in 1930: Juan Herelia. Herelia was one of three Spanish-surnamed men (Frank Rodrigues and Louis Torres for rape and Herelia for sodomy) charged with sex crimes in the county in 1930. Herelia was also one of the few men who appeared in both county criminal records and the US census. In 1930, Herelia was listed in the census as an inmate in Oakland's Alameda County Jail. He was thirty-eight and a widower who had been married at the age of eighteen. He was a native of Puerto Rico and listed his occupation as "Mariner." While Herelia was described in the census as "White," he was also clearly of Puerto Rican descent—both his parents had been born in Puerto Rico and "Spanish" was written under the category "language spoken at home before coming to the United States." While the above men were arrested on sodomy charges, it is not clear if any were subsequently convicted of the crime and none appear in appeals records. Nonetheless, their fleeting appearances in criminal and census records in California suggest that the policing, and likely demonization, of Mexican (and Puerto Rican) same-sex sexual intimacy extended beyond the Gomez and Muñoz cases.[21]

Elsewhere in the West, local arrest records from San Antonio reveal that twelve men were charged with sodomy between 1900 and 1930. The charges occurred sporadically, with spans of several years in which no one in San Antonio was charged with the crime. There were no sodomy charges in 1890 or in the years 1900–1904. One man was charged in 1905, another in 1906, and two more in 1908, 1914, and 1915, respectively. The highest total was in 1917, when three men faced sodomy charges. Only one man was charged in the next year, with an additional two in 1919 and one in 1920. In two cases during those years, the charges were repeated— Hal Brumbley was charged twice in 1917 and 1918, as was Thomas Irving in 1919 and 1920. Between 1921 and 1930, there was not a single charge of sodomy filed in San Antonio. Two of the twelve men charged with sodomy in Bexar County had Spanish surnames: Fred Trevino, charged with two counts in 1905, and Donaciano Garcia, also charged twice in 1908.[22]

Texas census records help clarify this glimpse into Mexican same-sex intimacy in the West. According to the US census, in 1900, the only individual with a name similar to the first man, Fred Trevino, in Bexar County was Frederico Trevino, who was the newborn child of Pedro and Simona Trevino. There were five other men with the same name scattered throughout Texas that year, with ages ranging from two to fourteen to forty. In 1910, a man named Fred A. Trevino, thirty-four, lived in nearby Bee County.[23] The second Spanish-surnamed individual charged with sodomy in Bexar County was Donaciano Garcia, who was charged in 1908. In 1900, the only individual named Donaciano Garcia in Texas was eighteen and lived with his widowed mother, Mercedes, in Starr County along the US-Mexico border in South Texas. Ten years later, in 1910, and two years after Donaciano Garcia was charged with sodomy in Bexar County, an eighteen-year-old named Donaciano Garcia appeared as an inmate at the Texas state "lunatic asylum" in Austin. According to the census, Garcia was born in Texas, with both parents born in Mexico, and the word "Mexican" was scribbled in the margins of the census page, one of two such annotations on the page (the other was written alongside the name of forty-one-year-old Concepcion Martínez). It seems likely that the Donaciano Garcia charged with sodomy in San Antonio in 1908 was the same Donaciano Garcia imprisoned in a Texas asylum in 1910. Curiously, Garcia was also listed on the 1910 census schedule as a female inmate of the asylum. There are, of course, several possible explanations for Garcia's appearance as a female in the census schedule. Mundanely, a typographical error may have occurred, or there may have been two individuals with the same name, one charged with sodomy in San Antonio in 1908, another incarcerated in 1910. Or, it is possible that the census enumerator recorded a fascinating moment of Mexican gender ambiguity and transgression. Donaciano Garcia's appearance in the census would not have been the only appearance in the historical record of nonnormative gender identity in the early twentieth century, but Garcia's presence is, like that of many other Mexicans, fleeting, leaving little but speculation as to her/his life. In any case, it is clear that Juan Muñoz and A. Gomez were not the only Spanish-surnamed men, or women, to face a legal apparatus committed to policing and punishing same-sex sexual acts.[24]

The determination by Gomez and Muñoz to confront this legal apparatus and appeal their convictions—and the subsequent trial record that their appeals processes produced—also reflects ongoing colonial tensions in the region, as well as Mexicans' vexed position as colonial subjects. American settler colonialism in the West had for many decades in the nineteenth century defined Anglo newcomers as natives to the land, as "Americans," and Mexican inhabitants as "foreigners." As I've noted, this process accelerated in the early twentieth century, and Mexicans—regardless of ancestry, duration in the United States, or citizenship status—found avenues to inclusion increasingly blocked or constricted. Tensions emerged in both trials between exclusive, taxonomic visions of citizenship ("Americans" incompatible with and separated by a rigid, unbending divide from "Mexicans" or "foreigners") and a more inclusive model of citizenship in which "Mexicans" were considered potential, if not immediate, citizens.[25]

In certain respects, both men were far removed from citizenship. Juan Muñoz, for instance, was not an English speaker. He spoke predominantly Spanish, so much so that his confession ("Yo le mame a Carlos Myers") had to be written in Spanish in order for him to sign it. Muñoz also literally traversed the US-Mexico border on a regular basis in order to care for his parents. Such border crossings, as historians have pointed out, were highly charged, and suspect, events in early twentieth-century Texas.[26] As in the case of A. Gomez, Juan Muñoz was similarly rendered invisible in the US census records. No Juan Muñoz appears in Laredo or larger Webb County in either 1920 or 1930.[27] Like A. Gomez, Juan Muñoz thus faced a host of challenges upon his arrest on the charge of sodomy. He was accused of performing oral sex on another male twenty years his junior and, based on the surname (Myers) of his partner, had also engaged in cross-cultural intimacy. Both forms of sexual activity (cross-cultural and same-sex) were heavily policed and punished in early twentieth-century America.[28]

At the same time, Juan Muñoz made several attempts to highlight his citizenly attributes during the trial. While the legal system, namely the prosecution and appeals court, depicted Muñoz as sexually aberrant and seemed to emphasize his distance from Americanness in both his utterances and his legal maneuvers, Muñoz crafted a competing vision of himself. He described himself as financially responsible and dutiful to his parents ("I have a mother and a father who are dependent on me") as well as law-abiding ("I have never been convicted of a felony in this state of Texas or any other state"; "I have never been in court before for any trouble"). It is also worth recalling that Juan Muñoz actually won his appeal to the Texas Court of Criminal Appeals on the charge of sodomy. While the coercive power of the state (the power to compel a confession and enforce incarceration) undoubtedly weighed heavily on Muñoz, he ultimately proved capable of defending himself and producing another form of power: a narrative in which he confessed to being a Spanish-speaking Mexican man who performed oral sex on another man, and did so in what was, in the end, judged noncriminal behavior. *Texas v. Muñoz* suggests, then, that even the policing of Mexican men's nonnormative sexual behaviors had the capacity to authorize multiple, even competing visions of Mexican civic inclusion.

While Mexican men involved in same-sex intimacies, such as A. Gomez and Juan Muñoz, appear only rarely in the historical record, Mexican women's understandings of sex and sexuality are even harder to trace. Throughout this book, Mexican women have appeared in court records and at times have spoken publicly and candidly on the witness stand about their sexual lives. Unsurprisingly, however, given the compulsion in the legal setting to portray oneself as respectable and worthy of the rights of full citizenship, such rare testimony by Mexican women is for the most part voiced within a heterosexual and reproductive framework. The case of *California v. Jesse Martínez* highlights both this adherence to established sexual norms and the demonization of nonnormative sexual practices.

In 1919, in Oakdale, California, Jesse Martínez was convicted of raping his neighbor, twelve-year-old Catharine Medina, both in the home of her family and in an abandoned chicken coop behind the house. During the trial, Medina's stepmother, who had adopted the girl ten years earlier, contradicted her stepdaughter's account and actually testified in support of Martínez's innocence. According to Evaline Medina, her stepdaughter had tried to hide her clothes from her parents and when confronted with the soiled laundry, "just soaked from head to foot with puss [sic]," had claimed that a man named Joe Paris had assaulted her. Medina then asked the girl whether Jesse Martínez had attacked her and, according to Evaline Medina, Catharine Medina replied, "No, honest to God Lena, he never did." Medina went on to testify that the girl frequently lied to others and was in general "a very bad girl."[29]

At a most basic level, the trial reveals once again the unequal status of Mexican women and girls. Somebody, after all, sexually assaulted twelve-year-old Catharine Medina, and her family proved unable, or unwilling, to protect her. Evaline Medina also testified in some detail about Catharine Medina's acts of masturbation dating back a full decade. Asked to describe what the girl's "habits [were] in regard to abusing herself," Medina replied, "she has always abused herself." Barely a week after she joined the Medina family, according to Medina, the three-year-old girl was discovered "abusing herself" with "a stick." She supposedly continued the practice for years to come. "I saw her do it afterwards," Medina said, "lots of times." Asked whether she attempted to prevent the girl's masturbation, Medina answered, "I sent for the doctor at one time." In her account, it is important to note that Evaline Medina does not frame Catharine Medina's masturbation as a religious problem or a sin (or, frankly, as a sign of possible early sexual abuse). Instead, Medina approaches masturbation largely as a medical issue. In doing so, she joins the numerous other Mexican women and men in the West who turned to medicine for answers to their sex-related questions. As discussed earlier in the book, medical modernity seems to have made significant inroads into Mexican communities, whether those inroads took the form of seeking medical advice for a stepdaughter's masturbation or consulting a doctor during childbirth or when a loved one fell into poor health.[30]

More striking is Medina's condemnation of her stepdaughter's supposed sexual excesses. Female masturbation is associated with lies and deception, rendered pathological and medically unhealthy ("I sent for the doctor at one time"), and placed in direct opposition to heterosexual sexual intimacy. By denouncing Catharine's sexual transgressions, Evaline Medina emerges by contrast as sexually continent and "normal." Medina was certainly not among California's Mexican elite class in the early twentieth century, yet her testimony drew a sharp divide between the sexual activities of her stepdaughter and what she alluded to as normal sexual behavior within the Mexican community. Given the primacy of sexual propriety in claims of citizenship ("Chinese American activists," Nayan Shah notes, "plac[ed] the viability of the nuclear family at the center of entitlement claims . . . All other social relations and networks were rendered deviant and decidedly un-American"), it is worth contemplating the extent to which a wider segment of the Mexican community fashioned claims to citizenship from assertions of sexual norms and respectability.[31]

At the same time, while no one in the courtroom rose to defend Catharine's acts of masturbation, the absence of such a public defense should not be taken as proof that Catharine's actions fell entirely on disapproving ears. Rather, trial testimony may have emboldened some within earshot, potentially validating their sexual inclinations rather than denigrating them. Public censure and disapproval is not, after all, as straightforward as it would often seem. Denunciations of transgressive sexual behavior could in fact, for some, suggest new sexual possibilities rather than closing the doors, as the authors of such pronouncements surely hoped, to sexual aberrance. Tightening sexual divisions in the early twentieth century increasingly pathologized and criminalized sexual practices like masturbation, and American colonial rule offered few rewards to those unable, or unwilling, to follow established sexual norms. Still, the case, and this chapter in general, suggests that American courts, despite a commitment to smothering nonnormative sexual activity and desire, could offer spaces to articulate the notion that Mexican sexual expressions—and perhaps even sexual pleasure—could expand beyond a heterosexual, reproductive context.

Traces of another form of transgressive sex—cross-cultural desire and intimacy—appear in other criminal cases from the West. Policing interracial sex was a high priority for law enforcement officials in the early twentieth century, and interracial intimacies were denounced and prohibited on multiple fronts. While prosecutions of interracial couplings sought to punish the accused and discourage others from committing similar offenses, the trials themselves could also offer the backdrop for the performance of alternative forms of desire.[32]

One such trial occurred in Southern California in the last decade of the nineteenth century. In 1891, twenty-five-year-old Juan Mesa was accused of attempting to rape Alice Westfall in Ventura, California. According to thirteen-year-old Westfall, she and Mesa were neighbors and had been close acquaintances for several months. "I have seen Juan Mesa a good many times," she testified, and they had even exchanged letters. "I have written a few notes to him, when he had written me," she said. On the night of May 31, 1891, Westfall and Mesa had been walking together along a fairly well-traveled street when Mesa, who in Westfall's words "did not have his arm around me, did not make any demonstration towards me, nor take any liberties with me," suddenly and without warning "simply pushed me off the sidewalk." Despite her strong resistance, Mesa then "raised [her] dress and tore [her] underdrawers" before Westfall told Mesa that she heard "someone was coming" and managed to escape. Juan Mesa's claims of innocence apparently were unpersuasive to the jury and he was convicted of attempted statutory rape. He was sentenced to a ten-year term in the California state prison.[33]

Facing a decade in jail, Juan Mesa and his lawyers sought to obtain a new trial. New evidence, they argued, had now come to light that could exonerate Mesa. His legal team produced affidavits from several individuals who all reported seeing Mesa and Westfall at the time of the alleged attack walking along a street a half mile from the site of the attack. One man, Joseph Taylor, explained that he had not come forward with the information earlier because "he did not want to be mixed up in a rape case." Another man, Alfredo Ortega, asserted that his brother, Charles Ortega, had been "against the advice and consent of [his brother] for some time going with and keeping company with the said Alice Westfall" and that Westfall had told Charles Ortega "that Juan Mesa had not done anything to her." In response, Alice Westfall produced an affidavit stating that her original testimony had been truthful and accurate. The court subsequently turned down Mesa's petition for a new trial.[34]

Undeterred, Mesa pressed his case to the California Supreme Court. His appeal argued first on technical grounds that court documents had been improperly and vaguely worded. Second, he contended, the evidence presented in the trial had not been "sufficient" to sustain a conviction. Finally, he pointed to the newly obtained affidavits as evidence warranting a new trial. Unsurprisingly, the higher court found little of substance in Mesa's first contention about the wording of the charge against him and duly dismissed it. The second claim, that the evidence presented in the trial was insufficient to support a guilty verdict, was no more persuasive. "It is said that an inspection of the record will show that she was not a credible witness," the court wrote, "but we are unable to find anything to warrant this conclusion." Other witnesses even corroborated aspects of Alice Westfall's story, the court continued, despite the fact that a conviction could have been "had upon the uncorroborated testimony of the prosecutrix."

Finally, the court ruled that the affidavits contradicting Alice's testimony were merely "cumulative" of the testimony of the defendant and did not "constitute good ground for granting a new trial." In the end, Juan Mesa's appeal was denied and his original ten-year prison sentence was upheld.[35]

The interracial relationship between Juan Mesa and Alice Westfall was a central, and contested, feature of the trial. While Alice and her mother, Mary Westfall, contended that their courtship was far from serious, Mesa and his defenders, including his own mother, viewed their intentions as more substantial. The couple's attraction to each other is evident from the trial transcript. They had known each other for several months, according to Westfall, and Mesa had once accompanied her home from a holiday dance at his mother's house. Westfall twice mentioned writing letters to Mesa and recounted his declarations of love for her. "He has told me at times before this affair," she testified, "that he loved me better than he loved any other, but I didn't believe him." Moreover, her recollection of conversations with Mesa about "a girl by the name of Simosa" are echoed by Mesa's assertion that on the night in question the two argued about another young woman ("We had some words over a Spanish girl," he later testified). Though over a century old, Westfall's testimony still resonates today: "I told him lots of times not to mention it. I didn't want to know anything about her. She is pretty dark. She wasn't, from what I heard, a girl of very good character. Juan has mentioned her to me a great many times and I told him I didn't want to know anything about her." Though she disavowed love for him, Westfall's biting and racially charged testimony can be read to reveal an abiding romantic attachment to Juan Mesa.[36]

Like Westfall, Juan Mesa placed their relationship firmly within a normative framework of heterosexual, marital love. "My intention was to marry her," he said during direct examination, "provided she would be a good girl and behaved herself." "I always thought good of her," he continued, "and thought she was a good girl." Recounting an argument between the two that he claimed occurred on the night of the attack, he recalled telling her "I loved her and I thought I would marry her." He repeated the same claim under cross-examination, adding, "I had good intentions towards her."[37]

Talk of marriage and respectability notwithstanding, Juan's relationship with Alice was anything but conventional. Racial differences and the fact that their intimacy crossed racial boundaries were raised throughout the trial. Alice Westfall's mother testified that she had seen Mesa "go home occasionally with a Spanish girl." "The Spanish girl named Simosa . . . is very good looking," she said, "very Mexican." Juan Mesa spoke of "trouble between me and Alice . . . about a Spanish girl." Mesa also noted during his appeals process that his mother was unable to assist him in defending himself against the charges brought because "she does not speak English." Although the trial transcript does not mention whether his mother testified through the use of a translator, her limited English proficiency would likely have been clear during her testimony. Furthermore, as Alice Westfall pointed out, Juan Mesa was a member of a different, and, to her mind at least, inferior race. "We weren't enemies by any means," she said, but "I never put confidence in him." "I never put confidence in anybody of that race," she added. Given the severity of her charges against Mesa and the difficulty that women traditionally have faced in pursuing rape charges, Westfall surely had an incentive to portray their relationship as friendly, but not romantic. She also, again perhaps unsurprisingly, accentuated his racial otherness ("I never put confidence in anybody of that race") and her own whiteness as a factor in the stalled romance. Anglos, she cannily suggested to the jury, were credible and trustworthy, while Mexicans like Mesa were not to be "put in confidence" or trusted.[38]

Once established, such racial differences could easily be paired during the trial with other, more pernicious social distinctions. E. H. Ireland, a police officer who encountered first a sobbing Alice Westfall and then Juan Mesa minutes after the alleged attack, testified that Mesa had approached him and asked if he planned to place him under arrest. "What should I prosecute you for?" Ireland asked. "For f-k-g the girl," Juan supposedly answered. "I said, 'have you been f-k-g the girl?'" "Yes, I f-k-d her and have been f-k-g her for the last two months," the officer reported that Mesa had said. Though Ireland admitted under cross-examination that during their conversation, he had been "rather pressing [Mesa] into making some kind of statement" and that he may have "been mistaken from his exact words that he used at the time," the repeated use of "f-k-g" in front of the jury portrayed Mesa as exceedingly vulgar and uncouth. Such individual failings, as a jury was likely to have known, were commonly associated with Mexican and other marginally white communities. Likewise, when Mary Westfall observed that she "would rather send Juan Mesa to the penitentiary than have him marry my daughter," she, knowingly or not, invoked the common association between Mexicans and criminality. Well aware of the potency of such racialized understandings, Mesa's lawyer was quick to step in when the prosecution broached the subject of Mesa's criminal past. During cross-examination of Mesa's mother, the prosecutor asked her to explain her son's recent absence from home. "We admit that he came home from the penitentiary," his lawyer interjected. "I don't know why we need to put the question to the old lady," he continued, "save her the pain of answering."[39]

A convicted criminal on trial for the attempted rape of a white thirteen-year-old, Juan Mesa was in a tight spot. Mesa could hardly have been unaware of negative depictions of Mexicans that had permeated civic life in Southern California since the early nineteenth century. A central feature of his defense strategy, in fact, was to portray himself as a respectable and hardworking member of the community. His legal team, for example, solicited testimony about his gentlemanly behavior toward Westfall previous to the night of May 31, 1891, and his gainful employment as a quarry worker was noted on several occasions. One of the witnesses to testify in Mesa's defense was Charles Levy, who testified that Mesa was "in my employ at the stone quarry in Casitas, on or about the 31st day of May." "I saw him when he got to the quarry on the morning of the 1st of June," Levy added. Mesa and his defenders also sought to distance him from Mexico and Mexicans. His mother, recall, described him as a "Californian," while he recounted an argument with Westfall about a "Spanish" (not a "Mexican") young woman. As an employed, English-speaking native "Californian," Mesa could make certain plausible claims to citizenship. His subsequent appeal of his conviction was further evidence that he considered himself to be entitled to certain rights and legal prerogatives within the American judicial system.[40]

Mesa articulated both his love for Alice Westfall and his intention to marry her from this context of his claims to the rights of citizenship. "I loved her," he said, "and I thought I would marry her." In effect, Mesa suggested that his sexual transgression, his love for a "white" female, framed as potentially marital and reproductive, be granted as much legitimacy as his other claims to citizenship. Surely desperate not to be convicted of attempted rape, Mesa was also unambiguous, and unapologetic, about his desire for Alice Westfall. While jurors and other members of the courtroom may have been unconvinced and may have found little to redeem romantic intimacy across racial boundaries, Mesa's proclamation is hardly insignificant. It is a deposition of alternative desire authored by a Mexican through cracks in the emerging racial order in the Southwest.[41]

Discussions of normal and abnormal sex also offered Mexican witnesses an opportunity to present themselves as members of decent families. During the trial, the distaste that Dolores de Valenzuela, Mesa's mother, held for both Westfall and her mother was barely concealed as she recounted a conversation between the families one evening before the attack. "Mrs. Westfall said it was good for them to marry," she recalled. "I told my son," she testified, "it was better for us to go home." But Valenzuela was not opposed to marriage. She was opposed to her son marrying Alice Westfall. She remembered telling her son: "This lady wants you to marry her daughter and you are a poor Californian, and I don't want you to marry her because she goes out nights and goes around; that is all I have to say." Though, as mentioned earlier, the transcript does not indicate that Valenzuela testified in Spanish, "Californian" was likely the English version of the Spanish *californio*, the term identifying native Californians of Mexican, or Spanish-Mexican, descent. Through much of the nineteenth century in California, daughters of elite Mexican families had married male Anglo newcomers, forming family alliances and, in some cases, facilitating the transfer of land and wealth into the hands of Anglo men. Referring to her son as a "poor Californian" tidily reverses the scenario so that the family seeking an alliance for their daughter is Anglo and the prospective groom is Mexican.[42]

Of far greater concern for Valenzuela than cross-cultural romance is the sexual comportment of her potential daughter-in-law. Valenzuela tells her son that she objects to his marriage to Westfall "because she goes out nights and goes around." Westfall was sexually intemperate, in other words, refusing to stay at home at night, and promiscuous, in space as well as sex, "going around" to various locations and, presumably in Valenzuela's estimation, to various men besides her son. Of course, Valenzuela, who seemed to love and defend her son, had a considerable stake in portraying Alice Westfall as sexually profligate—namely, challenging Westfall's sexual reputation could undermine her rape accusation against Valenzuela's son. Still, Valenzuela actively upholds a sexual double standard that views female sexual freedom with special disdain. It is notable that the mother of a "poor Californian" would present herself and her family as sexually respectable (especially in accentuating the value of marital reproductive sex) and an Anglo like Alice Westfall as sexually aberrant.

California v. Mesa thus both reinforced racial dividing lines in the West and provided a space for challenging those divisions. During the trial, witnesses consistently highlighted racial categories like "Mexican" and "Spanish" and, with varying degrees of subtlety, alluded to the association between Mexicans and poor behavior and criminality. At the same time, the defendant, Juan Mesa, publically proclaimed his affection for a "white" woman and his plans to marry her. His mother, moreover, publically asserted her own family's sexual propriety, an assertion standing in stark opposition to turn-of-the-twentieth-century attacks on the domestic customs and home lives of Mexican communities. That Dolores de Valenzuela would identify her son and herself as "Californian" points to a history of American colonial rule in the region and Valenzuela's clear recognition of that history. Juan Mesa's subsequent appeal of his guilty verdict in the trial, though ultimately unsuccessful, reflects in part his attempt, and likely the attempt of his mother, to maintain Mexican legal rights in the United States and to challenge racial exclusions (like opposition to cross-cultural intimacy between Mexican men and Anglo women) and Mexican marginalization.

Juan Mesa, of course, was not the only Mexican to announce publicly affection that transcended racial or ethnic boundaries. Besides offering a rare glimpse at same-sex liaisons involving Mexicans, the two sodomy cases that began this chapter both offered evidence of cross-cultural sexual intimacy in the Southwest. Before his motion to be tried individually, recall, A. Gomez had been a codefendant with William Heller on the sodomy charge. They had been charged with committing sodomy together, with no mention of force or the use of physical violence by either individual. Likewise, force does not appear to be an issue in the Muñoz case, in which Carlos Myers, or "Meyers," engaged in oral copulation.

Like a significant number of Mexicans across the region, Juan Mesa clearly considered it his prerogative in California to challenge his conviction to a higher court. Mesa's conviction of attempted rape was eventually affirmed by the California higher court, but many other Mexicans won their appeals cases in the West. Mexican success in the courts, of course, could be the result of multiple factors, including the performance and conduct, or misconduct, of trial judges, lawyers, and juries. Juan Muñoz, for instance, won his appeal because he was incorrectly charged with sodomy after engaging in oral sex, not anal sex, with Carlos Myers. Similar types of errors occurred in two other sodomy cases from Texas, neither of which involved a Mexican appellant. A year before Muñoz's legal victory, Fred Hamilton argued to the higher court that he had been wrongfully convicted of contributing to the delinquency of a minor in Tarrant County, in north central Texas, where Fort Worth is located. Hamilton had been discovered one night under a loading dock at a warehouse with a sixteen-year-old young man. The teenager was the prosecution's star witness, testifying that Hamilton had been "very drunk" and had "told him he wanted him to go down there [under the loading dock] with him and gave him a dollar to go with him." He also testified, however, that Hamilton never actually mentioned sexual activity and in fact "did nothing to him after they got to the place." Hamilton, he said, "did not touch him."[43]

According to the higher court's written decision, Hamilton's accuser simply assumed that "the appellant wanted him to go down there for the purpose of engaging in an act of sodomy." "This testimony is not sufficient," the court stated, "under our law, a party cannot be convicted on the mere surmise or supposition of a witness." "It takes testimony to overcome the presumption of innocence and reasonable doubt," the court added, "and the record in this case fails to disclose any evidence that would do either." The decision concluded by throwing out Hamilton's $250.00 fine and sentence of six months in prison and sending the case back to the Tarrant County court.[44]

In a second sodomy case—a rare appeals case involving an African American defendant—John Lee Berry appealed a sodomy conviction, and a five-year prison term, from Taylor County, Texas, in 1910. During the trial, several witnesses testified that they observed Berry committing sodomy with a cow. Berry, according to the appeals record, was arrested and "asked a great many questions" before signing a written confession to the crime. During the trial, his defense apparently attempted to exclude the confession and to convince the judge to offer detailed instructions to the jury regarding the credibility of the confession. In both cases, the defense argued that Berry lacked the "mental capacity and competency as a witness" and thus the confession was invalid. The appeals request, and subsequent ruling, rested heavily on this argument about Berry's mental capacity. "Appellant," the higher court noted, "is an unlearned and illiterate negro, and some of the testimony shows that he is crazy to the extent that he did not know the difference between right and wrong, or the nature of the act with which he was charged." Berry, the court continued, "was considered sort of a fool, half-witted and hardly a responsible creature." The court ruled that the trial judge should have instructed "the jury with reference to appellant's insanity" and thus overturned Berry's conviction and returned the case to Taylor County.[45]

Like Mexicans, African Americans faced pervasive and growing discrimination and violence in early twentieth-century Texas.[46] The appeals decision in the Berry case provides scarce details to help explain how John Lee Berry, who seemed, at best, to have few available resources, managed to finance a successful appeals process. As in the Hamilton case—and the other sodomy cases of Juan Muñoz and A. Gomez—the higher court in Berry's appeal focused more on errors in the trial proceedings (jury instructions not delivered, or delivered improperly) and paid little attention to the extent to which each man qualified for, or fell short of, citizenship. As I have addressed at various points in this book, trial transcripts and court decisions can be exceedingly murky documents. Certain lawyerly strategies or judicial decisions could owe as much to an attorney's eagerness to craft a winning argument for a client or a higher court's determination to correct and discipline a wayward local judge than they could represent recognition of the rights of ordinary Mexicans in the legal system.

Nonetheless, questions of citizenship and belonging are deeply embedded in the legal process. In a landscape of increasing demonization and deprivation for Mexicans, as the early twentieth century surely was, trial transcripts and appeals decisions point in a different direction. In court settings, ordinary Mexicans had a rare opportunity to speak publically, in front of an audience of fellow Mexicans, as well as Anglos and other races, and to construct—even in the context of a courtroom, where the power of the state to humiliate, divide, and punish was certainly keenly felt— narratives of their own lives. There was also an opportunity to defend and speak well of themselves and their families and communities—once again for Mexicans a rare and rapidly vanishing opportunity. For defendants and appellants, the American legal system could also offer a chance for vindication and reversal of fortune. Some Mexicans who were convicted of crimes in the West never appealed their cases and likely served their sentences in relative anonymity. Others, however, including those profiled in this book, appealed their convictions and on occasion won their cases. As this chapter has observed, some of those Mexicans, like Juan Muñoz, A. Gomez, and Juan Mesa, were convicted of crimes that were seen as especially heinous in turn-of-the-century America, like sodomy and sexual attacks by nonwhite men on "American" women.

That Mexicans, even Mexicans associated with nonnormative sexual desires and activity, could find success in American courts speaks as much to Mexican persistence as it does to judicial benevolence. Neither these cases nor the procedural errors and misconduct that could lead to a reversal would have even appeared before the courts in the first place if not for the insistence by Mexican defendants that their cases be appealed. Mexicans encountering American courts, whether as defendants, victims of crimes, witnesses in trials, or concerned relatives and friends, had few advantages. Many spoke little or no English, had few financial resources, and may have been unfamiliar with American laws and legal processes. The Mexicans mentioned in this chapter, from Juan Muñoz and A. Gomez to Catharine Medina and Juan Mesa to the men arrested on local criminal charges, remained socially marginal within broader Anglo society in the West. As this chapter has suggested, gender and sexual transgressions compounded such marginalization. At the same time, many Mexicans appeared capable of defending themselves in American courts. American colonial rule was an unstable blend of exclusion and inclusion, and ordinary Mexicans in the courts played an important, and often unacknowledged, role in promoting their own inclusion in the early twentieth century. Through pretrial motions, courtroom testimony, and appeals briefs, such Mexicans asserted their right to be treated justly and fairly within the American legal system.

SIX

Courtship and the Courts

There are two main versions of how sixteen-year-old Josefita Martínez came to be pregnant in the small northern New Mexico town of Sabinoso in the fall of 1914. In one version, Josefita and Juan Lujan, who had grown up together in Sabinoso, had sexual intercourse one September evening in the home of Juan's parents while his sister painted the walls in the next room and his parents slept. Juan, according to this account, promised to marry Josefita if they had sex, and she agreed. In the other version, Josefita had been for several months the *novia*, or sweetheart, of Faustin Gutiérrez, also of Sabinoso. The lovers' ensuing sexual relationship, conducted along river beds and in secluded buildings, eventually produced the pregnancy.

Each version of events had its staunch defenders who would describe, in conflicting detail, the following nine months in Josefita's life. Josefita said that she told no one of her pregnancy, not Juan Lujan (who she claimed was the father of the child), not her sister Aurora, not her mother or her father. Aurora Martínez confirmed her sister's story. Asked later if she had "expected the arrival of the child to [her] sister," she answered, "No, I did not know nothing about it." The birth of the child was a complete surprise, she said. Even days before giving birth, nothing about her sister's appearance suggested to Aurora that Josefita was pregnant.[1]

Others related a much different account of the period between August 1914 and April 1915. Jesus Maria Montoya, a friend of Faustin Gutiérrez, said that he had accompanied Faustin on a visit to Josefita's home one night in March 1915, when Josefita would have been more than seven months pregnant. Josefita, he said, met Faustin at her window. "The night was very dark," Montoya remembered, "and I stood behind him and he was right up behind the sash." Josefita was "by the window, sitting on a chair," and on her lap was a small pile of clothes. "I saw little clothes," he said, "four or five little dresses and a long robe" that Josefita was making for her expected child. According to Montoya, Faustin asked Josefita who the clothes were for and she answered in a low voice "for your child." Further refuting Josefita's claim that she told no one about her pregnancy, Montoya added that two of Josefita's sisters, Aurora and Francisquita, were also in the room at the time.[2]

While opinions varied as to the circumstances of Josefita's pregnancy, there was little doubt about its unfortunate conclusion. On April 13, 1915, Josefita Martínez gave birth alone in a bedroom in her family's home. Her mother was outside in a field planting chiles and her sister Aurora was in the next room. "I was the only one there," Josefita said. She described giving birth, "sitting down in a chair," and then calling out to her sister. The child, Josefita said, was dead. She held the child briefly in her arms before Aurora entered. The two sisters stared at the child for a moment before Aurora picked it up and carried it from the room. According to both Josefita and her sister, Aurora proceeded to dig a hole behind the house and bury the corpse. Aurora said later that she never told her parents, or anybody else, about the death of Josefita's child or the location of its grave.[3]

Several months later, Josefita Martínez officially accused Juan Lujan of the crime of seduction: "by the means of the promise of marriage [inducing] Josefita Martínez to have sexual intercourse with him." The trial began in November 1916 in the San Miguel County courthouse in Las Vegas, New Mexico. San Miguel County had a population of 23,000 in 1910. Ten years later, it was once again at 23,000 and grew only slightly in the following decades. Despite its relatively small population, San Miguel County was a central player in nineteenth- and twentieth-century New Mexico, due largely to the influence of its county seat, Las Vegas, which ranked alongside Albuquerque and Santa Fe as a cultural center and an economic and political hub in New Mexico. Mexicans also possessed a significant degree of authority in Las Vegas, and elite Mexican men served as prominent politicians and business leaders. This relative political and economic power of Mexicans in New Mexico differed sharply from many other regions of the West.[4]

Mexican civic authority, in fact, was highlighted on multiple occasions during the trial of Juan Lujan, including during the prosecution's opening argument. In his brief statement to the jury, W. G. Ward, the district attorney representing the prosecution, noted that Juan Lujan and Josefita Martínez were cousins and had lived in the same house for several years during their childhood. The house, he added, was "the house of the grandfather—Don Ramón Martínez." "Don," as a signal of respect and deference, was used often during the trial to identify Ramón Martínez and other high-status Mexicans. In fact, Mexican men on both sides of the aisle were assigned the title "Don." Rafael Crespín, the first witness called for the defense, stated that he worked for Cipriano Lujan, the father of the defendant. He was asked to describe an incident that occurred "at the Cañada de los Tipleys, during the lambing of Don Cipriano's sheep." Faustin Gutiérrez, testifying for the prosecution, recalled a conversation that he held with Juan Lujan that occurred, according to Gutiérrez, "at Don Cipriano Lujan's store." Don Ramón Martínez himself referred to the father of Juan Lujan as "Don Cipriano Lujan." While Anglos elsewhere in the West could at times appear respectful toward Mexicans during criminal trials, New Mexico was exceptional in the high level of deference paid to elite Mexicans in courtrooms and other public places.[5]

New Mexico v. Juan Lujan was less exceptional, however, in its treatment of Mexican women. Of the recurring themes of this book, one of the most common has been to point out the hazards and impediments facing Mexican women in the West. A main focus of this chapter will be on the hardships faced by Josefita Martínez and her resilience in the face of such adversity. The years 1915 and 1916 were not easy ones for Martínez. Apparently fearful of her family's disapproval, she hid her pregnancy for many months from both her parents and grandparents. She gave birth alone in a small room to a stillborn child whose corpse was soon buried behind her home. Furthermore, she was compelled to recount these stories in detail in public on several occasions.[6]

Martínez was also rendered marginal by a system of patriarchy whereby older elite men, Anglo and Mexican alike, assumed the authority to make decisions about important aspects of her life. In fact, during his opening statement, Ward likely used the title "Don" Martínez to attempt to compensate for perceived shortcomings in the reputation of Josefita Martínez, Martínez's granddaughter and the state's main witness. "We will show to you by evidence that we believe to be entirely credible, the evidence of the young woman herself," Ward stated, "that the seduction was accomplished as a result of a promise of the defendant to marry this young lady." Ward then outlined the state's case against Juan Lujan and finished with a curious admission. "There will be a great deal of detail, and I think probably quite a number of conversations," he told the jury, "and there will no doubt be some contradictions, which appear in almost every case." That is, Ward found the evidence of Josefita Martínez to be credible, but acknowledged to the jury the existence of contrary accounts. Contradictions notwithstanding, Ward appealed to the men of the jury, "I know you gentlemen will pay, as you have done in other cases, the most careful attention to the evidence." In other words, jurors may find reasons to doubt the full story put forth by Josefita Martínez, but as "gentlemen" they would decide the case correctly.[7]

New Mexico v. Lujan in this sense illustrates another important aspect of colonial rule in the West. As in other colonial regimes, Mexican claims of citizenship depended on adhering to particular norms of conduct and behavior. Among those norms in the US context was a commitment to heteropatriarchy—heterosexual, marital reproduction and the ultimate authority of men over women. Colonial rule rewarded adherents to heteropatriarchal mandates, and Anglo-dominated courts greeted with greater respect those families that carefully supervised their daughters and more closely resembled nuclear arrangements, with men, preferably fathers, as heads of household and with dependent women and children.[8]

In *New Mexico v. Lujan*, patriarchal power was pronounced, as were condemnations of sex, even heterosexual, reproductive sex, outside of marriage. The case in this respect points to some important continuities in the region, namely persistent gender and sexual inequalities in both Mexican communities and the broader West. Patriarchy was a powerful institution under Mexican (and previously Spanish) rule and, as many of the cases discussed throughout the book have suggested, Mexican women, especially young women, and those incapable of adhering to sexual norms (or choosing to transgress them) could face dire consequences. Recall the female rape victims, young and otherwise, whose accused attackers eventually went free, or the endurance of sexual double standards in which female sexual desire was condemned and male (hetero)sexual desire was tolerated. While Mexican women undoubtedly sought to protect other, more equitable gender dynamics, such as women's legal rights (the presence of notable numbers of Mexican female appellants in the early twentieth century suggests the resilience of this sense of entitlement both over time, stretching back to the mid-nineteenth century and earlier, and in space, across the border into Mexico), Mexican female subordination persevered in New Mexico and elsewhere in the region. As *New Mexico v. Lujan* and the experience of Josefita Martínez make clear, *Mexicanas* in fact suffered disproportionately under colonial rule.[9]

The trial of Juan Lujan opened with the testimony of Josefita Martínez. Martínez began her testimony by describing her family, beginning with her father, Cruz Martínez, and then turning to her grandfather, Ramón Martínez. She said that her grandfather, "Don Ramón," had raised her and that she had lived her entire life in Sabinoso. Prompted by Ward, Martínez next described her relationship with Juan Lujan. "My grandfather Don Ramón and my mother Juanita raised Doña Magalita," she explained. Magalita, she said, married "Don Cipriano Lujan," and the two were the parents of Juan Lujan. Josefita called Juan Lujan, the man accused of seducing her, her *primo*, or cousin, and the two had grown up together, even living for a time in the same house. Nevertheless, she exclaimed to the court, "we are *not* related" (emphasis in original). [10]

On that fateful night in August 1914, Josefita recalled that Juan's mother had asked her to come to the nearby Lujan home. Magalita Lujan, she said, had been in the kitchen, while Juan was working in an "inside room" of the small three-room house. Juan beckoned to Josefita to join him in the room. "He said, 'If I would let him use my person he would marry me '," Josefita recalled. "I would consent to it," she testified that she replied, "if he would marry me." Juan reportedly agreed and the two had sex on a bed in the room. While Josefita and Juan had sexual intercourse that night, Josefita claimed that they did not have sex again. Nor, she stated, had she "ever [had] sexual intercourse with anybody else." Josefita's direct testimony ended with her account of the birth in April 1915 of her stillborn child. [11]

Juan Lujan's defense attorney was O. A. Larrazolo, a prominent attorney who would eventually become governor of New Mexico. Larrazolo had several goals in mind when he began his cross-examination of Josefita Martínez. In the first place, he wanted to poke holes in her story of seduction by Juan Lujan. Second, he wanted the jury to believe that another man, not Juan Lujan, may have been the father of Josefita's child. Larrazolo opened the cross-examination by pressing Josefita to remember the precise date in August 1914 when she had sex with Juan Lujan. Josefita answered that she did not remember the exact date, but that "it was before or after the 15th" of that month. Larrazolo, perhaps sensing an opportunity to discredit the prosecution's star witness, continued to pursue the matter and returned at several points during the cross-examination to Josefita's memory of the exact date of her sexual liaison with Juan. [12]

During his questioning, Larrazolo also introduced the jury to the name of Faustin Gutiérrez, the man that he hoped to prove was both Josefita's longtime boyfriend and the father of her child. "During the years 1912, 1913, 1914, and 1915," he asked Josefita, "was [Faustin] your sweetheart or your lover?" Josefita said no, and added that she had never "had any private conversation" with Faustin or "met that boy alone." Larrazolo proceeded to ask Josefita about a specific event that, he suggested, had occurred one morning three years earlier outside the Martínez home. Two men, he said, Filaberto Chavez and Valentine Baca, who were passing by the Martínez home had come upon Josefita and Faustin—"you standing on the inside of the water-closet, at your father's premises and house and Faustin on the outside." Faustin fled upon seeing the men, but Josefita stood her ground. According to Larrazolo, Filberto Chavez quipped, "It seems that these people have an office here." "It is none of your business what I do," Josefita supposedly snapped back. "No," Chavez replied, "it is none of our business, but we say what we see."[13]

Asked by Larrazolo if the incident had occurred, Josefita was curt. "No," she said. Larrazolo pressed on, turning to another alleged romantic encounter between Josefita and Faustin Gutiérrez. "Sometime in the month of December, 1914," he suggested, Josefita and Aurora had climbed down the banks of the Red River near their home in Sabinoso, "carrying tin cans or buckets for water." Faustin soon appeared on the riverbank, he said, and while Aurora climbed to the top of the bank, away from the couple, Josefita and Faustin "commenced hugging and kissing." "Is not that a fact?" Larrazolo demanded. Once again, Josefita was unswayed. "No sir," she answered, "it is not." Larrazolo thus clearly challenged both Josefita Martínez's account of sex with Juan Lujan and, more importantly, her claim that her only sexual liaison had been with Lujan.[14]

In what may have been an attempt to weaken one of the defense's main arguments (that Faustin Gutiérrez, not Juan Lujan, was the father of Josefita's child), the prosecution also called Faustin Gutiérrez to the stand. Faustin testified that he was a native of northern New Mexico and had worked at several jobs, including cattle ranching, in the area for the past few years. He had worked for Cipriano Lujan, he stated, and had also known Juan Lujan "for a long time." Under questioning from the prosecution, Gutiérrez recounted a conversation that he claimed to have had with Juan Lujan in a corral in the early fall of 1914. "In August, or September, about the 28th or 29th," he remembered, Lujan told him "that he had business with that girl." "That girl," according to Gutiérrez, was Josefita Martínez. Asked to clarify, Gutiérrez stated to the court that Lujan had told him "that he had personal business with the girl, but that he was not going to marry her." Gutiérrez thus bolstered the prosecution's argument that Juan Lujan, though interested in sexual relations with Josefita Martínez, had no plans to marry her.[15]

During cross-examination, O. A Larrazolo wasted little time before accusing Gutiérrez of impregnating Josefita Martínez. "Is it not true," he asked, "that *you are* the father of that child." Faustin answered "No sir," and

Larrazolo asked him to explain his relationship with Josefita Martínez.[16] Faustin told the court that he was unmarried and would at times go to the small town of Sabinoso to attend a *baile*. He denied ever dancing with Josefita at the *bailes*, but acknowledged that he "knew her a little." Faustin also denied being Josefita's "lover or sweet-heart" or ever having sexual intercourse with her. Asked if he knew what sexual intercourse was, Faustin hesitated. "Maybe I do," he answered, prompting Larrazolo to reply, "it is the act by which a man and a woman get together, the man penetrates the private parts of the woman with his private sexual male organ." According to the court transcript, Faustin laughed and answered, "Yes sir."

"There is nothing to laugh about this, Faustin," Larrazolo scolded, "I am just giving you an explanation." "You say you never had sexual intercourse with Josefita," he asked again.

"Never," Faustin answered.[17]

Larrazolo also used his cross-examination of Gutiérrez to introduce several specific incidents to the jury that, he hoped, would further convince them that Gutiérrez was the father of Josefita's child. These incidents, which would be described in detail by defense witnesses later in the trial, included a conversation between Faustin and two coworkers, Rafael Crespin and Luis Lujan. Recounting the conversation and the words Faustin was said to have used to describe Josefita's pregnancy, Larrazolo stated that he wanted to translate the phrase into Spanish for Faustin in order to avoid misinterpretation. "I will put this in Spanish," he said, "and the interpreter can interpret into English." The trial record does not include Larrazolo's Spanish translation of the subsequent phrase ("I had struck it right and made a baby"), and it is unclear if Larrazolo continued to examine Faustin in Spanish rather than English, but the incident is suggestive nonetheless. Larrazolo was clearly comfortable speaking both English and Spanish and made a special point of Faustin's lack of facility with English, perhaps as a further attempt to discredit an important witness for the prosecution.[18]

Larrazolo pressed Faustin to explain, or confirm or deny, other conversations with friends and coworkers. In one, Faustin supposedly promised to hire friends after Josefita's baby was born, the couple married, and Ramón Martínez's sheep and property came into Faustin's possession. In another conversation, Faustin reportedly told a friend that he knew what had happened to Josefita's baby ("they buried him in the garden"). In a third conversation, which Faustin denied had occurred, just as he denied that any of the conversations or incidents mentioned by Larrazolo had occurred, Faustin reportedly told Valentine Baca that he "was the guilty party and the father of that child" and that Josefita's father ("Don José de la Cruz"), Ramón

Martínez, and his own father had met to discuss how to lay the blame on Juan Lujan, rather than Faustin, for Josefita's pregnancy. Faustin also denied a string of incidents that Larrazolo claimed to have transpired, including Faustin nearly being discovered one night by José de la Cruz outside Josefita's house, the previously mentioned meeting between Faustin and Josefita during which she showed him clothes she had made for the baby, and another meeting between the couple one night in a back room of the Martínez home. Faustin Gutiérrez's cross-examination ended with yet another denial on his part of a sexual relationship with Josefita Martínez.[19]

The final witness for the prosecution was Josefita Martínez's grandfather, Ramón Martínez. Ramón described his relationship with both Juan Lujan and his granddaughter and told the court that while they had both lived in his home at certain points, they never lived there at the same time. He added that Josefita, described by attorney Ward as "the little girl," frequently visited the Lujan home, which was located less than a hundred yards away. "She got the habit of going over there in the day and night," he said, "lots of time she used to go there to sleep with Don Cipriano's little girl." Ramón Martínez's direct testimony was relatively brief, and when O. A. Larrazolo declined to cross-exam the seventy-four-year-old, the state rested its case.[20]

During the trial, O. A. Larrazolo conducted a vigorous defense for his client, calling witness after witness to testify that Faustin Gutiérrez was in fact the father of Josefita Martínez's child. Larrazolo also argued that Gutiérrez and Martínez frequently conspired to meet each other. The first witness for the defense was Rafael Crespin. Crespin, who lived in Sabinoso and worked for Cipriano Lujan, testified that "during the lambing of Don Cipriano's sheep" in May of 1915 he spoke with Faustin Gutiérrez about Josefita Martínez. Larrazolo asked Rafael if Faustin had made the following statement to him: "since the year 1912, Josefita had been his *novia*; that in the month of August previous she told him, to use his language in Spanish 'that he had struck it right and made a child,' and now they want to put the blame on my *compadre*, Juan."

"Yes sir," Rafael answered, Faustin had indeed made such a statement to him. During the same conversation, Rafael added, Faustin showed him a present that he said had been given to him by Josefita. It was "a small braid of hair," Rafael stated, "the hair of Josefita Martínez."[21]

The prosecutor hoped to return the jury's focus to Juan Lujan and to undercut testimony by defense witnesses regarding Faustin Gutiérrez's relationship with Josefita Martínez. He began his cross-examination of Rafael Crespin by reminding the jury that Rafael was a longtime employee of Juan Lujan's father and thus may have had an interest in supporting Juan's case. Rafael testified that he had worked for Cipriano Lujan for the past eight years, largely handling Lujan's sheep herd, but occasionally working with cattle as well. Prosecutor Ward also pressed Rafael to describe in greater detail his conversation with Faustin about Josefita Martínez. The conversation occurred at five in the afternoon, Rafael testified, after dinner, outside of the tent the men had set up for themselves while they tended to the Lujan flock. Frank and Luis Lujan were also present, Rafael said, when Faustin told them that he "had made a boy" with Josefita Martínez. With so much of the defense's case resting on conversations involving Faustin Gutiérrez, Ward's scrutiny of Rafael's testimony about their conversation was a strategy that would be repeated at several points throughout the trial.[22]

Valentine Baca, the second witness for the defense, described several encounters between Faustin and Josefita. Valentine described seeing the couple together in a riverbed near his home in December 1914. "It looked like they were playing or wrestling or something like that," he said.[23] Valentine also told the court that during two separate conversations, Faustin had admitted to being the father of Josefita's child. One conversation occurred in April 1915, according to Valentine, when Faustin promised to hire Valentine and another man, Simon Aragon, after he married Josefita and received sheep and property promised to him by her grandfather. A month later, Valentine testified, Faustin told him the following: "I am the guilty party, and the father of that child, and the truth is she [Josefita] is to blame for it. I did not want to use her person, but she told me that if I did not use her person, she would not marry me, because her parents did not like me, and that if I used her person they would be compelled to agree to our marriage." During the same conversation, Faustin also supposedly told him that "they were trying to get Juan Lujan to marry Josefita Martínez."[24]

During cross-examination Valentine was asked to recount a conversation with Leandro Jimenez from March 1915, while both men were "working on a building at Cipriano Lujan's place" (another attempt by the prosecution to highlight a conflict of interest in an employee of Cipriano Lujan testifying in defense of Lujan's son). According to Ward, Valentine had said, "the poor Martínez's" and that Juan Lujan was "the wrongdoer." Valentine agreed that the conversation had occurred, but denied identifying Juan Lujan. "Leandro Jimenez asked me how I thought that the Martínez's felt with what had happened to Josefita," he remembered. "I told him I supposed they felt rather sorry," he continued, "and I told him I thought if Don Ramón Martínez had any shame he would not bring this matter up before the courts."[25]

According to Simon Aragon, the defense's next witness, Faustin had also boasted to friends of knowing what had occurred after the birth of Josefita's child. In April 1915, Simon recalled, while he, Faustin, and Valentine Baca worked together mending an *acequia* in Sabinoso, the conversation supposedly turned toward Josefita's pregnancy. "Let us bet that you don't know what was done with the baby," Simon said to Faustin, apparently unaware of their relationship. "Yes, I do," Faustin informed them, "they buried him in the garden." During the same conversation, Simon testified that Faustin described a clandestine late night visit to Josefita's home during which he narrowly escaped being discovered by Josefita's father. As he "stood on the outside of the house," evidently conversing with Josefita through a window, Faustin was startled when "Don José de la Cruz, the father of Josefita came out of the house." Faustin scrambled out of view and into the nearest hiding spot, under a nearby wagon. Huddled there, he told Simon, he watched Josefita's father approach his hiding place. Standing beside the wagon, and apparently unaware that a suitor of his daughter hid nearby, José de la Cruz began to urinate. "He nearly wet him," he added, but, fortunately for Faustin, never discovered him.[26]

The next witness, Luis Lujan, who was described by Larrazolo as "related to the defendant, Juan Lujan," confirmed the previous testimony of Rafael Crespin, in which Rafael had described a conversation during which Faustin Gutiérrez admitted to being the *novio* of Josefita Martínez and the father of her child.[27] Luis Lujan's testimony is also notable for an exchange that occurred between O. A. Larrazolo and Judge Leahy, in which Leahy seems to have lost his temper with Larrazolo and chastised him in public. Well into the trial, Larrazolo asked Leahy if it might be possible to halt the day's proceedings and commence again the next morning. After calling Luis Lujan to testify for the defense, Larrazolo asked the judge for a recess. "I have two more witnesses," he said, "but I do not care to put them on at this time." "Don't the court think we should have a little rest," he continued, "we have been here since nine o'clock this morning, and it is now twenty minutes to ten at night?"

"I presume we have worked pretty long," Leahy replied, "but if I did not think it necessary I would not do it."

Larrazolo, unwilling to concede, said, "It seems to me the people are entitled to some rest; we are working here all day and a part of the night."

"Call your next witness," the judge ordered, "I think we will get through with another witness."

Larrazolo then tried another tactic. "I cannot work any more tonight," he said, "I am sick and have been sick all day."

"Very well," Leahy agreed, but added, "when you are sick, be fair to the court and inform the court, and let that be your first excuse."

Larrazolo, apparently unwilling to let the matter rest, somewhat lamely explained, "I thought the court was sleepy also," earning a curt answer from the judge.

"No sir," Leahy told him, "the court is not sleepy," before excusing the jury and suspending the trial until nine o'clock the next morning.

The next morning, an apparently refreshed Larrazolo resumed his defense of Juan Lujan. While Larrazolo seemed confident in his witnesses' ability to convince the jury that another man besides Juan Lujan may have impregnated Josefita Martínez, he pursued other strategies as well. A smaller portion of Lujan's defense focused on the conversation that Josefita and the prosecution contended had occurred immediately prior to their sexual intercourse. Larrazolo called to the stand Louis Ilfeld ("*Luis* Ilfeld," the witness corrected him), a fellow lawyer from Las Vegas who had previously represented Juan Lujan in a preliminary hearing of the case. Referring to the notes he had taken during the hearing, Ilfeld testified that Josefita had stated the following: "that the proposition was made by him [Juan Lujan] to have sexual intercourse, and she said 'she would allow it, if he would comply with his contract.'" Josefita testified, according to Ilfeld, that Juan "promised to marry her if anything should happen." In other words, Martínez testified that Juan Lujan had promised to marry her if she became pregnant.[28]

Ilfeld's notes, in English, had been translated by him (he was apparently relatively fluent in Spanish) from Josefita's testimony in Spanish, and there was some dispute about the actual words Josefita used in her testimony. Later, while questioning a court stenographer about Josefita's testimony, Larrazolo would claim that she had said, "in *todos modos*, he promised me." Under cross-examination, however, the prosecution challenged the accuracy of both Ilfeld's memory and his transcription. "She might have used the word 'also' in Spanish," Ilfeld admitted, "and in writing it down quickly, I may have used the word 'any.'" "I would not like to testify to the exact word she used in Spanish," he added, "my memory is not good enough for that." At issue was whether Juan Lujan promised to marry Josefita Martínez regardless of whether she became pregnant or not, or *only* if she became pregnant. The difference, while subtle, would in fact make its way into the subsequent appeals case.[29]

Larrazolo's last witness was Juan Lujan himself. Juan denied either ever having sexual intercourse with Josefita Martínez or promising at any point to marry her. He told Larrazolo and the jury that he had never been "sweethearts" with Josefita or "ever entertained any relations of love with her."[30] Larrazolo was also eager to have Juan discuss his relationship with Faustin Gutiérrez. Like so many in Sabinoso, Juan and Faustin had known each other for years. Nearly the same age, they attended school together and had been, according to Juan, "good friends" before the trial. Juan claimed that Faustin spoke to him about Josefita Martínez. "While we were at school in Sabinoso," Juan said, "he told me that Josefita was his girl." He said that "he would use her any place he wanted to." Lujan thus both denied sexual involvement with Josefita Martínez and pointed to Faustin Gutiérrez as her *novio* and likely the father of her child. When Lujan left the stand, the defense rested their case.[31]

On November 28, 1916, both lawyers presented their closing arguments, and Judge Leahy gave his instructions to the jury before they began their deliberations. One of the several instructions said, in effect, that a conviction must be based on the jury's belief, beyond reasonable doubt, that Juan Lujan had seduced Josefita Martínez. The judge included in this instruction the phrase "unlawfully, willfully, and feloniously, and under and by means of the promise of marriage" to describe the crime of seduction. O. A. Larrazolo, however, objected to the wording of the instruction and asked the judge instead "to instruct the jury that a promise of marriage conditioned upon pregnancy from the intercourse would *not* amount to seduction" (emphasis mine). In other words, building upon the argument that he had introduced previously in Luis Ilfeld's testimony, Larrazolo argued that the promise of marriage "must be an absolute and unconditional" promise, not a promise based on whether or not a pregnancy resulted from subsequent acts of sexual intercourse. According to this position, Lujan would have committed seduction if he promised to marry Martínez (an unconditional promise), but would not have committed seduction if he promised to marry her only if she became pregnant (a conditional promise). Judge Leahy, however, refused Larrazolo's request, contending that by using the phrase "under and by means of the promise of marriage," his instruction had addressed the issue satisfactorily.[32]

When the jury returned a guilty verdict and sentenced Juan Lujan to the New Mexico state penitentiary, Lujan promptly appealed his case to the New Mexico Supreme Court. He and O. A. Larrazolo, who remained his attorney during the appeals process, argued two main points. First, they contended that Lujan was convicted based on faulty and insufficient evidence. Second, they charged that Judge Leahy's instruction to the jury regarding seduction had been improper and prejudicial. In its decision, which was delivered in January 1918, over three years after Josefita Martínez became pregnant, the three-person supreme court agreed that the evidence presented in the trial was "extremely unsatisfactory" and that the "story told by the prosecuting witness [Josefita Martínez was] very improbable." More importantly, the court ruled that the judge had indeed failed to instruct the jury properly. Although Judge Leahy had claimed that his instruction had "covered" the premise that the "promise of marriage conditioned upon pregnancy resulting from the intercourse would not amount to seduction," the higher court disagreed. "The court was in error in this assumption," the decision stated, "the instruction given did not advise the jury that the promise must be an absolute and unconditional one." The court concluded that the guilty verdict must be reversed, the case returned to the local court, and Juan Lujan be granted a new trial.[33]

Juan Lujan had won his appeal and been granted a new trial. But there is no evidence that another trial occurred. In all likelihood, prosecutors chose not to pursue further seduction charges against him and he appears to have been freed from custody and cleared of all charges. Juan Lujan had the distinction of being the only New Mexican, Mexican or otherwise, to appeal his conviction on seduction charges to the New Mexico Supreme Court in the early twentieth century. During the same period, only two civil cases in New Mexico directly involving seduction, neither of them with Mexican defendants, reached the supreme court. New Mexico was not alone in the small number of seduction cases reaching higher courts in the West. Only three seduction appeals cases occurred in Arizona between 1900 and 1930, and none directly involved Mexicans. In California, nine men convicted of seduction appealed their cases to the supreme court. Only one of the nine men, Manuel Lima, had a Spanish surname. Lima was convicted of seduction in 1918 in Santa Clara County. In the words of the higher court, Lima was charged with "inducing the prosecuting witness to accompany him from her home in Alameda County to San Jose, and there seduc[ing] her upon his promise of marriage." Unlike Juan Lujan, Lima's arguments proved unconvincing to the higher court and his appeal was turned down. In Texas, only one seduction case appealed to the state's higher court involved a Mexican defendant. Eusebio Guerra was convicted of seduction in 1916 in the district court of Starr County. In his appeal, Guerra challenged his conviction for seduction based on the fact that one of the jurors in the trial was under the age of twenty-one, the minimum age for jury service in

Texas. The court, unswayed, affirmed both Guerra's original conviction and his two-year sentence in the state penitentiary.[34]

Like most Mexicans in the West, Mexicans involved in seduction cases outside of New Mexico appeared only sporadically in census documents. For instance, there were three Eusebio Guerra's listed in the 1910 census of Starr County, Texas. One of the three was a newborn child, but the other two men would have been in their twenties when the case reached the higher court in 1916. The first Eusebio Guerra was a farm laborer who lived with his widowed father and four brothers. Like his neighbors, Guerra was of Mexican descent (he was born in Texas of Mexican-born parents) and spoke predominantly Spanish. The other Eusebio Guerra was a twenty-three-year-old married "retail merchant." While the newborn Eusebio reappeared in the 1920 census with his mother, the other two Eusebios had disappeared. In fact the only other Eusebio in the entire state of Texas in 1920 was a nine-year-old boy. A decade later even these two children had disappeared from the census, and the closest Eusebio Guerra to the Southwest was Cuban-born Eusebio Guerra of Tampa, Florida.[35]

Like Eusebio Guerra, who appealed a criminal conviction to a higher court, yet appeared only fleetingly, if at all, in census records, the lives of *nuevomexicana/os* like Juan Lujan, Josefita Martínez, Faustin Gutiérrez, and O. A. Larrazolo reflected the complicated nature of Mexican citizenship in the West. For example, while all of the trial participants who appeared in the census were listed as "white," Spanish was a dominant language for many, if not most. Josefita Martínez clearly spoke through an interpreter, and others may have testified in Spanish as well. In census documents from six years earlier, Juan Lujan and Faustin Gutiérrez were both listed as Spanish speakers, as were many of their family members and neighbors. At the same time, Juan Lujan, and his lawyer, O. A. Larrazolo, appeared to have considerable access to the American judicial system, and many of the trial's Mexican participants could make persuasive claims to American citizenship. In New Mexico, significant numbers of *nuevomexicana/os* were landowners and civic leaders; a handful was among the region's wealthiest and most politically powerful individuals. As the attorney leading Lujan's successful appeal, O. A. Larrazolo convinced the New Mexico Supreme Court to overturn the verdict and grant his client a new trial. Testament to the presence of well-educated, professional Mexican elite in New Mexico is the fact that in less than a decade, O. A. Larrazolo would be elected governor of the state.[36]

Future governor Larrazolo was obviously well known beyond *New Mexico v. Lujan*. In contrast to most regions of the West, other Mexicans involved in the trial were also not rendered fully invisible by government documents; certain individuals in fact appeared with some regularity in US census schedules. In 1910, for instance, the families of Josefita Martínez, Faustin Gutiérrez, and Juan Lujan were all listed in the San Miguel County census. In fact, the Gutiérrez and Lujan families appeared on the same page of the census. Faustin Gutiérrez, fourteen at the time, lived with his parents, Manuela and José León, and three younger brothers and a younger sister. The family, all native New Mexicans, spoke predominantly Spanish. His father was a rancher and the family resided on what the census enumerator described as a "horse ranch." Next to the Gutiérrez family was another ranch family, the family of Vidal and Manuela Zamora, also born in New Mexico and also Spanish speakers. Two households away from the Zamora family were the Lujans. Unlike his neighbors, Cipriano Lujan was not a rancher, nor was he listed as a Spanish speaker. He was a "merchant" and ran a "general store." He lived with his wife of two decades, Miguela, and their seven children, including fifteen-year-old Juan. Like his father and older brother and sister—and unlike Faustin Gutiérrez two households away—Juan Lujan was proficient in English. According to census records, Josefita Martínez lived with her parents, José de la Cruz and Felicita, sister Aurora, and four brothers on their small ranch in 1900. Like Josefita and her siblings, her parents and their parents before them had all been born in New Mexico. Ten years later, in 1910, the family reappeared in the census. Josefita was twelve years old and was listed with her parents and nine brothers and sisters, including thirteen-year-old Aurora. While Josefita's three older brothers could speak English, she, her remaining siblings, and her mother and father were all described by the census enumerator as speaking only Spanish.[37]

This heightened visibility of *nuevomexicana/os* in the US census should not be overstated, however. Even a seemingly prominent family could at times appear only inconsistently in the decennial census records. Juan Lujan's family, for instance, was listed in the 1910 San Miguel County census, and there were two Juan Lujans in San Miguel County in 1930. One had been born in 1916, while the other was thirty-one years old. The latter Lujan worked on a farm and was married to a Mexican woman (his wife, Isabel, twenty at the time, was listed as not able to speak English) and was likely the same Juan Lujan who was convicted of seducing Josefita Martínez in 1916.[38] At the same time, in 1920, only three years after Juan Lujan appealed his case to the New Mexico Supreme Court, the only Juan Lujan living in San Miguel County was a thirteen-year-old boy, clearly not the same Juan Lujan. Despite the more regular appearance of Juan Lujan and other northern New Mexicans from the trial in census documents, gaps nonetheless remained in their presence in the historical record.[39]

Although Mexicans in New Mexico may have appeared with greater regularity in the census and may have achieved higher political and economic status, it is also worth noting that such claims to citizenship were largely staked by Mexican men in *New Mexico v. Lujan*, not by Mexican women.[40] This disparity resonates with current theoretical work on intersections between race, gender, and sex. Comments by Andrea Smith, following the lead of Cathy Cohen and others, on heteropatriarchy are especially instructive in this respect. Smith notes that advancement (political, economic, social) by members of a marginalized, or formerly enslaved or colonized, community often hinged on the exclusion and further marginalization of other members of that same community. Such internal marginalization often proceeds, according to Smith, along heterosexist and patriarchal lines, privileging those most able to position themselves atop a heteropatriarchal hierarchy. Good families (reproductive, marital, nuclear) with a clear and unambiguous distinction between men and women, where men are in positions of authority and ultimate influence, are critical to this equation.[41]

By claiming properly ordered families and domestic spaces, Mexicans challenged one of the foundations of colonial rule in the West: the notion that Anglo families were superior to Mexican and other non-Anglo families. At the same time, family was also a critical site in the maintenance of social divisions within Mexican communities. Hierarchies based on gender were among the most persistent of such divisions. The subordination of women was especially visible in matters related to sex. Trial transcripts suggest the existence of a powerful sexual double standard whereby the sexual practices and desires of women and girls were carefully monitored while male sexuality was left relatively unsupervised and unfettered.

Take, for instance, the practice of female chaperonage—the escorting, often by male family members such as uncles, brothers, or cousins, of young unmarried women to events outside the home. Throughout the region, Mexicans turned to the family to cushion themselves against the pernicious effects of Anglo rule. Chaperonage offered one such attempt to shield vulnerable members from perceived social dangers. As Vicki Ruiz and others have maintained, female chaperonage could also, however, mask imbalances of power within Mexican communities, especially inequities of gender. Mexican men and boys, after all, were not supervised by other men, or women, when they left the home. Female chaperonage constrained the sexual freedom of *Mexicanas*, and also, under the guise of protection from sexual danger, severely limited their movements geographically, underscoring the notion that the proper place for women was in the home. Finally, chaperonage allowed parents and guardians better control over the courtship and the marriage partners of young women, helping to screen out unacceptable candidates and reinforce the power of parents and kin in marital decisions.[42]

From the perspective of heteropatriarchy, it is thus possible to view events within *New Mexico v. Lujan* more broadly as attempts to reinforce male authority and to discipline the sexual activity and independence of Mexican women. During the trial, Mexican men like "Don" Ramón Martínez and "Don" Cipriano Lujan were accorded respect and authority as men of wealth and property who stood unquestioned at the head of their respective families. Their elite, citizenlike status was articulated during the trial by an interracial Anglo/Mexican group of elite men. This cross-cultural elite fraternity (which, I suggest, nicely aligns with theories of heteropatriarchy) also depended on the marginalization of other members of the Mexican community: those not properly subscribing to gender and sexual norms and expectations.[43]

Josefita Martínez, for instance, regardless of which story one chose to believe about her pregnancy, had acted with a considerable degree of sexual independence and agency. According to the prosecution, and Josefita herself, the following exchange had occurred after Juan Lujan beckoned her to join him in a bedroom (notice also that Josefita describes her agreement to sex based on an unconditional promise, a description defense attorney Larrazolo would later badger her to describe as conditional and based on an ensuing pregnancy):

Q (LARRAZOLO): And you immediately went in?
A (MARTÍNEZ): Yes, sir
Q: Now what was the first thing that Juan told you when you went inside?
A: He asked me, "if I would not let him make use of my person."
Q: And what did you say?
A: I told him, "I would consent to it, if he would marry me."
Q: What did he do?
A: He said, "Yes."
Q: And then what did he do?
A: He made use of my person.

In the account put forth by Juan Lujan's defense team, Josefita also seemed to take an active role in arranging sexual liaisons with Faustin Gutiérrez. According to Valentine Baca, Faustin told him that Josefita had initiated sex, apparently with the clear intent of forcing her parents to accept Faustin as their son-in-law. "I did not want to use her person," Faustin supposedly said, "but she told me that if I did not use her person, she would not marry me, because her parents did not like me, and that if I used her person they would be compelled to agree to our marriage." Josefita's sexual assertiveness was matched by her verbal confidence. When Filberto Chavez, after discovering Josefita and Faustin together, reportedly commented, "It seems that these people have their office here," he told the court that Josefita did not shrink from the confrontation. Refusing to concede the men's ability to criticize her or control her romantic associations, she reportedly told the men, "it is none of your business what I do."[44]

Trial participants in fact seemed willing to forgive sexual transgressions like sex before marriage, *provided* the transgressions were based on a promise of marriage. Amid the disputed events, accusations, and counteraccusations of the trial, lawyers notably declined to challenge the propriety of the young woman's actions, suggesting that she had engaged in proper behavior for a *Mexicana*. Within the disputed instruction that Judge Leahy read to the jury in fact was a description of Josefita Martínez: "at said time and place the said Josefita Martínez was an unmarried female person, under the age of 21 years, and was at said time, and previous thereto, of good repute for chastity." That is, in convicting Lujan of seduction, jurors decided that a promise of marriage could understandably lead a Mexican woman like Josefita, "of good repute for chastity," to agree to sexual intercourse.[45]

At the same time, Josefita's secrecy regarding her pregnancy suggests that she could not avoid the pressing weight of heteropatriarchy. In both prosecution and defense versions of events, Josefita concealed her pregnancy from the most powerful men, and women, in her life. She was thus clearly cognizant of the consequences of pregnancy outside of either marriage or the promise of marriage. During the trial, witnesses highlighted such consequences in conversations in which Josefita and her family were the subject of pity and where Josefita was viewed as a victim. Valentine Baca testified that he told Faustin Gutiérrez in April 1915 that "it seems the *novia* is in a bad condition." Leandro Jimenez recalled a similar conversation also involving Valentine Baca a month earlier. "The poor Martínez's," Leandro recalled Valentine saying to him. "It looks like Josefita is sick," Valentine continued, going on to claim that Juan Lujan was "the wrongdoer." "I felt sorry," Leandro added, "I had good sympathies for one side as for the other."[46]

Sympathy, of course, is a far cry from acceptance and approval. Framed as a "choice" between marriage (that is, fulfilling the heteropatriarchal imperative to exchange subordination to a father or another male relative like a grandfather or an uncle for subordination to a husband) or bringing "shame" on her family, Josefita in reality had few real choices available to her. Her dependence and subordination to men were emphasized by witnesses, mostly by Mexican and Anglo men, throughout the trial, and the trial was in fact only one of the many hardships Josefita faced from the moment she became pregnant. With the possible exception of Juan Lujan, who was convicted of a felony (though he was later granted a new trial and may have never been retried), Josefita Martínez, not her grandfather or father or other members of her family, suffered the greatest harm. Court records only hint at the trauma involved. Her story is rendered even more poignant if one believes Jesus Maria Montoya, who described a visit to Josefita's home, where he witnessed Josefita showing baby clothes to Faustin Gutiérrez, or Rafael Crespin, who said that Faustin had shown him a braid of hair that Josefita had supposedly given him as a token of their love.

Like many of the women and girls described in this book, Josefita Martínez found the home to be a source of both comfort and tragedy. Other trials from across the region highlight the Mexican home as a similarly conflicted site, including both sexual danger and the protection of loved ones. Take, for example, the trial of Rudolfo Rodríguez from early 1920s Texas. Rodríguez was convicted of raping his fourteen-year-old daughter Natalia Rodríguez and was sentenced to five years in the Texas state penitentiary. According to the trial transcript, several months after the original attack, Natalia Rodríguez married José Mata, and six months later gave birth to a child. At that point, Rodríguez accused her father of raping her. While Natalia Rodríguez asserted that her father was the father of the child, the defense claimed that Rodríguez and her eventual husband, José Mata, had had sex before their marriage and that Mata was the father.[47]

Testimony on both sides of the aisle explored notions of proper courtship and chaperonage. Natalia Rodríguez told jurors that she had only met José Mata in person on a handful of occasions and had communicated with him largely through letters left for each other in the hollow trunk of an oak tree. Even when the couple met in person, Rodríguez testified that they were never alone with each other. On one occasion, Rodríguez and Mata met at a fence along the road outside her home. "My sisters could see where I was," Rodríguez stated, "I did not go anyplace where they could not see me."[48]

Rudolfo Rodríguez, on the other hand, told jurors that he had discovered his daughter and José Mata "close to the house, about ten yards, he was on the outside of the wire fence, and she was on the inside." "I don't know what they were doing," he continued, "probably talking as they were close together." Rodríguez had admonished Mata for not coming directly to the house, but instead leaving his horse on a nearby road and walking across a pasture to meet the young woman. "I told him these actions of his were dishonoring my home," Rodríguez recalled. "I told him," he continued, "if that was the way he was going to do toward that young lady, that he would not make a good husband for her, that he was trying to dishonor her, that if he wanted to speak to her, for him to come by way of the road and come to the house, and if I was there he could talk to her, but if I was not there, no." Rodríguez also added that he told his daughter "that any time I would catch either of the grown girls talking to any one out in the pasture, I would not permit them to be in the house any longer." Divided over the origins of Rodríguez's pregnancy, both sides shared an understanding of female chaperonage and supported its attempts to limit the sexual freedom and mobility of Mexican women.[49]

As in *New Mexico v. Lujan*, men in *Texas v. Rudolfo Rodríguez* also assumed the authority to make important decisions about women's lives. Across the West, Mexican women approached the courts from multiple angles. *West of Sex* has highlighted ordinary Mexican women's triumphs in the courts—some small, like women's stout defense of their homes on the witness stand, and some large, like the overturning of a guilty verdict and the achievement of a new trial. Such victories represent important challenges to growing exclusionary tendencies in American colonial rule in the early twentieth century. As colonial rule shifted in the American West and forces of racial exclusion sought to redraw and reinforce racial dividing lines, ordinary Mexicans struggled mightily to prop open the window of colonial inclusion and the promise of citizenship.

In promoting heteropatriarchy and condemning nonnormative sexual intimacies, however, even claims of inclusion—claims that themselves opposed the growing marginalization of Mexicans in the United States—could depend on a deeply corroded foundation, one that disavowed, even denigrated nonmarital, nonreproductive, nonheterosexual sexual desire and acts. As the wrenching experiences of Josefita Martínez and Natalia Rodríguez make clear, the effects of these disavowals—the exclusions at the heart of claims of inclusion—reverberated, at times tragically, throughout the lives of Mexican women in the West.[50]

From the Outskirts of Citizenship

There are few more durable borderlands icons than Gregorio Cortez. He is the star of a famous and enduring *corrido*, a groundbreaking book by border scholar Américo Paredes, and a movie starring Edward James Olmos (not to mention the namesake of Antonio Banderas's character in the *Spy Kids* movie series). Cortez's early 1900s Texas gunfight with local law enforcement, his skilled flight from Anglo authorities, and his capture, imprisonment, and eventual release have inspired generations with his daring and determination.[1]

Few chroniclers of Cortez, however, note that it was in the legal realm where Cortez fought some of his most notable, and most successful, battles. Convicted of murdering local sheriffs in separate incidents in both Karnes County and Gonzales County in 1901, Cortez appealed his convictions to the Texas Court of Criminal Appeals. In 1902, the court issued rulings on both cases. In the Karnes County case, Cortez and his lawyers argued that he should have been allowed to change the venue of his trial. The court agreed, noting that "many influential citizens subscribe[d] to a fund to secure defendant's arrest" and that "no lawyer in the county could be procured to represent defendant but that a number volunteered to prosecute." Thus, the court concluded, it would be "difficult for him to secure a fair and impartial trial there." In the Gonzales County appeal, the higher court also sided with Cortez, noting that the trial judge should have permitted a continuance in the trial to allow an important witness for the defense to testify. Moreover, the higher court stated, "the trial court erred in failing to instruct the jury that they should discern whether defendant's confession was voluntarily and freely made."[2]

In both cases, the convictions were overturned and the cases returned to the local courts. Two years later, Cortez, who had been convicted a second time of murdering the Gonzales County sheriff, returned to the higher court with another appeal. He was less successful on this third attempt, where he argued that the attempted arrest (which precipitated the gunfight and death of the sheriff) had been unlawful, and the court affirmed his conviction on first degree murder and sentenced him to life in prison.[3]

Gregorio Cortez was not alone among Mexican women and men in the early twentieth-century West in turning to the American courts—and the appeals process specifically—with a degree of confidence. In 1902, the year Cortez successfully appealed his two murder convictions, the Texas Court of Criminal Appeals heard seven cases (of 163 total) involving Spanish-surnamed appellants. The next year, there were nine Mexican appellants before the court, four of whom were successful—Antonio Trijo for murder, D. C. Luna for perjury, Benito Orta for murder, and Silvester Tarrango for theft. In 1904, Cortez's unsuccessful third appeal joined ten other Mexican appeals cases, including Aniseto Guerrero's successful appeal of a theft charge in which he was originally convicted of stealing a hog from an Anglo neighbor.[4]

Indeed, Gregorio Cortez was one of over a thousand Mexican men and women who appealed criminal convictions to higher courts in the American West between 1900 and 1930. These appeals cases—with convictions of crimes ranging from alcohol possession to assault to prostitution to murder, sodomy, and rape, and with varying degrees of success and failure—occurred in the midst of a series of punishing and humiliating attacks on Mexican communities across the West during the same years. American colonial rule in the West was shifting, and proponents of Mexican fitness for citizenship and eventual inclusion in the nation were losing ground as forces of immigration restriction gathered strength and anti-Mexican campaigns swept the region. Attacks, rhetorical and literal, on Mexicans in the United States crested in the 1930s with repatriation drives and newly instituted racial dividing lines—like the US census, which for the first time defined ethnic Mexicans as "Mexican" rather than "white"—that relocated Mexicans physically and symbolically to the outskirts of citizenship.[5]

The lives of a great many Mexicans were unhinged in those years, tens of thousands deported every year, Mexican neighborhoods stripped and shuttered. But a great many also survived the onslaught. Enduring as well was a vibrant tradition of ordinary Mexicans calling upon the American legal system for full rights and treatment as citizens. While Mexican American civil rights activism is often traced to the post–World War II era and landmark legal cases like *Mendez v. Westminster*, *Perez v. Sharp*, and *Hernandez v. Texas*, such triumphs did not emerge fully formed and unprecedented. They were, in fact, a product of colonial struggles, of efforts by ordinary Mexicans to reanimate a form of colonialism (a more inclusionary colonialism) that was calcifying, and becoming increasingly rigid in the early twentieth century. *West of Sex* has argued that ordinary Mexicans' claims of inclusion in appeals cases represent a significant example of opposition to colonial rule in the early twentieth-century West.[6]

This perspective can also help explore an important question in twentieth- and twenty-first-century America: how is social inequality maintained in a regime of legal equality? Like Puerto Ricans elsewhere in the country, who had been US citizens since 1917, Mexicans' vexed position in the early twentieth-century West (compelling a relative degree of respect in the courthouse, yet widely reviled elsewhere) derived from the disjuncture between their legal citizenship and their cultural marginalization. The status of Mexicans differed in this respect from that of African Americans, who suffered far more severe legal and cultural disenfranchisement over much of the twentieth century.[7] When the African American freedom struggle of the mid-twentieth century finally succeeded in abolishing many forms of legal inequality, the status of African Americans came to bear a striking resemblance to that of other American colonial subjects like Mexicans, Puerto Ricans, Filipinos, and even Native Americans: legally equal, yet perceived by "white" Americans as culturally inferior. This convergence suggests that American colonialism has perhaps expanded as much inward (domestically, as it were) as outward in the last half century. The post–civil rights era in America, in other words, may have opened a door to new, expanding forms of colonial order and domination, occurring as much within the nation as in foreign and distant lands.

West of Sex has also suggested that sex proved as critical to American colonial rule in the West as it did to other colonial regimes. Talk of sex could break in many directions, upholding colonial hierarchies in some respects, challenging them in others. Mexican prostitutes could frame themselves as properly domestic and fallen women, poor *Mexicanas* could speak defiantly of their homes and their "couch[es] of a married couple," *nuevamexicanas* could announce to snooping neighbors, "it is none of your business what I do." Even the most severely marginalized Mexicans, those convicted of same-sex crimes, could posit alternative spaces of sexual desire and activity. At the same time, adherence to sexual norms—especially in terms of the celebration of heteropatriarchal families, long one of the principal requisites toward the inclusion of colonial subjects into positions of status and authority—could have debilitating, even disastrous effects on less powerful members of Mexican families and communities. Inequities of gender, sexual double standards, heightened authority and supervision of women and girls persisted in Mexican America throughout the early twentieth century. So too could Mexican homes, so often safe and nurturing, on occasion fail to protect their most vulnerable members and become spaces of sexual danger and violence.

A final case, *New Mexico v. Amado Ancheta*, reflects several such themes. In Cuervo, New Mexico, in 1913, the July heat drove the family of six-year-old Maria Inéz Lucero to sleep outside their home. The family—Lucero, her mother, father, and two siblings—had gone to sleep in the same bed, but at three in the morning, her mother discovered that her daughter had disappeared. "I woke up," she said, "and turned around to cover them and I didn't find her." A frantic search ensued, enlisting friends and relatives. At first light, a group of men discovered and then followed a set of footprints leading away from the Lucero home. They tracked the footprints to a spot under a cedar tree, where they found "ground [that] looked like it had been freely trampled and a little pool of blood." Two sets of tracks, one large and one small, led in opposite directions away from the cedar tree, and the group split up.[8]

The men following the smaller set of footprints soon came upon Maria Inéz Lucero, alone, "standing mute." The Lucero family summoned Dr. Joseph Spector to examine their daughter later that day. "I found the little girl badly frightened at first," he said, "and I found some blood stains on her undergarments and the child was very tender to the touch." Ten days later, he was again called to the home by the Lucero family and examined the girl a second time. "[I] found that a discharge had developed which probably is gonorrhea," he said.[9]

Another man, a Laguna Indian named Teodoro Bautista, had followed the larger set of tracks in the opposite direction from the girl. He described tracking the footprints from the woods into a small village and eventually to the house of Amado Ancheta. Convinced that Ancheta was the man who had attacked Lucero, Bautista continued searching the area until he found Ancheta standing outside a nearby home. "He was very excited," Bautista testified in the trial, "and his chin was trembling." "Then I think this is the one," he added. Another man testified that he had seen Ancheta at six o'clock on the same morning and that Ancheta had blood on his shirt.[10]

Amado Ancheta argued in his defense that on the night of the attack he had been in the town of Cuervo with two friends attending a local show and visiting a saloon. Around midnight, he and the other men parted ways. "I went over to the house of Mrs. Pilar Baca," he said. "From there," he continued, "I went out and went to the house of my uncle Teofilo Sarracino." Sarracino, who testified that he had known Amado Ancheta "nearly ever since he was born," confirmed Ancheta's story. At "about one o'clock in the morning," he stated, "he was laying down there in the bed that they put up for him in my house." The next morning, he said, Ancheta appeared as "natural as I have ever seen him" while he ate breakfast with the family.[11]

Ancheta's alibi, however, did not convince the jury, which convicted him and sentenced him to a twenty-year prison term. His appeal argued, among other things, that the court should not have allowed the footprint evidence to be presented to the jury because, according to the appellant brief, Teodoro Bautista "had no experience or knowledge which would enable him to speak intelligently and enlighten the court and jury." The New Mexico Supreme Court agreed that in weighing such testimony "great caution should be exercised," but went on to state that "we believe in this case the facts justify the admission of this particular evidence." Other arguments were no more successful, and the court decided against Ancheta and upheld his conviction.[12]

As with several of the cases mentioned in this book, *New Mexico v. Ancheta* highlights sexual dangers faced by Mexican girls in and around the home. At the same time, the Lucero family was treated with considerable respect and deference during the trial. Their home was not portrayed as disheveled or dirty, their sleeping arrangements (outside the house, the entire family sleeping together) were not criticized or condemned. The fact that the Lucero household was nuclear, with a father, mother, and children, is not unimportant in this respect. Heteropatriarchal tendencies were strong in the West, including in Mexican communities, and the rewards—such as arresting and convicting the rapist of one's six-year-old daughter—could be all too tangible. Amado Ancheta, of course, may still have been arrested and convicted, and his appeal rejected, if Maria Inéz Lucero's parents were separated, or her home life was disordered and improper. Nevertheless, by portraying themselves as fulfilling sexual norms, the Lucero family likely improved their chances of finding success in the courts.

Recognizing the legal activism of ordinary Mexicans in the early twentieth century is an important goal of this book, as is accounting for the place of sex and sexual discourses in challenging, as well as reinscribing, Mexican marginalization. No less critical, however, is acknowledging persisting inequities within Mexican communities. In promoting heteropatriarchy and disavowing nonnormative sexual intimacies, Mexican communities silenced and hobbled some of their most vulnerable members. This emphasis on good citizenry and traditional sexual norms also runs the risk of obscuring an alternative vision of desire and belonging that some of the Mexicans in this book articulated and defended. The tradition of nonnormative sexual desire is in fact faint but discernible in the historical record, emerging in Juan Muñoz's successful appeal of his sodomy conviction in 1920s Laredo and Juan Mesa's announcements of love and plans to marry Dorothy Westfall in turn-of-the-century Southern California.

Among the legacies of Mexican legal activism in the early twentieth century, that is, is also an alternative vision of sex and sexual desire. This vision, though it may be now maddeningly elusive to historians, is one that does not depend upon or reinforce traditional sexual norms. Historians have unearthed—and undoubtedly will continue to explore—evidence of transgressive sexual acts and desires in the history of Mexican communities in the United States. An important goal for further research would be to link such excavations of desire with the emergence in the second half of the twentieth century of Chicana feminist critiques of the Chicano movement and the subsequent work of Gloria Anzaldúa, Cherríe Moraga, and others. As historians continue to explore the histories of *la frontera*, it is worth remembering that the history of the borderlands includes the colonial, the anticolonial, and the queer.[13]

NOTES

CHAPTER ONE

1. A century ago, like today, people of Mexican origin in the United States identified themselves in a variety of ways. References to region (*nuevomexicano, tejano, californio*) were common, as were terms like "Spanish," "Spanish American," "Latin American," and, of course, "Mexican." "Chicana/o" was not in common usage and I use it sparingly here. At the same time, I fully recognize the important continuities in the history of Mexicans in the United States. Like their mid- to late-twentieth-century counterparts, Mexicans around the turn of the century had both an intimate relationship with Mexican culture (Spanish language, food, family, and friends in Mexico) and deep attachments to their lives in the United States (homes and communities in the United States, social and political organizations, and employment opportunities, though poorly paid and at times unreliable). Moreover, in both time periods, individuals of Mexican ancestry frequently found themselves excluded from full participation in the American body politic.

2. I will use the term "Anglo" to identify men and women of largely Northern European descent who by the early twentieth century were politically and economically dominant in the West. Most were native to the United States, though many were newcomers to the West, and most tended to refer to themselves as "Americans." I will use both terms in the book.

3. Peter Boag, *Same-Sex Affairs: Constructing and Controlling Homosexuality in the Pacific Northwest* (Berkeley: University of California Press, 2003); Peggy Pascoe, *What Comes Naturally: Miscegenation Law and the Making of Race in America* (New York: Oxford University Press, 2009); Sharon R. Ullman, *Sex Seen: The Emergence of Modern Sexuality in America* (Berkeley: University of California Press, 1997); Mary E. Odem, *Delinquent Daughters: Protecting and Policing Adolescent Female Sexuality in the United States, 1885–1920* (Chapel Hill: University of North Carolina Press, 1995); Barbara Berglund, *Making San Francisco American: Cultural Frontiers in the Urban West, 1846–1906* (Lawrence: Kansas University Press, 2007); Nayan Shah, "Adjudicating Intimacies on U.S. Frontiers," in *Haunted by Empire: Geographies of Intimacy in North American History*, ed. Ann Laura Stoler (Durham: Duke University Press, 2006), 116–39; Nayan Shah, "Between 'Oriental Depravity' and 'Natural Degenerates': Spatial Borderlands and the Making of Ordinary Americans," *American Quarterly* 57, no. 3 (September 2005): 703–25.

4. Lauren L. Basson, *White Enough to Be American?: Race Mixing, Indigenous People, and the Boundaries of State and Nation* (Chapel Hill: University of North Carolina Press, 2008); Gail Bederman, *Manliness and Civilization: A Cultural History of Gender and Race in the United States, 1880–1917* (Chicago: University of Chicago Press, 1995); Margot Canaday, *The Straight State: Sexuality and Citizenship in Twentieth-Century America* (Princeton: Princeton University Press, 2009); Lionel Cantú, Jr., *The Sexuality of Migration: Border Crossings and Mexican Immigrant Men*, ed. Nancy A. Naples and Salvador Vidal-Ortiz (New York: New York University Press, 2009); Lisa Lindquist Dorr, *White Women, Rape, and the Power of Race in Virginia, 1900–1960* (Chapel Hill: University of North Carolina Press, 2004); Lisa Duggan, *Sapphic Slashers: Sex, Violence, and American Modernity* (Durham: Duke University Press, 2000); Rosa Linda Fregoso, *meXicana Encounters: The Making of Social Identities on the Borderlands* (Berkeley: University of California Press, 2003); Martha Hodes, *White Women, Black Men: Illicit Sex in the Nineteenth-Century South* (New Haven: Yale University Press, 1997); Susan Koshy, *Sexual Naturalization: Asian Americans and Miscegenation* (Stanford: Stanford University Press, 2004); Mary Ting Yi Lui, *The Chinatown Trunk Mystery: Murder, Miscegenation, and Other Dangerous Encounters in Turn-of-the-Century New York City* (Princeton: Princeton University Press, 2007); Eithne Luibhéid, *Entry Denied: Controlling Sexuality at the Border* (Minneapolis: University of Minnesota Press, 2002); Eithne Luibhéid and Lionel Cantú, Jr., eds., *Queer Migrations: Sexuality, U.S. Citizenship, and Border Crossings* (Minneapolis: University of Minnesota Press, 2005); Pascoe, *What Comes Naturally*; Paul R. Spickard, *Mixed Blood: Intermarriage and Ethnic Identity in Twentieth-Century America* (Madison: University of Wisconsin Press, 1989).

5. I use "colonialism" here as opposed to "imperialism" following Lanny Thompson, who "distinguish[es] between colonialism (the expansion of a people through settlement), and imperialism (the expansion of a state through political domination)." While the extensive involvement of the United States in Mexican politics and economic development in the late nineteenth and early twentieth centuries appears decidedly imperial in nature, Mexican immigrants encountered what I believe to have been a distinctively colonial landscape when they crossed into the United States. See Lanny Thompson, "The Imperial Republic: A Comparison of the Insular Territories under U.S. Dominion after 1898," *Pacific Historical Review* 71, no. 4 (November 2002): 535–74; quotation on 540n10. See also Patrick Wolfe, "Land, Labor, and Difference: Elementary Structures of Race," *American Historical Review* 106 (June 2001): 866–1006.

6. I am following the lead of other historians who have remarked on this lingering colonial presence in the region in the twentieth century. Vicki Ruiz, for instance, describes Mexicans in the early twentieth century as "inheriting a legacy of colonialism wrought by Manifest Destiny," that is, stretching back to the middle of the nineteenth century; Vicki L. Ruiz, *From Out of the Shadows* (New York: Oxford University Press, 1998), 7. See also Amy L. Fairchild, *Science at the Borders: Immigrant Medical Inspection and the Shaping of the Modern Industrial Labor Force* (Baltimore: Johns Hopkins University Press, 2003), 150; Gilbert G. Gonzalez, *Guest Workers or Colonized Labor?: Mexican Labor Migration to the United States* (Boulder: Paradigm Press, 2006), 5; Linda Gordon, "Internal Colonialism and Gender," in Stoler, *Haunted by Empire*, 427–51; Ramón A. Gutiérrez, "Internal Colonialism: An American Theory of Race," *Du Bois Review* 1, no. 2 (2004): 282; Mae M. Ngai, *Impossible Subjects: Illegal Aliens and the Making of Modern America* (Princeton: Princeton University Press, 2004), 29;

Nayan Shah, "Cleansing Motherhood: Hygiene and the Culture of Domesticity in San Francisco's Chinatown, 1875–1900," in *Gender, Sexuality, and Colonia Modernities*, ed. Antoinette Burton (London: Routledge, 1999), 19–34; Alexandra Minna Stern, "Buildings, Boundaries, and Blood: Medicalization and Nation-Building on the U.S.-Mexico Border, 1910–1930," *Hispanic American Historical Review* 79, no. 1 (1999): 41–81; Elliott Young, "Imagining Alternative Modernities: Ignacio Martínez's Travel Narratives," in *Continental Crossroads: Remapping U.S.-Mexico Borderlands History*, ed. Samuel Truett and Elliott Young (Durham: Duke University Press, 2004), 164.

7. See Margaret D. Jacobs, *White Mother to a Dark Race: Settler Colonialism, Maternalism, and the Removal of Indigenous Children in the American West and Australia, 1880–1940* (Lincoln: University of Nebraska Press, 2009); Sally Engle Merry, *Colonizing Hawaii: The Cultural Power of Law* (Princeton: Princeton University Press, 2000); Laura Briggs, *Reproducing Empire: Race, Sex, Science, and U.S. Imperialism in Puerto Rico* (Berkeley: University of California Press, 2002); Eileen J. Suárez Findlay, *Imposing Decency: The Politics of Sexuality and Race in Puerto Rico, 1870–1920* (Durham: Duke University Press, 1999); Paul A. Kramer, *The Blood of Government: Race, Empire, the United States, and the Philippines* (Chapel Hill: University of North Carolina Press, 2006); Craig Calhoun, Frederick Cooper, and Kevin W. Moore, eds., *Lessons of Empire: Imperial Histories and American Power* (New York: W. W. Norton, 2006); Stoler, *Haunted by Empire*.

8. Myron P. Gutmann, Robert McCaa, Rudolfo Gutiérrez-Montes, and Brian J. Gratton, "The Demographic Impact of the Mexican Revolution in the United States," Texas Population Research Center Papers 1999–2000, 4, 6; Elliott Robert Barkan, *From All Points: America's Immigrant West, 1870s–1952* (Bloomington: Indiana University Press, 2007), 199; Gabriela F. Arredondo, *Mexican Chicago: Race, Identity, and Nation, 1916–39* (Urbana: University of Illinois Press, 2008), 97. Despite the seeming fixity and accuracy of census categories and census counts, Mexicans and other communities of color, not to mention poor people of all races, were consistently undercounted. See chapter 2 for an example of this undercounting of ethnic Mexicans.

9. Tomás Almaguer, *Racial Fault Lines: The Historical Origins of White Supremacy in California* (Berkeley: University of California Press, 1994); Katherine Benton-Cohen, *Borderline Americans: Racial Division and Labor War in the Arizona Borderlands* (Cambridge, MA: Harvard University Press, 2009); William Deverell, *Whitewashed Adobe: The Rise of Los Angeles and the Remaking of Its Mexican Past* (Berkeley: University of California Press, 2005); Edward J. Escobar, *Race, Police, and the Making of a Political Identity: Mexican Americans and the Los Angeles Police Department, 1900–1945* (Berkeley: University of California Press, 1999); Neil Foley, *The White Scourge: Mexicans, Blacks, and Poor Whites in Texas Cotton Culture* (Berkeley: University of California Press, 1997); Laura E. Gómez, *Manifest Destinies: The Making of the Mexican American Race* (New York: New York University Press, 2007); Andrew R. Graybill, *Policing the Great Plains: Rangers, Mounties, and the North American Frontier, 1875–1910* (Lincoln: University of Nebraska Press, 2007); Benjamin Heber Johnson, *Revolution in Texas: How a Forgotten Rebellion and Its Bloody Suppression Turned Mexicans into Americans* (New Haven: Yale University Press, 2003); Stephanie Lewthwaite, *Race, Place, and Reform in Mexican Los Angeles: A Transnational Perspective, 1890–1940* (Tucson: University of Arizona Press, 2009); Eric V. Meeks, *Border Citizens: The Making of Indians, Mexicans, and Anglos in Arizona* (Austin: University of Texas Press, 2007); Natalia Molina, *Fit to Be Citizens?: Public Health and Race in Los Angeles, 1879–1939*

(Berkeley: University of California Press, 2006); F. Arturo Rosales, ¡Pobre Raza!: Violence, Justice, and Mobilization among México Lindo Immigrants, 1900–1936 (Austin: University of Texas Press, 1999); Ruiz, From Out of the Shadows; George Sánchez, Becoming Mexican American: Ethnicity, Culture, and Identity in Chicano Los Angeles, 1900–1945 (New York: Oxford University Press, 1993).

10. For recent discussions of these events see Benton-Cohen, Borderline Americans; Fairchild, Science at the Borders; Johnson, Revolution in Texas; Molina, Fit to Be Citizens?; Ngai, Impossible Subjects; Pascoe, What Comes Naturally; Courtney Q. Shah, "'Against Their Own Weakness': Policing Sexuality and Women in San Antonio, Texas, during World War I," Journal of the History of Sexuality 9, no. 3 (September 2010): 458–82. Italian Americans, for instance, unlike Mexicans, were never reclassified as nonwhite in the 1930 US census or elsewhere; Thomas A. Guglielmo, White on Arrival: Italians, Race, Color, and Power in Chicago, 1890–1945 (New York: Oxford University Press, 2003), 87. Denigrations of the homes of a variety of non-Anglo groups as dirty and unhealthy occurred throughout the country in the early twentieth century. See Jacobs, White Mother to a Dark Race; Phyllis Palmer, Domesticity and Dirt: Housewives and Domestic Servants in the United States, 1920–1945 (Philadelphia: Temple University Press, 1989); Lynn Sacco, Unspeakable: Father-Daughter Incest in American History (Baltimore: Johns Hopkins University Press, 2009); Nayan Shah, Contagious Divides: Epidemics and Race in San Francisco's Chinatown (Berkeley: University of California Press, 2001).

11. http://www.mexica.net/guadhida.php (accessed July 30, 2010).

12. Between 1850 and 1859, Spanish-surnamed individuals were involved in 51 civil and criminal cases (of 2,346) appealed to the Texas Supreme Court, 66 of the 1,985 total cases appealed to the California Supreme Court, and 18 of the 34 appealed to the New Mexico Supreme Court. Two of the 38 total cases appealed to the Arizona Supreme Court during the years 1865 to 1880 involved Spanish-surnamed individuals. In 1880, there were 19 Spanish-surnamed appeals (of 587) in Texas, 14 (of 543) in California, and 1 (of 6) in New Mexico. Two cases from 1880 in Texas exemplify these tensions between colonial exclusion and differentiation and potential inclusion. In a murder case from Bee County, Texas, the court's decision reversing the guilty verdict of Felipe Greta noted "the homicide was instigated by conjugal jealousy—an emotion which is generally assumed to be potent among the Mexican race, to which all the parties belonged." In a theft case from Travis County that was also overturned, the court ruled that Antonio Jorasco merited a new trial and stated "to deprive a citizen of his liberty, the law demands that his conviction shall be based upon legal evidence of such force and character as to satisfy the minds of his peers beyond a reasonable doubt; and without this amount of legal evidence, his condemnation shall not stand." Stark racial differentiation, in the first case, stands in contrast to a strong assertion in the second case of the rights of Spanish-surnamed Antonio Jorasco and the ultimate success of his appeals case. LexisNexis Legal Database, accessed December 2009–November 2010; Texas v. Felipe Greta, Supreme Court of Texas, 1880; Texas v. Antonio Jorasco, Supreme Court of Texas, 1880.

13. For other examples of subjects of American colonial rule using the American legal system, see Ned Blackhawk, Violence over the Land: Indians and Empires in the Early American West (Cambridge, MA: Harvard University Press, 2006); Christian W. McMillen, Making Indian Law: The Hualapai Land Case and the Birth of Ethnohistory (New Haven: Yale University Press, 2007); Sally Engle Merry, Colonizing Hawaii: The Cultural Power of Law (Princeton: Princeton University Press, 2000); Marsha

Weisiger, *Dreaming of Sheep in Navajo Country* (Seattle: University of Washington Press, 2009); Tisa Wenger, *We Have a Religion: The 1920s Pueblo Indian Dance Controversy and American Religious Freedom* (Chapel Hill: University of North Carolina Press, 2009).

14. LexisNexis Legal Database, accessed December 2009–June 2011. The online LexisNexis legal database supplied an incomparable research tool for this project. For every year between 1900 and 1930, I identified cases involving Spanish-surnamed appellants from a longer list of criminal cases appealed to higher courts in the region (Texas Court of Criminal Appeals, California Supreme Court, California Court of Appeals, New Mexico Supreme Court, Arizona Supreme Court). Eliminating duplicate cases resulted in a total of 1,076 Spanish-surnamed criminal appeal cases for Texas, California, New Mexico, and Arizona between 1900 and 1930.

     Though individuals of Spanish, Chilean, Puerto Rican, Cuban, and other Latin American ancestry long resided in the West, the vast majority of those with Spanish surnames in the region were of Mexican descent. There is a possibility, given the previous centuries of Spanish colonialism in the Southwest and the mixture of Spanish, Mexican, and Native American cultures and peoples, that some of the Spanish-surnamed appellants were Native American individuals. Court records, however, tended to identify "Indians" who appealed cases, and I have not included those cases in the above count. The same is true of Filipino appellants with Spanish surnames (see note 27, this chapter), who appear on occasion in California appeals cases. Appellants of mixed heritage with Mexican ancestry and non-Spanish surnames also do not appear in these totals. I have also excluded, as best as possible, individuals with names that are less obviously of Mexican origin, unless the appeals case specifically described the appellant as "Mexican." Neither Daisy Mayo, for instance, who appealed a conviction for sale of liquor (Court of Criminal Appeals of Texas, 1928), nor Willie Sola, who appealed a conviction of assault (Court of Criminal Appeals of Texas, 1916), are included in the above count of Spanish-surnamed appeals cases.

15. For discussions of the use of legal sources, see Katherine Elaine Bliss, *Compromised Positions: Prostitution, Public Health, and Gender Politics in Revolutionary Mexico City* (University Park: Pennsylvania State University Press, 2001); Robert M. Buffington, *Criminal and Citizen in Modern Mexico* (Lincoln: University of Nebraska Press, 2000); Pablo Piccato, *City of Suspects: Crime in Mexico City, 1900–1931* (Durham: Duke University Press, 2001); Stephen Robertson, *Crimes against Children: Sexual Violence and Legal Culture in New York City, 1880–1960* (Chapel Hill: University of North Carolina Press, 2005). For early twentieth-century legal transformations, see Jeffrey S. Adler, *First in Violence, Deepest in Dirt: Homicide in Chicago, 1875–1920* (Cambridge, MA: Harvard University Press, 2006); Laura F. Edwards, *The People and Their Peace: Legal Culture and the Transformation of Inequality in the Post-Revolutionary South* (Chapel Hill: University of North Carolina Press, 2009); Morton J. Horwitz, *The Transformation of American Law, 1870–1960: The Crisis of Legal Orthodoxy* (New York: Oxford University Press, 1994); Michael Willrich, *City of Courts: Socializing Justice in Progressive Era Chicago* (Cambridge: Cambridge University Press, 2003). The legal system in the American West is discussed in Gordon Morris Bakken, "Becoming Progressive: The California Supreme Court, 1880–1910," *Historian* 64, no. 3 (Spring/Summer 2002): 551–65; Paul T. Heitter, "A Suprising Amount of Justice: The Experience of Mexican and Racial Minority Defendants Charged with Serious Crimes in Arizona, 1865–1920," *Pacific Historical Review* 70, no. 2 (May 2001): 183–220; and Linda S.

Parker, "Statutory Changes and Ethnicity in Sex Crimes in Four California Counties, 1880–1920," *Western Legal History* 6, no. 1 (Summer/Fall 1993): 69–91.

16. Edwards, *The People and Their Peace*, 199.

17. See, for instance, Ramón A. Gutiérrez, *When Jesus Came, the Corn Mothers Went Away: Marriage, Sexuality, and Power in New Mexico, 1500–1846* (Stanford: Stanford University Press, 1991); Linda Heidenreich, *"This Land Was Mexican Once": Histories of Resistance from Northern California* (Austin: University of Texas Press, 2007); Pablo Mitchell, *Coyote Nation: Sexuality, Race, and Conquest in Modernizing New Mexico, 1880–1920* (Chicago: University of Chicago Press, 2005); Emma Pérez, *The Decolonial Imaginary: Writing Chicanas into History* (Bloomington: Indiana University Press, 1999); Shah, "Adjudicating Intimacies on U.S. Frontiers"; Mark Wild, *Street Meeting: Multiethnic Neighborhoods in Early Twentieth-Century Los Angeles* (Berkeley: University of California Press, 2005).

18. Some notable examples are Peter Boag, *Same-Sex Affairs: Constructing and Controlling Homosexuality in the Pacific Northwest* (Berkeley: University of California Press, 2003); George Chauncey, *Gay New York: Gender, Urban Culture, and the Making of the Gay Male World, 1890–1940* (New York: Basic Books, 1994); John D'Emilio and Estelle Freedman, *Intimate Matters: A History of Sexuality in America* (New York: Harper and Row, 1988); Duggan, *Sapphic Slashers*; John Howard, *Men Like That: A Southern Queer History* (Chicago: University of Chicago Press, 1999); Kevin P. Murphy, *Political Manhood: Red Bloods, Mollycoddles, and the Politics of Progressive Era Reform* (New York: Columbia University Press, 2008); Sacco, *Unspeakable*; Jennifer Terry, *An American Obsession: Science, Medicine, and Homosexuality in Modern Society* (Chicago: University of Chicago Press, 1999).

19. See Fregoso, *meXicana Encounters*; Ruiz, *From Out of the Shadows*.

20. Odem, *Delinquent Daughters*, 15–17, 96, 172; Carolyn E. Cocca, *Jailbait: The Politics of Statutory Rape Law in the United States* (Albany: State University of New York Press, 2004); Ruiz, *From Out of the Shadows*; Lui, *The Chinatown Trunk Mystery*; Bederman, *Manliness and Civilization*; D'Emilio and Freedman, *Intimate Matters*, 210; Robertson, *Crimes Against Children*; Ullman, *Sex Seen*; Willrich, *City of Courts*.

21. Odem, *Delinquent Daughters*; Cocca, *Jailbait*; Ruiz, *From Out of the Shadows*.

22. Sánchez *Becoming Mexican American*; Monica Perales, "'Who Has a Greater Job Than a Mother?': Defining Mexican Motherhood on the US-Mexico Border in the Early 20th Century" (unpublished manuscript); David Wallace Adams, *Education for Extinction: American Indians and the Boarding School Experience: 1875–1928* (Lawrence: Kansas University Press, 1997); K. Tsianina Lomawaima, *They Called It Prairie Light: The Story of Chiloco Indian School* (Lincoln: University of Nebraska Press, 1995).

23. Edwards, *The People and Their Peace*. For examples of studies of Chicana/o civil rights movements, see Ernesto Chávez, *"¡Mi raza primero!": Nationalism, Identity, and Insurgency in the Chicano Movement in Los Angeles, 1966–1978* (Berkeley: University of California Press, 2002); Ignacio M. García, *White but Not Equal: Mexican Americans, Jury Discrimination, and the Supreme Court* (Tucson: University of Arizona Press, 2008); Gómez, *Manifest Destinies*; Ariela Gross, "Texas Mexicans and the Politics of Whiteness," *Law and History Review* 21, no. 1 (Spring 2003): 195–205; David G. Gutiérrez, *Walls and Mirrors: Mexican Americans, Mexican Immigrants, and the Politics of Ethnicity* (Berkeley: University of California Press, 1995); Ian Haney Lopez, *White by Law: The Legal Construction of Race* (New York: New York University Press, 2006); Cynthia E. Orozco, *No Mexicans, Women, or Dogs Allowed: The Rise of the Mexican*

American Civil Rights Movement (Austin: University of Texas Press, 2009); and F. Arturo Rosales, *Testimonio: A Documentary History of the Mexican American Struggle for Civil Rights* (Houston: Arte Público Press, 2000).

24. Frances R. Aparicio, "Jennifer as Selena: Rethinking Latinidad in Media and Popular Culture," *Latino Studies* 1 (2003): 90–105. See also Gómez, *Manifest Destinies*; Lopez, *White by Law*.

25. United States Census Bureau, available at http://www.census.gov/population/www/documentation/twps0056.html. See also Myron P. Gutmann et al., "The Demographic Impact of the Mexican Revolution in the United States," 6; Almaguer, *Racial Fault Lines*, 130.

26. Alameda County Criminal Records; Los Angeles County Criminal Records; *Texas v. Louis Basquez*, Court of Criminal Appeals of Texas (1930); *California v. Marina Torres*, Supreme Court of California (1924); *California v. Juanita Casanova*, Court of Appeal of California (1921); *California v. Juan Mesa*, Supreme Court of California (1891). Thanks to Beth McLaughlin for her invaluable assistance in conducting research in county criminal records.

27. In 1929, for instance, two Filipino Americans appealed criminal convictions to the Court of Appeal of California (*California v. Rufo Sotelo, California v. E. Garcia*) (LexisNexis Legal Database, accessed June 2011). While African Americans did not appear as frequently in the appeals record as Mexicans, a handful of African Americans did appeal criminal convictions in the West in the early twentieth century. In California, for instance, there were at least twenty-one appeals by African American defendants to California's Court of Appeal and Supreme Court between 1900 and 1930 (LexisNexis Legal Database, accessed February 2011; these appeals cases do not include cases that may have involved African American defendants when the race of the defendant ["negro," "colored," "black"] was not noted). Among those cases was an appeal by an African American woman, Fay Alma Smith, who (unsuccessfully) appealed a murder conviction to the Court of Appeal of California in 1923. In the state of Georgia, by comparison, there were ten cases (of several thousand total) involving African Americans appealed to the Court of Appeals of Georgia between 1900 and 1930 (LexisNexis Legal Database, accessed February 2011). For examples of the use of the American legal system by members of other racially marginalized groups, see Molina, *Fit to Be Citizens?*; Shah, "Adjudicating Intimacies on U.S. Frontiers" and "Between 'Oriental Depravity' and 'Natural Degenerates'"; Basson, *White Enough to Be American?*; Diana L. Ahmed, *The Opium Debate and Chinese Exclusion Laws in the Nineteenth-Century American West* (Reno: University of Nevada Press, 2007); McMillen, *Making Indian Law*; Wenger, *We Have a Religion*.

28. Mexican witnesses could also make explicit certain forms of discrimination and exploitation that were often left obscure in Anglo accounts. Anglos, for instance, often failed to mention that some of the circumstances surrounding migration, especially American-style modernization programs within turn-of-the-twentieth-century Mexico and the increased monitoring of the US-Mexico border, could lead to alternative family formations once in the United States. The fact that a lack of adequate housing for Mexicans could lead to residence in rooming houses that also functioned as spaces of commercial sex was similarly left unsaid, as was the role of employment discrimination in leading to job instability and geographic mobility, once again creating alternative domestic situations; or the role of poverty in forcing families to rent out rooms to boarders, opening greater possibilities for sexual intimacy and violence in the home. Mexican witnesses drew such linkages into the

open, providing structural explanations to decisions and choices often framed by Anglos as individual and tied to inadequacies in Mexican culture.

29. Canaday, *The Straight State*. For some examples of the central role of courts and legal institutions in colonial rule, see Alfred W. McCoy, *Policing America's Empire: The United States, the Philippines, and the Rise of the Surveillance State* (Madison: University of Wisconsin Press, 2009); Mary A. Renda; *Taking Haiti: Military Occupation and the Culture of U.S. Imperialism, 1915–1940* (Chapel Hill: University of North Carolina Press, 2001); essays in Stoler, *Haunted by Empire*.

CHAPTER TWO

1. *California v. Álvaro Fernández*, Court of Appeal of California (1906), 45. Unless otherwise noted, throughout the book, page numbers refer to the location in the original trial transcript.

2. *California v. Fernández*, 43.

3. *California v. Fernández*, 33–34.

4. See Tomás Almaguer, *Racial Fault Lines: The Historical Origins of White Supremacy in California* (Berkeley: University of California Press, 1994); Edward J. Escobar, *Race, Police, and the Making of a Political Identity: Mexican Americans and the Los Angeles Police Department, 1900–1945* (Berkeley: University of California Press, 1999); Stephanie Lewthwaite, *Race, Place, and Reform in Mexican Los Angeles: A Transnational Perspective, 1890–1940* (Tucson: University of Arizona Press, 2009); Natalia Molina, *Fit to Be Citizens?: Public Health and Race in Los Angeles, 1879–1939* (Berkeley: University of California Press, 2006); George Sánchez, *Becoming Mexican American: Ethnicity, Culture, and Identity in Chicano Los Angeles, 1900–1945* (New York: Oxford University Press, 1993).

5. US Census Population 1900; US Census Population 1910.

6. Thanks to Elizabeth Supp for research assistance on surnames and countries of origin in the US Census Population 1900, and US Census Population 1910.

7. See Ann Laura Stoler, ed., *Haunted by Empire: Geographies of Intimacy in North American History* (Durham: Duke University Press, 2006); Margaret D. Jacobs, *White Mother to a Dark Race: Settler Colonialism, Maternalism, and the Removal of Indigenous Children in the American West and Australia, 1880–1940* (Lincoln: University of Nebraska Press, 2009); Sally Engle Merry, *Colonizing Hawai'i: The Cultural Power of Law* (Princeton: Princeton University Press, 2000); Laura Briggs, *Reproducing Empire: Race, Sex, Science, and U.S. Imperialism in Puerto Rico* (Berkeley: University of California Press, 2002); Eileen J. Suárez Findlay, *Imposing Decency: The Politics of Sexuality and Race in Puerto Rico, 1870–1920* (Durham: Duke University Press, 1999); Paul A. Kramer, *The Blood of Government: Race, Empire, the United States, and the Philippines* (Chapel Hill: University of North Carolina Press, 2006).

8. US Census 1900; US Census 1910; John Outcalt, *A History of Merced County, California* (Los Angeles: Historic Record Co., 1925), http://www.cagenweb.com/merced/Merced.Outcalt.pdf.

9. US Census 1900, US Census 1910 (ancestry.com, last accessed February 22, 2011); "Golden Harvest," 30; Outcalt, *A History of Merced County*; http://www.mariposaresearch.net/DISVIT3.html;http://freepages.genealogy.rootsweb.com/~ostrander/3722.htm. Less evidence remains of the life of prosecuting attorney E. H. Hoar. Six years earlier, in 1900, a Henry Hoar lived in Merced with his wife, Jane, and infant son, Frederick. Then twenty-eight, Hoar was a court reporter; however, it is unclear whether Henry Hoar, the court reporter in 1900, became E. H. Hoar, the Merced

County district attorney in 1906. In 1910, an attorney named Elizah H. Hoar lived one hundred and fifty miles away, in Bakersfield, California (US Census 1900, US Census 1910, ancestry.com, last accessed February 22, 2011).

10. According to Linda Kerber, women began serving on juries in California in 1911; Kerber, *No Constitutional Right to Be Ladies: Women and the Obligations of Citizenship* (New York: Hill and Wang, 1998), 137. See also Gretchen Ritter, "Gender and Citizenship after the Nineteenth Amendment," *Polity* 32, no. 3 (Spring 2000): 345–75. While no women served on the jury in the Fernández trial, other trials in the period included female jurors. See *California v. Anastacio Ruiz*, Court of Appeal of California (1920), *California v. Louis Geonzelis*, Court of Appeal of California (1930), and *California v. Luz Cabrera*, Court of Appeal of California (1930). Thanks to Donna Schuele for her timely assistance in questions about women and jury duty.

11. US Census Schedule, Merced County, California, 1910.

12. *California v. Fernández*, 32–35.

13. *California v. Fernández*, 50–51.

14. Outcalt, *A History of Merced County*, http://www.cagenweb.com/merced/Merced .Outcalt.pdf (last accessed May 2011); US Census, Merced County, California, 1910.

15. *California v. Fernández*, 176.

16. *California v. Fernández*, 190–94.

17. *California v. Fernández*, 193.

18. See Thomas A. Guglielmo, *White on Arrival: Italians, Race, Color, and Power in Chicago, 1890–1945* (New York: Oxford University Press, 2003).

19. *California v. Fernández*, 200–211.

20. *California v. Fernández*, 214–16. For a similar tendency toward the homogenization of Spanish-speaking communities in Texas, see Cynthia E. Orozco, *No Mexicans, Women, or Dogs Allowed: The Rise of the Mexican American Civil Rights Movement* (Austin: University of Texas Press, 2009).

21. *California v. Fernández*, 270–71.

22. *California v. Fernández*, 288–92.

23. *California v. Fernández*, 348–49.

24. *California v. Fernández*, 351–56.

25. *California v. Fernández*, 351–56.

26. *California v. Fernández*.

27. *California v. Fernández*. See Jacobs, *White Mother to a Dark Race*; Orozco, *No Mexicans, Women, or Dogs Allowed*; Adams, *Education for Extinction*; Jacqueline Fear-Segal, *White Man's Club: Schools, Race, and the Struggle of Indian Acculturation* (Lincoln: University of Nebraska Press, 2007). Significant numbers of Mexicans in trials across the West needed interpreters in the courtroom. Though the courts provided interpreters, inability to speak English undoubtedly accentuated Mexicans' distance from claims of full citizenship. Other legal institutions also sought to address language differences. Courtney Shah notes that some policewomen appointed in San Antonio in 1917 spoke Spanish; Shah, "'Against Their Own Weakness,'" 475.

28. *California v. Fernández*.

29. United States Census Schedule, Merced County, California, 1910.

30. See Almaguer, *Racial Fault Lines*; Lewthwaite, *Race, Place, and Reform in Mexican Los Angeles*; Molina, *Fit to Be Citizens?*

31. This tendency toward homogenization occurred elsewhere in Mexican America. In matters of voting in 1920s Texas, for instance, Cynthia Orozoco notes that "most European Americans apparently saw little difference between Mexican citizens and

México Tejanos, often racializing 'the Mexican' voter" (Orozco, *No Mexicans, Women, or Dogs Allowed*, 36). For a similar dynamic in Arizona, see Katherine Benton-Cohen, *Borderline Americans: Racial Division and Labor War in the Arizona Borderlands* (Cambridge, MA: Harvard University Press, 2009), 22. See also Lauren L. Basson, *White Enough to Be American?: Race Mixing, Indigenous People, and the Boundaries of State and Nation* (Chapel Hill: University of North Carolina Press, 2008).

32. *Texas v. Pablo Villafranco*, Court of Criminal Appeals of Texas (1918), 4.

33. *California v. Fernández*, 169.

34. Historian Pablo Piccato, for instance, offers numerous examples of women in turn-of-the-century Mexico City asserting rights in legal settings; Pablo Piccato, *City of Suspects: Crime in Mexico City, 1900–1931* (Durham: Duke University Press, 2001). Jeffrey Adler also points to the increased use of the courts by women in turn-of-the-century Chicago; Jeffrey Adler, *First in Violence, Deepest in Dirt: Homicide in Chicago, 1875–1920* (Cambridge, MA: Harvard University Press, 2006).

35. Morton Horwitz notes of the period: "After the trauma of the American Civil War, amid heightening social conflict produced by immigration, urbanization, and industrialization, orthodox legal thinkers and judges sought ever more fervently to create an autonomous legal culture as part of their search for order. Through a process of systemization, integration, and abstraction of legal doctrine, they legally refined and tightened up what had previously been a loosely arranged, ad hoc system of legal classification"; Morton J. Horwitz, *The Transformation of American Law, 1870–1960: The Crisis of Legal Orthodoxy* (New York: Oxford University Press, 1994), 10. See also Laura Edwards, *People and Their Peace*, for similar efforts from an earlier period to standardize local courts.

36. Vicki L. Ruiz, *From Out of the Shadows* (New York: Oxford University Press, 1998), 6.

37. See Neil Foley, *The White Scourge: Mexicans, Blacks, and Poor Whites in Texas Cotton Culture* (Berkeley: University of California Press, 1997); Lewthwaite, *Race, Place, and Reform in Mexican Los Angeles*.

38. *California v. Fernández*, 50. See Foley, *The White Scourge*, and Lewthwaite, *Race, Place, and Reform in Mexican Los Angeles*, for discussions of Mexicans and the racialization of mobility.

39. *California v. Fernández*, 113. The following chapter will explore similarly conflicting views of Mexican homes in more detail. For supposed links between non-Anglo homes and dirt, see Phyllis Palmer, *Domesticity and Dirt: Housewives and Domestic Servants in the United States, 1920–1945* (Philadelphia: Temple University Press, 1989); Lynn Sacco, *Unspeakable: Father-Daughter Incest in American History* (Baltimore: Johns Hopkins University Press, 2009); Nayan Shah, *Contagious Divides: Epidemics and Race in San Francisco's Chinatown* (Berkeley: University of California Press, 2001); Nancy Tomes, *The Gospel of Germs: Men, Women, and the Microbe in American Life* (Cambridge, MA: Harvard University Press, 1998).

40. *California v. Alexander Avila*, Court of Appeal of California (1920), 118–119.

41. *California v. Avila*, 109, 113. Another case in which the military service of a Mexican witness is discussed is *California v. Anastacio Ruiz*, Court of Appeal of California (1920).

42. *California v. Avila*, 108, 117, 120.

43. *California v. Avila*, 117.

44. *Texas v. Ignacio Muñoz*, Texas Court of Criminal Appeals (1927).

45. *Texas v. Anesetto Guerrero*, Texas Court of Criminal Appeals (1904); *New Mexico v. Malaquias Cortez*, Supreme Court of New Mexico (1909).

46. *Texas v. Saturina Garza*, Texas Court of Criminal Appeals (1905); *Texas v. Blazeo Pedro*, Texas Court of Criminal Appeals (1905); *Texas v. Pedro Barstado*, Texas Court of Criminal Appeals (1905).

47. *Texas v. Garza*; *Texas v. Pedro*; *Texas v. Barstado*. See also *New Mexico v. Sotero Trujillo*, Supreme Court of New Mexico (1921), a case in which Sotero Trujillo was ordered to be released from custody after his manslaughter conviction in the death of Luke Casamoff was overturned.

48. *People, on Behalf of Guadalupe and Elvira Gutiérrez, Alleged Wards, etc., Respondent v. Tomás Gutiérrez*, Court of Appeal of California (1920). In another case from California, *California v. Selso Rodriguez*, (Supreme Court of California, 1919), an Anglo woman testified that a Mexican family "seemed to be good people" (59).

49. *California v. Gutiérrez*.

50. *Texas v. Beneficio Tendia*, Texas Court of Criminal Appeals (1929). In reversing a grand larceny conviction against Federico Merino and Brigido Lira in 1914, the Arizona Supreme Court made a similar statement: "the courts are simply insisting that no man, whatever his station in life, shall be unlawfully tried and punished. This duty of protecting the meanest as well as the most exalted person from the invasion of a substantial right, and forbidding the conviction of one charged with crime, except upon the well-settled rules of the criminal law, is a duty imposed upon us by the law, and our oaths as judges." "The defendant," the court continued, "has been denied a trial wherein his substantial rights have been respected and conserved, and by reason thereof this case is reversed." *Arizona v. Federico Merino*, Supreme Court of Arizona (1914).

51. Benton-Cohen, *Borderline Americans*; Foley, *The White Scourge*; Benjamin Heber Johnson, *Revolution in Texas: How a Forgotten Rebellion and Its Bloody Suppression Turned Mexicans into Americans* (New Haven: Yale University Press, 2003); Lewthwaite, *Race, Place, and Reform in Mexican Los Angeles*; Molina, *Fit to Be Citizens?*; F. Arturo Rosales, *¡Pobre Raza!: Violence, Justice, and Mobilization among México Lindo Immigrants, 1900–1936* (Austin: University of Texas Press, 1999); Ruiz, *From Out of the Shadows*; Sánchez, *Becoming Mexican American*.

CHAPTER THREE

1. *Texas v. Tanis Cabana*, Texas Court of Criminal Appeals (1927), 16–17. Cabana was accused of statutory rape in the attack on Estraca. In 1927, the age of consent in Texas was eighteen. According to Mary Odem, "by 1920, nearly every state in the country had raised the age at which a woman could legally consent to sexual relations to either sixteen or eighteen years"; Mary E. Odem, *Delinquent Daughters: Protecting and Policing Adolescent Female Sexuality in the United States, 1885–1920* (Chapel Hill: University of North Carolina Press, 1995), 37.

2. In Hawai'i, for instance, Sally Engle Merry notes, "the willingness of early missionaries and the government they created to welcome all peoples who were willing to transform their bodies and their lives—their cultural selves—in accordance with principles of Christian piety and comportment into the community of the 'civilized'"; Merry, *Colonizing Hawai'i*, 23. See Shah, "Adjudicating Intimacies," for a discussion of "racial taxonomies."

3. *California v. Alma Carrillo*, Court of Appeal of California (1929), 13; *California v. Alvino Méndez*, Supreme Court of California (1924). For similar descriptions of Mexican homes as "shacks," see Lewthwaite, *Race, Place, and Reform in Mexican Los Angeles*, 25; Jacobs, *White Mother to a Dark Race*.

4. *California v. Cruz Vicunia*, Court of Appeal of California (1930), 239.
5. *California v. Frank Rameriz*, Court of Appeal of California (1911), 174.
6. María Cristina García, "Agents of Americanization: Rusk Settlement and the Houston Mexicano Community, 1907–1950," in *Mexican Americans in Texas History: Selected Essays*, ed. Emilio Zamora, Cynthia Orozco, and Rudolfo Rocha (Austin: Texas State Historical Association, 2000), 121–37. For more recent discussions of Anglo views of Mexican domesticity, see Perales, "'Who Has a Greater Job Than a Mother?'"; Ruiz, *From Out of the Shadows*; Lewthwaite, *Race, Place, and Reform in Mexican Los Angeles*; Benton-Cohen, *Borderline Americans*; and Molina, *Fit to Be Citizens?*
7. *California v. Eulogio Castro*, Supreme Court of California (1901), 30, 31, 38. An example of Mexican women literally defending their homes occurred in *New Mexico vs. Telesforo Gallegos and Felix Borrego*, New Mexico Supreme Court (1912), when Manuela Trujillo de Sisneros shot her gun at two men who were trying to break into her home (20).
8. *Texas v. Domingo Brown*, Texas Court of Criminal Appeals (1922), 28.
9. Orozco, *No Mexicans, Women, or Dogs Allowed*. See also Foley, *The White Scourge*; Johnson, *Revolution in Texas*; and David Montejano, *Anglos and Mexicans in the Making of Texas, 1836–1986* (Austin: University of Texas Press, 1987). On juries, see Clare Sheridan, "'Another White Race': Mexican Americans and the Paradox of Whiteness in Jury Selection," *Law and History Review* 21, no. 1 (Spring 2003): 112. Women were similarly not allowed to serve on juries in Texas until 1954, http://www.tsl.state.tx.us/exhibits/suffrage/aftermath/page1.html (accessed January 28, 2010). Thanks to Crista DeLuzio for bringing up this point. See also Gretchen Ritter, "Jury Service and Women's Citizenship before and after the Nineteenth Amendment," *Law and History Review* (Fall 2002): http://www.historycooperative.org/journals/lhr/20.3/ritter.html (accessed January 28, 2010).
10. *Texas v. Cabana*, 2.
11. *Texas v. Cabana*, 3–4.
12. *Texas v. Cabana*, 4–6.
13. *Texas v. Cabana*, 7–8.
14. *Texas v. Cabana*, 8–10.
15. *Texas v. Cabana*, 10.
16. Molina, *Fit to Be Citizens?*; Sánchez, *Becoming Mexican American*; Lewthwaite, *Race, Place, and Reform in Mexican Los Angeles*; Ruiz, *From Out of the Shadows*.
17. *Texas v. Cabana*, 14–15.
18. Earl Lewis and Heidi Ardizzone, *Love on Trial: An American Scandal in Black and White* (New York: Norton, 2001).
19. In *California v. Tony Flores*, California Supreme Court (1911), where Flores was convicted of enticing Ruby Emerson into prostitution, Emerson's mother also testified with a child, her son and the victim's brother, on her lap (93).
20. *Texas v. Cabana*, 17–18. Women in Mexico also testified confidently about sexual attacks committed against them. See Piccato, *City of Suspects*, 121, 128.
21. *Texas v. Cabana*, 18–19.
22. *Texas v. Cabana*, 20–21.
23. *Texas v. Cabana*, 21–24. See, for example, Sacco, *Unspeakable*, 166.
24. *Texas v. Cabana*, 26, 29–30.
25. *Texas v. Cabana*, 26–29.
26. *Texas v. Cabana*, 31–36.

27. *Texas v. Cabana*, 31–38.
28. *Texas v. Cabana*, 41–42.
29. *Texas v. Cabana*, 42–43.
30. *Texas v. Cabana*, 45.
31. *Texas v. Cabana*, 45.
32. *Texas v. Cabana*, 45–46.
33. *Texas v. Cabana*. The judge's sharp words provide another example of judges disciplining and ordering trial courts.
34. *Texas v. Cabana*.
35. *Texas v. Cabana*.
36. *Texas v. Cabana*.
37. *Texas v. Cabana*, 45, 33, 35, 30.
38. *Texas v. Cabana*, 18.
39. United States Census Schedule, Karnes County, Texas, 1930; United States Census Schedule, Texas, 1910, 1920, 1930.
40. *Texas v. Cabana*, 31–39.
41. *Texas v. Cabana*, 31–39. For descriptions of anti-Mexican campaigns in 1920s Texas, see Foley, *The White Scourge*; Orozco, *No Mexicans, Women, or Dogs Allowed*; Montejano, *Anglos and Mexicans in the Making of Texas*; Johnson, *Revolution in Texas*.
42. Mexican boys at times also faced dangers of sexual assault. In Arizona, Pablo Soto was convicted of raping "Amilio" Sherman, who is described in court documents as "a Mexican boy of about the age of four years." Mary Sherman testified that she had sent her son to buy "chili and candy" at a store several blocks from their home and that he had returned "crying and very pale." She examined him and discovered that he had been sexually assaulted. Emilio subsequently told his mother that Pablo Soto had attacked him. Soto was arrested on the charge of committing "the crime against nature" and eventually convicted for his attack on the boy. Soto appealed the case, arguing that Mary Sherman should not have been allowed to describe her son's description of the attack to the jury. The Arizona Supreme Court disagreed and affirmed Soto's original conviction. *Arizona v. Pablo Soto*, Supreme Court of Arizona (1908). Lynn Sacco's *Unspeakable* includes other examples involving Spanish-surnamed individuals drawn from newspaper accounts.
43. Lynn Sacco, "Sanitized for your Protection: Medical Discourse and the Denial of Incest in the United States, 1890–1940," *Journal of Women's History* 14, no. 3 (2002): 80–104; Stephen Robertson, *Crimes against Children: Sexual Violence and Legal Culture in New York City, 1880–1960* (Chapel Hill: University of North Carolina Press, 2005), 2. Katharine Bliss notes that mothers in Mexico used the courts to prosecute men who sexually assaulted their daughters; Bliss, *Compromised Positions*, 136–37.
44. See Odem, *Delinquent Daughters*, 15–17, 96, 172; Cocca, *Jailbait*.
45. *Texas v. Santiago Martínez*, Court of Criminal Appeals of Texas (1923), 1, 6, 17. As Lynn Sacco notes, there was a common belief that men could not transmit gonorrhea to girls.
46. *Texas v. Martínez*, 21, 22.
47. *Texas v. Martínez*, 23, 26.
48. *Texas v. Martínez*, 4, 8, 19, 20.
49. *Texas v. Martínez*, 11, 12, 13, 15.
50. *Texas v. Martínez*, 25, 5, 18.
51. *Texas v. Pablo Villafranco*, Court of Criminal Appeals of Texas (1918), 12, 20. Mi-

chele T. Moran's *Colonizing Leprosy: Imperialism and the Politics of Public Health in the United State* (Chapel Hill: University of North Carolina Press, 2007) notes that leprosy was at times racially differentiated by region. See also Alexandra Minna Stern, "Buildings, Boundaries, and Blood: Medicalization and Nation-Building on the U.S.-Mexico Border, 1910–1930," *Hispanic American Historical Review* 79, no. 1 (1999): 41–81; Shah, *Contagious Divides:*; Molina, *Fit to Be Citizens?*; Duggan, *Sapphic Slashers*; Terry, *An American Obsession*.

52. *Texas v. Cabana*, 27. For example, William Bassett, a doctor from northeastern New Mexico, claimed that his advanced age prevented him from having sex four times in one night, as his accuser alleged; *New Mexico v. William Bassett*, New Mexico Supreme Court (1921).

53. *Texas v. Cabana*, 4–5, 13, 18; Ruiz, *From Out of the Shadows*.

CHAPTER FOUR

1. *California v. Marina Torres*, California Supreme Court, (1924), 7, 155.
2. *California v. Torres*, 51.
3. *California v. Torres*. According to Mark Wild, the area around 1217 Temple Street was identified with commercial sex in the early twentieth century. See the wonderful map on page 129 of Wild's *Street Meeting: Multiethnic Neighborhoods in Early Twentieth-Century Los Angeles* (Berkeley: University of California Press, 2005). A decade before the Torres trial, the *Los Angeles Times* reported a prostitution sting at 1247 Temple Street; *Los Angeles Times*, October 15, 1914, ProQuest Historical Newspapers *Los Angeles Times*, 1881–1987, accessed October 28, 2010.
4. Sánchez, *Becoming Mexican American*, 88–90; Molina, *Fit to Be Citizens?* For other recent studies of early twentieth-century Los Angeles, see Deverell, *Whitewashed Adobe*; Linda España-Maram, *Creating Masculinity in Los Angeles's Little Manila: Working Class Filipinos and Popular Culture, 1920s–1950s* (New York: Columbia University Press, 2006); and Wild, *Street Meeting*.
5. *California v. Torres*, 6, 13.
6. *California v. Torres*, 64, 65–66, 73.
7. *California v. Torres*, 72, 75, 100.
8. *California v. Torres*, 162, 166–67, 176, 179, 183.
9. *California v. Torres*, 254–55, 261–62, 264–65.
10. *California v. Torres*, 269, 275. Katherine Bliss offers a similar example from Mexico City, where prostitutes defined themselves as good mothers, Bliss, *Compromised Positions*, 196, 198–99, 202–3. See also Willrich's *City of Courts*.
11. *California v. Torres*.
12. Molina, *Fit to Be Citizens?*; Wild, *Street Meeting*; Lewthwaite, *Race, Place, and Reform in Mexican Los Angeles*; Sánchez, *Becoming Mexican American*.
13. *California v. Torres*, 2, 4, 13, 125.
14. *California v. Torres*. For an account of the centrality of white domesticity to notions of white supremacy, see Duggan, *Sapphic Slashers*.
15. *California v. Torres*, 245, 247.
16. *California v. Torres*, 250–51, 253, 38–39.
17. *California v. Torres*, 270, 272, 274. Though Mexicans were commonly linked with overcrowding living conditions in 1920s Los Angeles, the fact that five people lived in a single room in a boarding house was not commented upon directly during the trial. See Molina, *Fit to Be Citizens?*; Lewthwaite, *Race, Place, and Reform in Mexican Los Angeles*.

18. *California v. Torres*, 173, 195.

19. Briggs, *Reproducing Empire*, 44, 53. See also Findlay, *Imposing Decency*.

20. Briggs, *Reproducing Empire*, 44.

21. Merry, *Colonizing Hawai'i*, 220.

22. Philippa Levine, *Prostitution, Race, and Politics: Policing Venereal Disease in the British Empire* (New York: Routledge, 2003), 222. See also Findlay, *Imposing Decency*; Bliss, *Compromised Positions*.

23. *California v. Torres*, 114, 120. Courtney Shah notes that Mexican and African American women in prostitution in World War I–era San Antonio were often portrayed as chronic offenders, not curable victims of unfortunate circumstances, Shah, "'Against Their Own Weakness,'" 468–69. In Mexico City, by contrast, prostitutes on occasion depicted themselves, like Josephine Verdugo, as "fallen women"; Bliss, *Compromised Positions*, 198.

24. *California v. Torres*, 162, 204–5. See España-Maram, *Creating Masculinity in Los Angeles's Little Manila*.

25. In Texas, during the same period, of the nearly two hundred (192) cases involving prostitution that were appealed to the Texas Court of Criminal Appeals, four were appeals by Spanish-surnamed individuals (LexisNexis Legal Database, accessed December 2009–November 2010). For a case from Texas involving prostitution see, *Texas v. Alberto Davila*, Court of Criminal Appeals of Texas (1927). Historian Ann Gabbert similarly observes that 30 percent of prostitutes in El Paso were Mexicans in 1900; Ann R. Gabbert, "Prostitution and Moral Reform in the Borderlands: El Paso, 1890–1920," *Journal of the History of Sexuality* 12 (2003): 575–604.

26. *California v. Juanita Casanova*, Court of Appeal of California (1921).

27. *California v. Casanova*.

28. See Wild, *Street Meeting*; Shah, "'Against Their Own Weakness,'" 478–79, for other recent examples of interracial mingling in commercial sex work in the West.

29. US Census 1920. See Duggan, *Sapphic Slashers*, for the association between women in the theater and prostitution.

30. *Los Angeles Times*, June 8, 1924, A3. ProQuest Historical Newspapers *Los Angeles Times*, 1881–1987 (last accessed October 28, 2010).

31. *Texas v. Ida Ott*, Court of Criminal Appeals of Texas (1920), 51–66; *Texas v. Ida Ott*, Court of Criminal Appeals of Texas (1921).

32. *New Mexico v. Pearl Snyder*, Supreme Court of New Mexico (1923). See also the case of Lizzie McGrath, which I discuss in *Coyote Nation*.

33. *Texas v. Louis Basquez*, Court of Criminal Appeals of Texas (1929), 1, 11, 3, 10–11, 13–14. For another appeals case involving an African American prostitute, see *New Mexico v. William Hall*, Supreme Court of New Mexico (1900).

34. *Texas v. Basquez*, 35, 38.

35. United States Census 1900, 1930. See Wild, *Street Meeting*; Berglund, *Making San Francisco American*.

36. In Mexico City, Katherine Bliss notes that prostitutes organized in the 1930s to demand rights. They argued, she says, for "more inclusive ideas of motherhood, nationalism, and citizenship"; Bliss, *Compromised Positions*, 186. Accusations of pimping against men also allowed Mexican women the chance to denounce the poor behavior of Mexican men; Bliss, *Compromised Positions*, 147, 149–51.

37. See Adler, *First in Violence, Deepest in Dirt*; Bliss, *Compromised Positions*, 38–40; Odem, *Delinquent Daughters*; Piccato, *City of Suspects*; Robertson, *Crimes against Children*; Sacco, *Unspeakable*; Willrich, *City of Courts*.

38. Evidence of the role of African American women in initiating appeals to higher courts is unfortunately quite limited. See Dorr, *White Women, Rape, and the Power of Race in Virginia, 1900–1960*, for appeals of rape convictions by African American men in the turn-of-the-twentieth-century South.

39. *Texas v. Petra Lerma*, Court of Criminal Appeals of Texas (1917); *California v. Trixie Gonzales*, Court of Appeal of California (1928); *Texas v. Julia Fernández*, Court of Criminal Appeals of Texas (1917). For other appeals cases involving Mexican women, see *Texas v. Francisca Mendez de Alemán*, Court of Criminal Appeals of Texas (1926); *Texas v. Incarnación Garza de Aguirre*, Court of Criminal Appeals of Texas (1928); *Texas v. Bertha Álvarez*, Court of Criminal Appeals of Texas (1928).

40. *Texas v. Carmen Fonseca*, Court of Criminal Appeals of Texas (1905).

41. *New Mexico v. Guadalupe Quintana and Maud Peña*, Supreme Court of New Mexico (1925), 117, 67.

42. In northern New Mexico, unlike most regions in the early twentieth-century West, Mexican men routinely served on juries, a topic I will discuss in more detail in chapter 6. The presence of Mexican men on juries in New Mexico points to the unevenness of Mexican citizenship and inclusion, both across the region and in terms of gender; until the 1960s Mexican women were barred from jury service (Ruiz, *From Out of the Shadows*, 94).

43. *New Mexico v. Quintana*. For another case in which a Mexican woman successfully appealed a murder conviction, see *New Mexico v. Hilaria Martínez*, New Mexico Supreme Court (1922).

44. Levine, *Prostitution, Race, and Politics*; Merry, *Colonizing Hawai'i*; Findlay, *Imposing Decency*; Jacobs, *White Mother to a Dark Race*; Malathi De Alwis, "'Respectability,' 'Modernity' and the Policing of 'Culture' in Colonial Ceylon," in Burton, *Gender, Sexuality, and Colonial Modernities*; Sarah Carter, *The Importance of Being Monogamous: Marriage and Nation Building in Western Canada to 1915* (Edmonton: University of Alberta Press, 2008).

CHAPTER FIVE

1. *Texas v. A. Gomez*, Court of Criminal Appeals of Texas (1916).

2. *Texas v. Gomez*.

3. *Texas v. Juan Muñoz*, Court of Criminal Appeals of Texas (1926). Some notable works that address male same-sex desire and activity include Boag, *Same-Sex Affairs*; Peter Boag, "Go West Young Man, Go East Young Woman: Searching for the Trans in Western Gender History," *Western Historical Quarterly* (Winter 2005): 477–97; Shah, "Between 'Oriental Depravity' and 'Natural Degenerates'"; Chauncey, *Gay New York*; Murphy, *Political Manhood*; Howard, *Men Like That*.

4. Roderick Ferguson, "Of Our Normative Strivings: African American Studies and the Histories of Sexuality," *Social Text* 23, nos. 3–4 (Fall–Winter 2005): 85–100. In a like manner, Kevin Murphy explores the relationship between same-sex intimacy and turn-of-the-twentieth-century political culture in *Political Manhood*.

5. See Merry, *Colonizing Hawai'i*; Briggs, *Reproducing Empire*; Anjali Arondekar, *For the Record: On Sexuality and the Colonial Archive in India* (Durham: Duke University Press, 2009); Renda, *Taking Haiti*; Paul Kramer, "The Darkness That Enters the Home: The Politics of Prostitution during the Philippine-American War," in Stoler, *Haunted by Empire*. See also Sacco, *Unspeakable*. Sacco notes that turn-of-the-twentieth-century medical professionals viewed father/daughter incest as especially prevalent among "foreigners" and African American communities. She also observes that such accu-

sations could be leveled at poor and working-class communities regardless of race (108–9). Kevin Murphy also notes that in the United States, "sodomites" were seen as unfit for self-government and the full rights of citizenship, *Political Manhood*, 160, 164.

6. Canaday, *The Straight State*; Stern, "Buildings, Boundaries, and Blood"; Duggan, *Sapphic Slashers*; Pascoe, *What Comes Naturally*; Terry, *An American Obsession*; Murphy, *Political Manhood*; Chauncey, *Gay New York*.

7. *Texas v. Gomez*; United States Census Schedule, Austin County, Texas, 1910.

8. United States Census Schedule, Austin County, Texas, 1910.

9. *Texas v. Gomez*.

10. *Texas v. Gomez*.

11. United States Census Schedule, Austin County, Texas, 1910, 1920.

12. *Texas v. Gomez*.

13. *Texas v. Gomez*.

14. See Boag, *Same-Sex Affairs*; Shah, "Between 'Oriental Depravity' and 'Natural Degenerates'"; Chauncey, *Gay New York*; Murphy, *Political Manhood*.

15. United States Census Schedule, Austin County, Texas, 1910, 1920. Thanks to Elizabeth Supp for her assistance in census research. See García, *White but Not Equal*, for exclusion of Mexicans from jury service in early twentieth-century Texas.

16. *Texas v. Muñoz*, 1–2. See Beatriz de la Garza, *A Law for the Lion: A Tale of Crime and Injustice in the Borderlands* (Austin: University of Texas Press, 2003), for a detailed account of another criminal trial involving Mexicans in early twentieth-century Laredo.

17. The United States census offers a further glimpse at Myers's life. The first census in which Carlos would have appeared was the 1920 census, when he would have been nine years old. The 1920 census, in fact, included an individual named Carlos Myers living in Laredo. Carlos Ruben "Meyers" (not "Myers," as his name is listed in the trial documents) was nine years old and lived with his parents, Henry and Fela Meyers, on 917 Victoria Street in the city of Laredo. Ten years earlier, a man named Enrique Myers (probably Carlos's father) appeared in the 1910 census living in the city of Laredo. He was twenty-two and worked as a "transporter." He and his wife, Felicitas had one child, one-year-old Enriquè Jr. United States Census Schedule, Laredo, Texas, 1910, 1920.

18. *Texas v. Muñoz*, 2–3.

19. *Texas v. Muñoz*, 3–4.

20. *Texas v. Muñoz*.

21. United States Census Schedule, Alameda County, California, 1930. In 1910, in Alameda County, there was one charge each for sodomy, the "infamous crime against nature," placing one's wife in prostitution, or "pimping," and for a lewd act on a child, listed as violating section 288 of the California criminal code. In 1920, one attempted rape charge, two charges of committing a lewd act on a child, and one sodomy charge were filed, all against non-Spanish-surnamed men.

22. Bexar County Criminal Records, 1900–1930.

23. United States Census Schedule, Texas, 1900, 1910.

24. United States Census Schedule, Texas, 1910. See also Boag, "Go West Young Man, Go East Young Woman."

25. See Shah, "Adjudicating Intimacies on U.S. Frontiers," for a discussion of racial taxonomies of colonialism.

26. Johnson, *Revolution in Texas*; Elliott Young, *Catarino Garza's Revolution on the Texas-*

Mexico Border (Durham: Duke University Press, 2004); Stern, "Buildings, Boundaries, and Blood"; Sánchez, *Becoming Mexican American*; Kelly Lytle Hernández, *Migra!: A History of the U.S. Border Patrol* (Berkeley: University of California Press, 2010).

27. In contrast, Gordon Gibson, one of Muñoz's lawyers, appears in the 1930 US census in Laredo. Likewise, John A. Valls, the prosecutor, appears in the 1910 and 1930 census. Valls himself is a fascinating character; he was one of the most prominent Mexican-born lawyers and politicians in West Texas for decades. See de la Garza, *A Law for the Lion*.

28. See, for example, Martha Hodes, ed., *Sex, Love, Race: Crossing Boundaries in North American History* (New York: New York University Press, 1999); Pascoe, *What Comes Naturally*; Dorr, *White Women, Rape, and the Power of Race in Virginia, 1900–1960*; Boag, *Same-Sex Affairs*; Shah, "Between 'Oriental Depravity' and 'Natural Degenerates'"; Chauncey, *Gay New York*; Murphy, *Political Manhood*.

29. *California v. Jesse Martínez*, Court of Appeal of California (1919), 262–63.

30. *California v. Martínez*, 263–65. Other cases of masturbation appear in legal archives in the early twentieth-century West. *Texas v. Wayne Roper* (1930) has testimony about girls masturbating ("50% of girls abuse themselves," 59). In *California v. Louis Geonzelis* (1929), the mother of the victim catches the boy masturbating and he tells her about attacks (15–17). In *California v. George Fultz* from San Diego in 1895, the eleven-year-old victim of rape by her father described "playing with myself with a candle" (56, 65). Her father also testified that he discovered his daughter masturbating (82).

31. Scholars have recently attended more carefully to the establishment of sexual norms within marginalized communities (African Americans in the turn-of-the-twentieth-century South, Chinese Americans in early twentieth-century San Francisco); Ferguson, "Of Our Normative Strivings"; Shah, *Contagious Divides*, 245. Chapter 6 will explore similar topics in its discussion of heteropatriarchy.

32. Pascoe, *What Comes Naturally*; Dorr, *White Women, Rape, and the Power of Race in Virginia, 1900–1960*; Lewis and Ardizzone, *Love on Trial*; Hodes, ed., *Sex, Love, Race*. Another example of disapproval of interracial mixing from appeals records occurs in *Texas v. Tom Johnson*, Court of Criminal Appeals of Texas (1929), in which a witness describes a predominantly African American neighborhood as "a very undesirable place for white girls and boys to be," 430.

33. *California v. Juan Mesa*, Supreme Court of California (1892), 9, 11, 5, 7. According to the appeals decision, Mesa was charged with the following: "The said Juan Mesa . . . did unlawfully, feloniously, with force and violence, assault Alice Westfall, a female child under fourteen years of age, with intent to commit rape, and without her consent and against her will." In 1897, the age of consent in California was raised to sixteen, and in 1913 raised to eighteen. See Odem, *Delinquent Daughters*.

34. *California v. Mesa*, 36, 48.

35. *California v. Mesa*.

36. *California v. Mesa*, 10, 23.

37. *California v. Mesa*, 21, 22, 24.

38. *California v. Mesa*, 9, 17.

39. *California v. Mesa*, 13, 17, 21. See Lewthwaite, *Race, Place, and Reform in Mexican Los Angeles*; Ken Gonzales-Day, *Lynching in the West: 1850–1930* (Durham: Duke

University Press, 2006); Shah, "'Against Their Own Weakness'"; Fairchild, *Science at the Borders*; Arredondo, *Mexican Chicago*; Rosales *¡Pobre Raza!*; for evidence of link between Mexicans and criminality.

40. *California v. Mesa*, 20. See Arredondo, *Meixcan Chicago*; Molina, *Fit to Be Citizens?*; Gonzales-Day, *Lynching in the West*; Wild, *Street Meeting*; Lewthwaite, *Race, Place, and Reform in Mexican Los Angeles*.

41. *California v. Mesa*, 22.

42. *California v. Mesa*, 20. See María Raquél Casas, *Married to a Daughter of the Land: Spanish-Mexican Women and Interethnic Marriage in California, 1820–1880* (Reno: University of Nevada Press, 2007); Miroslava Chávez-García, *Negotiating Conquest: Gender and Power in California, 1770s to 1880s* (Tucson: University of Arizona Press, 2004); Louise Pubols, *Father of All: The de la Guerra Family, Power, and Patriarchy in Mexican California* (Berkeley: University of California Press, 2010).

43. *Texas v. Fred Hamilton*, Court of Criminal Appeals of Texas (1925).

44. *Texas v. Hamilton*.

45. *Texas v. John Lee Berry*, Court of Criminal Appeals of Texas (1910).

46. Foley, *The White Scourge*; Johnson, *Revolution in Texas*; Montejano, *Anglos and Mexicans in the Making of Texas, 1836–1986*.

CHAPTER SIX

1. *New Mexico v. Juan Lujan*, Supreme Court of New Mexico (1918), 31.

2. *New Mexico v. Lujan*, 98, 102.

3. *New Mexico v. Lujan*, 22–23.

4. See Sarah Deutsch, *No Separate Refuge: Culture, Class, and Gender on an Anglo-Hispanic Frontier in the American Southwest, 1880–1940* (New York: Oxford University Press, 1987); Mitchell, *Coyote Nation*; John M. Nieto-Phillips, *The Language of Blood: The Making of Spanish American Identity in New Mexico, 1880s–1930s* (Albuquerque: University of New Mexico Press, 2004); Charles H. Montgomery, *The Spanish Redemption: Heritage, Power, and Loss on New Mexico's Upper Rio Grande* (Berkeley: University of California Press, 2002); María E. Montoya, *Translating Property: The Maxwell Land Grant and the Conflict over Land in the American West, 1840–1900* (Berkeley: University of California Press, 2002); David A Reichard, "'Justice Is God's Law': The Struggle to Control Social Conflict and United States Colonization of New Mexico, 1846–1912" (PhD dissertation, Temple University, 1996).

5. *New Mexico v. Lujan*, 22, 57, 34, 55.

6. Mexican women suffered violence and marginalization in both Mexico and the United States. See Piccato, *City of Suspects*, 91–92, 105, 108–10, 116, 124; Bliss, *Compromised Positions*.

7. *New Mexico v. Lujan*, 22, 4. The jury in the trial was all male. Women, in fact, did not serve on juries in New Mexico until 1969; Ruiz, *From Out of the Shadows*, 94.

8. "Heteropatriarchy" summarizes an interrelated set of inequalities that are often left unrecognized or are seen as natural and eternal. The principle heteropatriarchal hierarchies are male over female, heterosexual over homosexual, married over unmarried, and reproductive sex over nonreproductive intimacy. Heteropatriarchal societies tend to see civic leadership, authority to distribute societal resources, and political and economic success as "naturally" belonging to those demonstrating a commitment to heterosexual marriage, reproductive sex, and ultimately the authority of men over women.

Both Mexican and dominant Anglo forms of heteropatriarchy value marital, reproductive sex, male authority, and limitations on female sexual activity. The two forms of heteropatriarchy are not identical, however. The appeals cases that I analyze in this book, for instance, suggest that Mexican communities tended to value domestic arrangements with extended families more than strictly nuclear family formation, one of the pillars of Anglo heteropatriarchy. Andrea Smith, "Heteropatriarchy and the Three Pillars of White Supremacy: Rethinking Women of Color Organizing," in *Color of Violence: The Incite! Anthology* (Cambridge, MA: South End Press, 2006), 66–73. See also Eithne Lubhéid, *Entry Denied*. See Lewthwaite, *Race, Place, and Reform in Mexican Los Angeles*, 83, for some of the supposed hazards of nonnuclear households.

9. Gutiérrez, *When Jesus Came, the Corn Mothers Went Away*; Deena González, *Refusing the Favor: The Spanish-Mexican Women of Santa Fe, 1820–1880* (New York: Oxford University Press, 1999); Casas, *Married to a Daughter of the Land*; Chávez-García, *Negotiating Conquest*; Montoya, *Translating Property*; Bliss, *Compromised Positions*; Piccato, *City of Suspects*. Note also the significant number of Mexican women running for office or in elected positions in New Mexico in the early twentieth century. See, for instance, Elizabeth Salas's "Adelina Otero Warren: Rural Aristocrat and Modern Feminist," in *Latina Legacies: Identity, Biography, and Community*, ed. Vicki Ruiz and Virginia Sánchez Korrol (Oxford: Oxford University Press, 2005), 135–47. Thanks to an anonymous reader of the manuscript for making this observation.

10. *New Mexico v. Lujan*, 5, 6.

11. *New Mexico v. Lujan*, 7, 8, 15.

12. *New Mexico v. Lujan*, 10.

13. *New Mexico v. Lujan*, 20–21.

14. *New Mexico v. Lujan*, 21–22.

15. *New Mexico v. Lujan*, 32–33.

16. *New Mexico v. Lujan*, 35 (emphasis in original), 42.

17. *New Mexico v. Lujan*, 38, 39.

18. *New Mexico v. Lujan*, 42.

19. *New Mexico v. Lujan*, 43–45.

20. *New Mexico v. Lujan*, 55.

21. *New Mexico v. Lujan*, 58–59.

22. *New Mexico v. Lujan*, 63.

23. *New Mexico v. Lujan*, 67.

24. *New Mexico v. Lujan*, 65–66.

25. *New Mexico v. Lujan*, 70–71.

26. *New Mexico v. Lujan*, 75.

27. *New Mexico v. Lujan*, 82.

28. *New Mexico v. Lujan*, 87. In the 1910 US census, thirty-four-year-old Luis Ilfeld appeared in Las Vegas with the occupation of lawyer. Though he corrected the pronunciation of his name in court and seemed bilingual in Spanish and English, Ilfeld was the child of two German immigrants (United States Census Schedule, San Miguel County, New Mexico, 1910, ancestry.com, last accessed February 15, 2011).

29. *New Mexico v. Lujan*, 87–88, 11.

30. *New Mexico v. Lujan*, 115.

31. *New Mexico v. Lujan*, 122–23.

32. *New Mexico v. Lujan*.

33. *New Mexico v. Lujan*.

34. LexisNexis Legal Database (Arizona, California, Texas). *California v. Manuel Lima,* Court of Appeal of California (1918); *Texas v Eusebio Guerra,* Court of Criminal Appeals of Texas, (1916). Other seduction cases involving Mexicans appear in local criminal records. In San Antonio, fourteen men were charged with seduction in 1920. Over half of the men, eight, had Spanish surnames. There were also twenty-four rape charges, ten of which charged men with Spanish surnames. In Los Angeles County between 1917 and 1920, two men were charged with seduction. In Oakland's Alameda County, there were zero seduction charges in 1920, and only eleven rape charges, though five of the eleven men charged with rape had Spanish surnames.

35. United States Census Schedule, Texas, 1910, 1920, 1930 (ancestry.com, last accessed February 15, 2011).

36. Montgomery, *The Spanish Redemption*; Nieto-Phillips, *The Language of Blood*; Mitchell, *Coyote Nation*; Montoya, *Translating Property*; Gómez, *Manifest Destinies.*

37. United States Census Schedule, San Miguel County, New Mexico, 1900, 1910 (ancestry.com, last accessed February 15, 2011).

38. According to 1910 census records, Juan Lujan was born in 1895, and thus would have been thirty-five, not thirty-one, in 1930. Four years, however, is a relatively small discrepancy in census documents.

39. United States Census Schedule, San Miguel County, New Mexico, 1920, 1930 (ancestry.com, last accessed February 15, 2011).

40. The same is true for most of the other cases in the book: Mexican men appeared far more likely than Mexican women to present themselves in public, and to be presented by others, as good citizens. Mexican men, of course, were also predominantly the defendants in the cases described, with a greater stake than most in portraying themselves with citizenlike attributes.

41. Smith, "Heteropatriarchy and the Three Pillars of White Supremacy."

42. Ruiz, *From Out of the Shadows,* 71.

43 See Orozco, *No Mexicans, Women, or Dogs Allowed,* 90; Murphy, *Political Manhood,* 202; and Briggs, *Reproducing Empire,* for discussions of fraternal bonding; "imperial brotherhood" (Murphy quoting Robert Dean) may be evident here as well in bonding between Anglo and Mexican men in New Mexico; Murphy, *Political Manhood,* 202. Also see fraternal bonding in male-oriented civil rights groups; Orozco, *No Mexicans, Women, or Dogs Allowed,* 90.

44. *New Mexico v. Lujan,* 65–67.

45. *New Mexico v. Lujan.*

46. *New Mexico v. Lujan,* 74, 129–30.

47. *Texas v. Rudolfo Rodríguez,* Texas Court of Criminal Appeals (1921), 9.

48. *Texas v. Rodríguez,* 39–41.

49. *Texas v. Rodríguez,* 9, 39–41.

50. Mexican women were not alone in this predicament. Other women in colonial settings, especially very poor women, faced similar obstacles and attacks. In Puerto Rico, for instance, "respectable" elites based their nationalist, and anti-American, claims to leadership on their distance from disreputable, poor, often Afro Puerto Rican women (Briggs, *Reproducing Empire*; Findlay, *Imposing Decency*). The centrality of sexual normativity to opposition to colonial rule was no less divisive in other colonial regimes. See, for instance, De Alwis, "'Respectability', 'Modernity' and the Policing of 'Culture' in Colonial Ceylon"; Carter, *The Importance of Being Monogamous*; and Merry, *Colonizing Hawai'i.*

CONCLUSION

1. Américo Paredes, *"With a Pistol in His Hand": A Border Ballad and Its Hero* (Austin: University of Texas Press, 1958), 96–98; *The Ballad of Gregorio Cortez* (Robert M. Young, director, 1982); Orozco: *No Mexicans, Women, or Dogs Allowed*; Hernández, *Migra!*, 20. See also Catrióna Rueda Esquibel, *With a Machete in Her Hands: Reading Chicana Lesbians* (Austin: University of Texas Press, 2006).

2. *Texas v. Gregorio Cortez*, Court of Criminal Appeals of Texas (1902); *Texas v. Gregorio Cortez*, Court of Criminal Appeals of Texas (1904).

3. *Texas v. Cortez* (1902); *Texas v. Cortez*, (1904).

4. *Texas v. Antonio Trijo*, Court of Criminal Appeals of Texas (1903); *Texas v. D. C. Luna*, Court of Criminal Appeals of Texas (1903); *Texas v. Benito Orta*, Court of Criminal Appeals of Texas (1903); *Texas v. Silvester Tarrango*, Court of Criminal Appeals of Texas (1903); *Texas v. Aniseto Guerrero*, Court of Criminal Appeals of Texas (1904).

5. LexisNexis Legal Appeals, accessed December 2009–May 2011. For discussions of hardening racial dividing lines during the period, see Benton-Cohen, *Borderline Americans*; Fairchild, *Science at the Borders*; Foley, *The White Scourge*; Johnson, *Revolution in Texas*; Lewthwaite, *Race, Place, and Reform in Mexican Los Angeles*; Molina, *Fit to Be Citizens?*; Ngai, *Impossible Subjects*; and Pascoe, *What Comes Naturally*.

6. See Chávez, *"¡Mi raza primero!"*; García, *White but Not Equal*; Gómez, *Manifest Destinies*; Gross, *"Texas, Mexicans, and the Politics of Whiteness"*; Gutiérrez: *Walls and Mirrors*; Ian Lopez, *White by Law*; Orozco, *No Mexicans, Women, or Dogs Allowed*; F. Arturo Rosales, *Testimonio: A Documentary History of the Mexican American struggle for Civil Rights* (Houston: Arte Público Press, 2000).

7. Recall from chapter 1 some of legal advantages that Mexicans possessed (generally not subject to anti-intermarriage laws; legal ability to sit on juries; broader, if still limited, political participation) and the significantly higher numbers of Mexicans bringing appeals cases in states like California.

8. *New Mexico v. Amado Ancheta*, Supreme Court of New Mexico (1915).

9. *New Mexico v. Ancheta*, 23–24, 51.

10. *New Mexico v. Ancheta*, 61, 68.

11. *New Mexico v. Ancheta*, 74–75, 90–91.

12. *New Mexico v. Ancheta*, 20, 22.

13. Gloria Anzaldúa, *Borderlands/La Frontera: The New Mestiza* (San Francisco: Spinsters/ Aunt Lute Book Company, 1987); Esquibel, *With a Machete in Her Hands*; Fregoso, *meXicana Encounters*; Cherríe Moraga, *Loving in the War Years* (Boston: South End Press, 1983); and Emma Pérez, *The Decolonial Imaginary: Writing Chicanas into History* (Bloomington: Indiana University Press, 1999).

714) – 657 – 8718

Nancy Alonzo

714) 992 – 4565   Target South